"If you're doing any kind of Web project, you need to have this book beside you. Its contents are so clearly drawn from real-world experience of what works and what doesn't that you'd be nuts to try to do your project without it. Add to that the real-life examples and templates and it'd be hard to see why any Web project manager wouldn't want to own this book."

—Fergus O'Connell, Chairman and CEO of ETP and author of
How to Run Successful Projects III: The Silver Bullet, Third Edition

"The authors achieve their implicitly stated purpose, which is to coach Web project managers on the theory, reality, and practice of their art form. The language and tone is easy to read. That makes the book approachable and nonthreatening."

—Russell Nakano, President, Navaha Inc.,
and author of *Content Web Development*

"The book is a very complete, impressive collection of insights and tips! I'd recommend this book especially to new project managers or other functional managers who want to understand how Web projects work."

—Tim Horgan, Senior Vice President/Online
CXO Media Inc., an IDG Company

"After experiencing scope creep on every project I have ever worked on, it was liberating to get the project manager's perspective on how a project should be managed. Applied to my recent projects, what I've learned from Real Web Project Management *has become core to the way in which I work, allowing me to liberate the other developers and actually meet deadlines with quality code. This book has become an essential part of my techie library."*

—David Kitchen, Senior Developer
Premium TV (NTL)

REAL WEB PROJECT MANAGEMENT

REAL WEB PROJECT MANAGEMENT

Case Studies and Best Practices from the Trenches

Thomas J. Shelford
Gregory A. Remillard

✦Addison-Wesley

Boston • San Francisco • New York • Toronto • Montreal
London • Munich • Paris • Madrid
Capetown • Sydney • Tokyo • Singapore • Mexico City

Many of the designations used by manufacturers and sellers to distinguish their products are claimed as trademarks. Where those designations appear in this book and Addison-Wesley was aware of a trademark claim, the designations have been printed in initial caps or in all capitals.

The authors and publisher have taken care in the preparation of this book, but make no expressed or implied warranty of any kind and assume no responsibility for errors or omissions. No liability is assumed for incidental or consequential damages in connection with or arising out of the use of the information or programs contained herein.

The publisher offers discounts on this book when ordered in quantity for bulk purchases and special sales. For more information, please contact:

U.S. Corporate and Government Sales
(800) 382-3419
corpsales@pearsontechgroup.com

For sales outside of the U.S., please contact:

International Sales
(317) 581-3793
international@pearsontechgroup.com

Visit Addison-Wesley on the Web: *www.awprofessional.com*

Library of Congress Cataloging-in-Publication Data

Shelford, Thomas J.
    Real Web project management : case studies and best practices from the trenches / Thomas J. Shelford and Gregory A. Remillard.
       p.   cm.
    Includes bibliographical references and index.
    ISBN 0-321-11255-5 (alk. paper)
    1. Web site development.   2. Project management.   3. Computer software development.
I. Remillard, Gregory A. II. Title.

TK5105.888.S485 2002
005.2'76--dc21

                                                                        2002026276

For information on obtaining permission for use of material from this work, please submit a written request to:

Pearson Education, Inc.
Rights and Contracts Department
75 Arlington Street, Suite 300
Boston, MA 02116
Fax: (617) 848-7047

ISBN 0-321-11255-5
Text printed on recycled and acid-free paper.
1 2 3 4 5 6 7 8 9 10—MA—0605040302
First printing, October 2002

To our wives, Jackie and Kirstin, for putting up with late nights and frayed nerves as we worked on obscure project management topics of no special interest to people at cocktail parties, and to the dedicated and passionate Web development professionals with whom we have worked over the years.

Contents

Foreword

I have been immersed in Web-based business initiatives for a long time.

I have worked closely with several (in fact, many) Web project managers, and I currently have the good fortune to work among the very best and brightest—Lydia Callaghan, Mike Jones, Michael Dugan, and Jeff Bauer. The role of project manager for a Web-based business is highly complex and often very misunderstood, most notably by project managers themselves.

This book characterizes and details the various roles that contribute to successful Web projects and also coaches the reader on how best to run projects, including "how to":

- Run productive meetings
- Win the confidence of key contributors and the whole team
- Deal, constructively, with conflict
- Manage expectations
- Win

Real Web Project Management will prove to be a valuable book to those new to the project management job because its goal is to mentor that group of readers. It's also aimed at giving seasoned project managers an opportunity to review and reflect on what they have already experienced while working to refine their skills in this increasingly important profession and discipline.

Our industry is reinventing itself and the limited people resources that Web projects have need to be managed judiciously. This means, simply, high productivity and low cost. It is absolutely critical for Web-based projects to be executed with precision in order to meet their business objectives.

A person who is well trained in Web project management is essential to the success of Web-based business initiatives, and I feel that *Real Web Project Management* is a very useful book, written by experienced artisans about their well-developed craft.

Michael E. Smith
Chief Technology Officer
Forbes.com

Preface

Like many of our fellow Web project managers, we came to the role, or rather the role came to us, suddenly and somewhat unexpectedly. Without really knowing it, we had been preparing for the role through our individual professional experiences for some time. We were familiar enough with the project lifecycle to be able to distinguish one end of a project from the other, but the more refined aspects of project management were as yet unknown when we assumed our new responsibilities. It was time to discover just what project managers actually are and what they actually do.

The search for knowledge began with Yahoo! At the time, our search turned up only a small handful of Web sites devoted to project management but nothing Web-specific. We did discover the *Project Management Body of Knowledge®* (*PMBOK®*) from the Project Management Institute (PMI). PMBOK, and other project management books, taught us basic, traditional project managment processes and methods that had been used in other industries for years. We felt reassured with this newfound knowledge but at the same time a little uneasy because we still could find nothing specific on Web project management. "That's all right," we thought. "A project's a project—right?"

As we set out to mimic our colleagues in the more mature branches of software project management, a dark, uneasy feeling entered the pits of our stomachs at the kickoff meeting of every new project. Somehow, in spite of everything we had recently read about process and methodology, we knew we were going to end up doing the one thing we felt sure would betray the very premise of project management: wing it.

The disconnect between the *correct* process and what happens in *real life* has been a source of growing unease among Web project managers. For a time, many people explained away the problem by pointing to the inexperience of the industry. It was assumed that once traditional software development processes and best practices were understood by immature Web professionals, the chaos would subside. Well, not quite. As we gained more experience, project by project, we discovered that the harder we tried to adhere to the use of the traditional project management methods, the more frustrated we became and the more chaotic the atmosphere seemed.

How do you hit a hard-and-fast completion date when the specifications for the project are changed and expanded daily by the very person who is mandating the completion date? In your project plan, how do you account for the time your star developer spends getting in the mood to work by shooting minibasketball free throws for a couple of hours, followed by a donut run, and then a few quick games of UNO with the graphic designer? This was our reality. Knowing when or how to implement overengineered or seemingly inapplicable project management techniques like "force field analysis" or "interrelationship digraphs"caused us to second guess our approach to the "science" of project management. We needed techniques and processes we could implement NOW that would garner us the greatest results in the shortest amount of time.

Because of the continued rapid growth of the Web, the constant changes to the technologies that support it, and the frenzied, media-driven expectations and mythologies that surround it, developing Web sites using only traditional project management methodologies adopted from other industries just was not enough to get the job done. Many traditional methodologies rely on the existence of a fixed scope and clear, measurable objectives. Web site design and development, however, is not like building a rocket or releasing an off-the-shelf software product. Web teams must collaborate in a continually unfolding creative process, which is often more of an art than a science.

Traditional methods will get you part way there. Basic process building blocks can be used with great success and should be. In this book, we demonstrate some of the basic methods as they relate to Web development. But we also demonstrate where traditional methods fail and discuss how the ability to improvise and think on your feet will serve you far better than a painstakingly constructed work breakdown structure or GANTT chart.

It all boils down to this: There is no accepted, proven, documented, or foolproof process for developing Web sites or Web applications. You use what works, and what works you glean from experience. We certainly don't think we have a patentable method, but we do have a lot of experience; and we know what has worked for us and our peers in the industry.

Our Approach

In writing this book, the goal was to spare the new project manager the pain of learning project management theories, processes, and terminology that would cause only confusion and frustration when they were applied to the Web development arena. We wanted to chronicle our experience and describe the methods and processes that have worked by showing them at work in real-world situations.

From the moment we embarked on this project, we decided that the best approach to recounting experiences was to be as lighthearted as possible without undermining the point of the lessons. We are the first to admit that project management for the Web, or any industry for that matter, is a pretty dry topic. We hope that a little humor mixed into the content will keep the material engaging. One thing we've learned from our experiences as project managers is that you must maintain a sense of humor—without it you will lose the ability to lead effectively, and your life at work will be tedious. By the same token, why should reading a book about your profession be tedious? Simple answer: It shouldn't.

The Use of Case Studies and Interviews

What's the use of a lot of theoretical mumbo jumbo without some illustrative material to prove or disprove the theory? In our early search for project management knowledge, we read many books that were long on theory but short on examples of real-life application. We wanted to see an example of a "force field analysis" in action. More to the point, we wanted to see an example of a "force field analysis" in action on a Web project in full meltdown mode with only two days to go before launch. While working our way through project after project, we discovered traditional methodologies that worked and many that did not. We found other methodologies and techniques that could be tweaked to fit into the Web environment. After a couple of years, it dawned on us that the hundreds of e-mail threads, scope documents, and project plans we had drafted contained our own project management body of knowledge. The basis for this body of knowledge was experience: the real-life projects we had managed.

As we interviewed colleagues and peers in the Web development industry for this book, we were provided with more case studies and stories that could be used to illustrate project managment methods. We found that the experiences that resonated the most with colleagues were not the huge successes but the dismal failures. To be truly helpful and instructive, we have chosen to publish case studies and interviews that illustrate things that can and often do go wrong during a Web development project. In order to avoid any legal difficulties from sensitive corporations and their attorneys, we have fictionalized the stories recounted here and changed the names to protect the not-so-innocent. But be assured: The stories herein are all based on real-life events; we couldn't have made up some of this stuff if we tried.

Who Should Read This Book

This book was written for people who are new to the project manager role in the Web development industry. *Real Web Project Management* will provide those of you who come to the role from more specialized expertise, such as programming or design, with an introduction to the world of Web development from a manager's or generalist's perspective. We also hope the book will provide a resource for fresh ideas and inspiration to veteran Web project managers who may recognize themselves in some of the case studies and situations described in the book.

Through frontline experience and during the many interviews conducted for this book, it became crystal clear that the role of the project manager in the Web development industry has come to be considered indispensable. This is true for both interactive agencies and internal Web development or IT departments. Web project management has become a crucial success factor for a huge variety of organizations. Having worked with many unfortunate companies that lack solid project management practices, we believe that reading this book will be worth your time. Please enjoy it, and send any feedback to *feedback@realwebprojects.com*.

Acknowledgments

The authors thank the following individuals for their support of this project.

- *Tracy M. Brown,* for contributing content to Chapters 6 and 8, as well as for her invaluable editorial feedback as a reviewer.
- *Rich Caccappolo,* for contributing content to Chapter 13.
- *Alicia M. Carey,* assistant editor, Addison-Wesley Professional, for her unwavering confidence in the vision and approach of this book.
- *Susan Dorward,* for contributing content to Chapter 13.
- *Stephanie Kip-Rostan,* literary agent at James Levine Communications Inc., for her advice and guidance throughout the complicated process of publishing a quality professional reference book.
- *William Webb,* for contributing content to Chapter 12.

About the Authors

Thomas J. Shelford is a partner in Project Calibrate™, a project management consulting firm focused on providing best practices for Web teams (*http://www.projectcalibrate.com*). Tom began his career on the Web as the technical production manager of a major content portal and has witnessed Silicon Alley's explosive dot-com lifecycle first-hand. He is also a senior consultant at SeaState Internet Solutions (*http://www.seastatesolutions.com*), a freelance Web development shop.

During his career, Tom has managed dozens of Web projects, including content sites, e-commerce sites, e-marketing campaigns, and internationalization efforts. These projects have led to an interest in content management systems and user interface design. Tom advocates an interdisciplinary approach to the Web, and his eclectic background includes mathematics and illustration in addition to project management.

Gregory A. Remillard has been managing Web development projects for more than five years. He was the technology manager at Parents.com and is currently a Web strategy consultant. Greg is also a partner in Project Calibrate™.

When not obsessively managing Web development projects or providing Web strategy to Fortune 500 companies, Greg can be found behind the mixing console indulging his other obsession: recording and mixing music.

CHAPTER 1

The Project Manager: Who You Are and What You Do

Who You Are

Project management for Web development projects is very similar to project management for other industries. The basic tasks are the same: write documentation, create timelines, manage deliverables and milestones, facilitate meetings, manage the team, and provide a single point of contact for everyone involved in the project. These are core skills you will learn over the course of your first few projects, and many are covered in this book. But how does the Web project manager differ from, say, the software development project manager? The difference lies not so much in the basic role itself but in the dynamics surrounding a Web development project and how you understand and deal with the expectations and situations that typically are present. What differentiates Web project managers is that they manage projects that, by their very nature, are forever in flux. The promise of the Web from a development perspective—easy to master and implement technology—can also be its biggest handicap. Client expectations still tend to be influenced by the notion that changes to specifications are simple to execute and the direction of the project can be turned on a dime.

When Moe's Construction Company builds a bridge, they work from a plan that has been engineered to a very fine level of detail. Moe knows what that bridge is going to look like and what it's going to do long before the first rivet is pounded home. If only you were as lucky as Moe. Rarely will a finished Web site or Web application resemble the final specification that was signed off at the beginning of the project. There are many factors that contribute to the huge variance in what was originally conceived and what was finally delivered. These are some of the more common factors.

- ◆ Changes in technology. Web technologies change about every six months.

- ◆ Increase or decrease in the project budget. If the budget is determining the scope of the project instead of the other way around, expect the scope to change as the client attempts to negotiate for more functionality or finds more funding. There will also be occasions on internal projects where the budget is reduced and the scope of the project must be scaled back appropriately.

- ◆ Competition in the marketplace. If AcmeWidgets.com is your client's competition, and they just rolled out an e-commerce engine that can read minds and completes the order process without requiring a single keystroke by the user, then be ready for your client to demand the same functionality.

- ◆ Personal agendas of team members. As mentioned before, advances in technology continually allow ways to do things better, faster, or just plain differently. Part of the fun of this industry is utilizing the ever-changing tools and methods. The problem is that on occasion someone will try out a new tool or method at the expense of the client and the project.

- ◆ Changes in the business model. There are still very few concrete, irrefutable models for turning a profit online. As the public's and Wall Street's perceptions of the Web change from positive to negative and back again, Web entrepreneurs are more apt to change their business model to match the business plan flavor of the week—even in the middle of the project build.

All of these factors not only weigh heavily on your projects but also influence who you are from a professional perspective. Because of the fluid nature of these factors, scope, expectations, and specifications will change as the project progresses. You have to be completely comfortable with change because that, more than anything else during your career as a Web project manager, is what you will be managing most often. Change is what this industry is all about.

The Best Seat in the House

Being the project manager on a pressure-filled, high-stakes Web development project is the professional equivalent of riding an out-of-control roller coaster day in and day out for months at a time. If this analogy turns you off, keep in mind that in addition to the adrenaline-fused ups and downs that make up your work day, you are also at the center of every major decision that influences the project and potentially the organization. You will be tapped by the decision makers to weigh in on key issues, and your opinion will be valued and constantly solicited.

At different points during the course of your projects you will have access to just about every level of your company or your client's company. In the space of half an hour you will talk business strategy with the CEO and also show the part-time HTML intern how to use style sheets. You will be trusted with sensitive information and know most of the project details before everyone else does. The insider status you maintain affords you the best seat in the house, and the knowledge and experience that come with this status will continually enrich your career.

What You Do

Summing up the project manager role in one tidy sentence that you can pull out at Thanksgiving to explain to Aunt Martha what you do for a living is not easy. The tasks you are charged with are widely varied and require skills ranging from the ability to write and speak well to understanding the principles of a relational database. When you tell Aunt Martha that you "manage Web development projects," chances are she'll respond with a kindly, "That's nice, dear" and return her attention to her glass of wine. However, Uncle Dick may not let you off the hook so easily and will want to know just what this "Web development" stuff is all about. In that case, here is a short list of the tasks that comprise the Web project manager role and provide a high-level view of what you do.

- Facilitating communication among members of the team and the client.
- Setting the technical, functional, and design scope of the project.
- Creating and maintaining project documentation, including creative briefs, functional specifications, and design style guides.
- Establishing and maintaining the project timeline.
- Managing the project milestones.
- Facilitating meetings.
- Managing the handoff of deliverables from one resource group to another.

◆ Managing internal and external conflicts.

◆ Providing motivation and leadership to the project team.

You will notice that these tasks require a widely varied range of skill sets. The Web project manager is considered a generalist with just enough knowledge of every disipline used on a Web project to be conversant with the people performing the work and the person paying for it.

These tasks require skills that are divided into two classes: hard and soft. Hard skills tend to be composed of specialized knowledge that allows you to perform a specific discipline-related task like design a user interface or write programming code. Soft skills, such as the ability to negotiate and motivate, allow you to collaborate with others and facilitate high-level performances from your team.

Each chapter in this book will cover one aspect of the project manager's duties during the course of a Web development project. Each chapter will be weighted toward a set of hard or soft skills, such as the steps involved in the technical build (Chapter 10) or managing the graphic design process (Chapter 9). What is important to keep in mind and what this book attempts to demonstrate is that for any given task the project manager is performing, a combination of both hard and soft skills is absolutely necessary to be successful.

The Enabler

During the course of managing a Web development project you will be enabling many things, both large and small, tangible and intangible, to occur. Before the project begins you will be enabling the project sponsor or the client to picture his or her idea or concept in the finished form. You will reveal their vision by relating their idea back to them verbally in nontechnical language or through the use of a creative brief, page map, or site map. During the course of the project you will be educating the client, which will help them to better understand and articulate their expectations and better comprehend each phase of the project.

During the course of a project you will also enable the people on your team to perform their jobs effectively and relatively free of stress. Through effective management, communication, and experience you grease the wheels of production and keep the team focused and on task. You provide the necessary answers to questions about the specification, the design, the timeline, and the client. You enable better interpersonal relationships among your peers by your ability to resolve conflict and smooth ruffled feathers.

The ability to enable others to do their jobs is an often overlooked and rarely mentioned aspect of the project manager's role. However, this very trait is what has many companies and organizations clamoring for more and better project management practices tailored to the Web development industry.

Summary

Good project managers who are capable of efficiently delivering Web development projects are in great demand. From a development and business perspective, project management is the most crucial determining factor of a project's success or failure. The focus on good project management in New Media and Web development companies has become so acute that when investors and potential clients alike are analyzing a company, the first thing they try to ascertain is whether the company has an established, mature, and utilized project management capability.

If you have just recently come to the role of Web project manager, then reading this book will hopefully save you a lot of frustration, worry, and embarrassment as you learn your craft. This book should not be used as a crutch, and it will not address every potentially difficult situation or obstacle you find yourself up against. This is not what this book is intended for, but reading it and absorbing the lessons in each chapter and case study will give you the necessary insight into the role of the Web project manager and the fundamental skills to grow and devise methods for overcoming the unique challenges you will face.

CHAPTER 2

Web Team Roles

Being a Web project manager means that you are coaching a diverse team of cross-functional experts whose talents range from banner buying to data modeling. Success depends not only on the project manager's familiarity with each team member's deliverable but also on the ability of this diverse group to work together. Leading a disparate band of talented, well-paid, and sometimes cranky experts into the white heat of a large-scale, expensive, and difficult development project is no picnic. The team will look to the project manager for leadership, solace, inspiration, and days off.

The project manager needs to understand everyone's job function, the contribution their deliverable makes to the project, what inspires them to perform, and their individual quirks and idiosyncrasies. The Web project manager needs to understand his or her team on the professional, personal, and cultural level in order to be the most effective coach and manager possible.

Common Web Team Roles

The composition of most development teams is a chance occurrence, usually determined by available staff, and you will rarely, if ever, be allowed the luxury of picking and choosing the people for the team. The project kickoff meeting will be the first time the team is assembled and your first opportunity to gauge the dynamics of this new amalgamation of talent. The internal dynamics of Web teams can be staggering in their complexity and scope. Managing the team, let alone the project itself, is an enormous task requiring energy and interpersonal skills.

Before you can manage a Web development team you have to know the players. It's important to note that team composition is different from organization to organization, project to project, and process to process. Your Web development team may not exactly mirror the type that is described in this chapter (see the diagram in Figure 2.1), but there will undoubtedly be many similarities. The basic roles on a typical Web development team remain relatively constant and typically include the following.

- Project stakeholder (also client or business owner)
- Project manager
- Producer
- Editor/copywriter
- Information architect
- Graphic designer
- HTML developer
- Developer
- Tech lead
- Database administrator
- Quality assurance engineer

The typical Web project team is divided into three distinct groups: content, graphic design, and technology. The project manager manages across all of these groups and manages the communication between the client or project stakeholder and the team. The stakeholder normally does not play a daily, hands-on role in the development of the project but is the person responsible for initiating the project, getting the budget allocated, and wresting free the necessary resources. The project manager is the conduit of communication between the stakeholder and the team. Keeping the stakeholder or client abreast of progress on the project is one of the project manager's primary tasks.

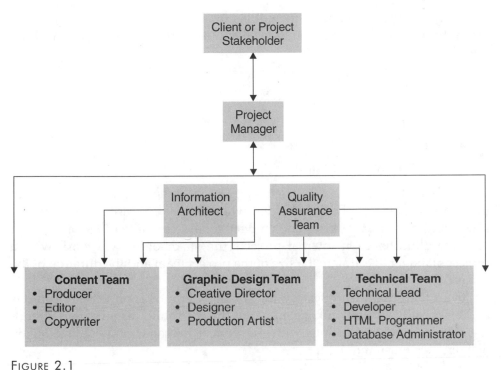

FIGURE 2.1
Diagram of a Web Development Team

The roles associated with the technology side of the project include tech lead, DBA, developer, and HTML developer. The roles associated with the content side of the project are producer, editor, and copywriter (who could also be the producer). The graphic design team consists of the creative director, designers, and production artists. Two roles that cross over between both the tech and content sides of the project are the information architect and the quality assurance engineer. The IA works closely with the developers on the site architecture and with the design and content teams on ensuring that the interfaces meet usability requirements. QA engineers are responsible for testing all the components of the product from a user perspective and generally look for both functionality and display flaws and bugs.

The Project Stakeholder

The project stakeholder, sometimes called the business owner, is the person responsible for initiating the project. This person could be from the marketing department, an external client, an editor, a producer, or even the CEO of the company. Some stakeholders are middle managers who must go to their boss for authorization of new costs. The stakeholder's deliverables could include the following.

- Project concept/idea
- Budget
- Marketing plan
- Page mockups
- Third-party content deals

Some of the stakeholder's deliverables are prepared with the help of the project manager. The stakeholder, when internal, is also responsible for presenting the creative brief and budget to the committee responsible for resource allocation. On internal projects the stakeholder will work with a project manager to estimate the size of the project team and the duration of the project.

Once the project is underway, the stakeholder moves on to other projects and tasks and is usually not a member of the core build team beyond attending regular update meetings with the project manager and signing off on deliverables when required.

The Stakeholder Is Your Customer

Very early in the project, even before the team has been put together, establish how you and the stakeholder will work together. Discuss issues such as communication, status reports, and conflict resolution. Typically you will be managing the team and the build; the stakeholder will be managing the business goals and marketing initiatives. There will be occasional overlaps during the process; but if the roles are clearly defined from the outset, your chances of success are greatly increased.

You will collaborate with the stakeholder on estimating and tracking the resource costs on the project. The more business knowledge you possess, the more you will be able to help the stakeholder early in the process with establishing the business goals of the project. Being integrated in all aspects of the project will give you a better understanding of the end product, allow you to experience a greater sense of ownership, and give the stakeholder piece of mind.

The stakeholder is your customer, and your goal is to provide exceptional customer service. The stakeholder empowers you with the responsibility to turn his or her vision into reality. It's a tall order, especially when little, if any, authority comes with the responsibility.

The Producer

The Web producer has myriad tasks and responsibilities to manage during the course of a project. The Web producer role is approached and interpreted differently and morphs from company to company and department to department. It's also important to note that the producer role may also exist on the client side in the form of a product manager. These are the typical deliverables and responsibilities associated with the producer.

- Project concept/idea
- Creative brief
- Page maps
- Site map
- Final specifications
- Project timeline
- Budget
- Design direction
- Editorial content/direction
- Editorial resource management
- Third-party content deals

Traditionally the producer is much closer to the content and display aspects of the project than the project manager. The producer tends to maintain the point of view of an end user or client when working on a project. Projects may be initiated by a stakeholder, but the producer gives the project its special flavor.

Working with the Producer

The producer/project manager relationship can be a delicate balancing act, a graceful waltz, or a full-blown rumble. Because of the overlapping of tasks and the occasional redundancy in resource management, the producer/project manager relationship can be difficult to master. You need to establish a clear understanding of who will be responsible and manage what tasks, deliverables, and resources in order to avoid problems down the road. Just as important as defining each other's roles and responsibilities is the communication of the details of the arrangement to other team members. Once the relationship has been clearly defined and communicated to everyone, be sure to stick to the plan, or you will risk confusing the team and undermining your chances for a smooth project.

♦ Producer and Project Manager Overlap

In some companies the producer manages the entire project and all resources without the help of a project manager. In other companies the producer works on developing the concept and then turns over the project to a project manager for the build phase.

Sometimes the producer is the stakeholder, sometimes not.

In some agencies the producer works closely with the client, and in others the producer's primary tasks are internal. Good Web producers have honed their project management skills and know how to work harmoniously with a project manager. Then again there are producers who find it necessary to micromanage every aspect of the build and make the project manager feel superfluous.

The producer is a vital role and crucial to the project hitting the content mark. It's a generalist role that can on occasion overlap with the project manager role. If you find yourself in this situation, just remember the old adage "Two heads are better than one."

When a producer and a project manager align themselves behind the common goal of exceeding all expectations, the odds of success are greatly enhanced. Think of Joe Torre and Don Zimmer winning multiple World Series, Steve Jobs and Steve Wozniak launching Apple Computers, or John Lennon and Paul McCartney collaborating on "Sgt. Pepper's Lonely Hearts Club Band," and you should get the idea.

The Editor

Depending on the size of the company or department, editorial functions such as writing, researching stories, and copy editing may involve several people or a single person wearing all of these hats. The editorial staff is responsible for creating or acquiring stories, articles, product descriptions, headlines, and other types of copy. The editorial staff is usually tightly woven with the producer's staff and can be managed by the producer if there is no managing editor on staff.

Most large, content-rich Web sites use an editorial tool to maintain the content on the site. The editorial tool allows the editorial staff to input copy and images throughout the site. Most editors will write the copy in a separate program like Microsoft Word and then transfer the copy to the editorial tool. In many cases the content entry is performed by production assistants who work on the production staff. Figure 2.2 illustrates the typical content creation workflow.

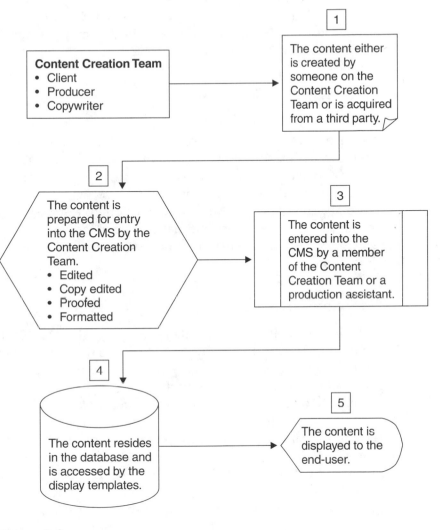

FIGURE 2.2
A Typical Web Content Creation Flow

The editorial staff's deliverables include the following.

- ◆ Story ideas
- ◆ Articles and stories
- ◆ Procurement of stories or articles
- ◆ Product descriptions and reviews
- ◆ Interviews

If there is a photo editor on staff, he or she will work closely with the editorial department on creating or choosing images and photographs to accompany stories. The photo editor will more than likely be part of the design group.

Working with the Editorial Staff

Watch out for friction between the Web site producer(s) and the editorial staff. Turf wars between producers and editors can flare up over the ownership of content and the responsibility for coming up with concepts and ideas. The producer may have an idea she loves, only to find stony opposition from the editor. The same situation can happen in reverse.

Also, because the production staff is often responsible for inputting the content, they depend on editorial to meet deadlines. It's the producer's job to chase down the content and hound the editors, and that can lead to confrontations.

The Information Architect

One of the most challenging and interesting roles on a Web development team is that of the *information architect,* or IA. The IA is the person who ensures that the Web site will be usable by human beings and ensures that the underlying structure of the Web site, including the design, content, and technology, will make sense to users. IAs come from either a technology or design background and are conversant in the finer points of both. IAs are usability experts and have logged many hours observing people interact with various types of graphical interfaces, computer hardware and software, and other objects that require quick comprehension by humans to be used successfully.

Depending on the company, IAs can wield a great deal of power on a Web initiative. They often take part in every aspect of the project build but especially in the early design and functionality planning stages. Having an IA on board helps all groups in the build process by providing a person solely dedicated to safeguarding against bad design or whacky functionality that will eventually be deemed unusable by the intended audience.

Working with the Information Architect

Working with an IA is always an interesting and educational experience. However, just like any other member of the team, IAs are not infallible and can make mistakes. Trust your experience and common sense. If the IA deems a design or piece of functionality unusable, but you believe otherwise, do not be afraid to challenge the IA on the point.

Another potential area of concern is the fact that the IA's role overlaps with so many others' in the process but none more so than the designer. Watch out for turf wars between the information architect and the designer. Normally their collaboration is fairly friction-free because their common goal is to achieve the best design possible for the client, but the relationship can occasionally be tested by disagreements that can lead to delays.

G   *Information Architect*   An information architect is an individual whose primary responsibility on a Web development team is to organize the Web site content or information into an intuitive, easy-to-understand structure from a visual, navigational, and technical perspective.

The Graphic Designer

Designers breathe life into a Web site. Typography, photography, iconography, color palettes, graphics, animation—these are the tools the designer uses to establish concept, expression, message, tone, feel, and quality. Usually the first stop for a producer working on an idea or concept, the designer provides an excellent sounding board and translates crude page mockups into beautifully polished works of art. Designers are also adept at working out thorny navigation problems that crop up in the early stages of development. While normally not bona fide information architects, good designers have an excellent grasp of how users approach Web sites and will design with the user experience foremost in mind. Designers often collaborate closely with the information architect on the page maps, site map, graphical interfaces, and navigation design.

Designers have higher profiles that add responsibilities and pressures other team members are spared. Because the graphic design and page layouts are the first tangible manifestations of the project, the designer is often trotted out before the stakeholder or client, page printouts in hand, to explain why fuchsia is the "right" color for the navigation bars and what the current standard is in "cool" Web design. Good with industry buzzwords, a designer can help sell a concept or influence the client.

Designers are long on creativity and talent but traditionally short on programming skills, but that is becoming more the exception to the rule as designers realize the value of technical knowledge. Depending on experience, they can be conversant in Web technology and understand the various components that comprise the back end of a Web site. They usually have basic HTML skills and can mock up Web pages for the browser or test how a design will translate to the screen. During the build phase the designer will work closely with the HTML resource as the final page designs are officially rendered for the screen.

Because Web design is a collaborative process, designers are good team players and understand the art of compromise. Internal clients consist of producers and stakeholders, and when working in an agency environment, they will work closely with the producer or account manager to realize the client's vision.

While being good team players and giving 100 percent on every project, designers often miss milestones and can add time to a project in their pursuit of perfection. Hovering over or badgering the designer (or any resource) as they work is not a good tactic for getting results. If a designer is consistently missing milestones and delaying projects, rather than risking an unpleasant and nonproductive confrontation, talk to the creative director about it and let him or her handle the problem. Also keep in mind that the client or stakeholder could be the culprit for the delays by going outside the normal channels of communication and inundating the designer with tweaks and last-minute changes.

Working with the Designer

Collaborating on the Web site design can be one of the most enjoyable experiences in the project life cycle. Working with the designer to chase down ideas and work out difficult user experience problems calls on your own creativity and is always a good learning experience. But don't get carried away. During the design meetings it will be your job to keep an eye on the technical scope as ideas begin flying fast and furiously. The design phase is when the scope of the project can grow exponentially. It's not the designer's fault—they're paid to be creative. And it's not necessarily the producer's fault—producers will push the design as far as they can and continue adding features beyond the original specifications until someone draws the line. The designer and the producer will be looking to you to speak up when things have gone too far and you suddenly find that the purple navigation bar with the four different user states has just added a week of DHTML and JavaScript programming to the project.

The HTML Developer

How many of the people working in the Web industry today cut their teeth on HTML? The most basic Web technology skill at the end of the 20th century has evolved into one of the most challenging and unsung skills at the beginning of the 21st. Where would the Web be without experts adept at table structure and style sheets? Browser compatibility, layout, alignment, frames, fonts, download time—these are just a few of the technical and display issues the HTML developer wrestles with daily. Working closely with designers and back-end developers—often simultaneously—the HTML developer must possess good design sensibility and technical prowess. Because he or she is often at the center of heated design and layout debates, it helps if the HTML developer also possesses good negotiating skills.

The HTML developer's deliverables and responsibilities can include the following.

♦ The HTML frameworks for all display templates
♦ The execution of smaller, nondynamic "flat" or HTML-only projects
♦ HTML mockups of proposed designs
♦ Style sheet implementation
♦ Image directory maintenance

The HTML developer is in constant demand in any Web company or department. Designers and back-end developers alike put great demands on the HTML developer's time. When you are working on a project that requires many templates to pass through the HTML developer's hands, take care that he or she is not being distracted by others. Designers can take advantage of the availability and good nature of the HTML person by asking for mockups or tweaks that are neither scheduled nor necessary. When you are on deadline, it's up to you to protect your team from such interruptions. Ask the HTML developers to funnel through you all requests for work that come directly to them. That way the requests will be channeled through the proper work request process.

Working with the HTML Developer

For the HTML developers to complete their tasks, you must be sure they have the necessary deliverables from the designer. These can include printouts, mockups, optimized images, and type and color specifications. Because the HTML developers may be working on several projects at once or just doing favors for others, be sure to track their milestones closely and when necessary intercept distracting work requests that could jeopardize the project timeline.

The Developer

The developer is your secret weapon, your go-to player and most trusted resource on the project team. He or she thrives on mental challenges, brainteasers, and puzzles—the more difficult and convoluted the better. Beyond being technically proficient, exceptional developers can also see the forest for the trees. They quickly grasp the business goals behind the project (assuming the goals are valid) and can usually determine if the project will be a boon or a bust. And, given the opportunity, the developer can help *you* understand the project better as well.

When you embark on a project and you are creating the early drafts of the specifications, the developer will help you crystallize and define the back-end requirements. If you are not very technical, then save yourself a lot of frustration and potentially wasted time. Block out some time with the developer and collaborate on the technical requirements and functionality.

Watching a programmer design an application on a white board or even a scrap of paper can be a confusing but ultimately rewarding experience. With near religious zeal they will leave no stone unturned as they pepper you with questions and potential user scenarios you never thought of. They might embarrass you a little in the process by exposing the gaps in your knowledge or ideas, but the project will be so much the better for going through this exercise. After a white board session with the developer (or tech lead), you will begin to see your project from a 360-degree vantage point and will be able to go back to the producer or stakeholder and get the clarification necessary to answer questions, make suggestions, and meet their expectations.

KEY POINT

Conduct a white board session with your programmer or tech lead (preferably both) early in the project. Using the first or second round of page mockups *and definitely before the design phase is underway,* diagram the application showing user inputs, decision processes, database interaction, application output, and display pages. A little bit of UML knowledge goes a long way in this exercise (see the UML reference in Appendix B). Mapping the application with the programmer will expose logic errors before they end up in the code and will provide you with a list of questions to take back to the stakeholder that should result in a better Web site.

Working with the Developer

Do your best to establish a strong rapport with your developers. Break through whatever barriers you feel may exist and forge a good working relationship. A developer's knowledge can be intimidating, but keep in mind that everyone has strengths, and while yours may not be solely in the technical area, you perform tasks on a daily basis that many people, including developers, find intimidating as well. It helps to tell your developer everything there is to know about the project: from the company objectives to background colors—hold nothing back. By divulging all the information you have about the project and asking for feedback, you are establishing a feeling of inclusion and trust.

A primary goal of establishing a solid bond with the developer is to allow for a free and clear exchange of information. You need to be able to describe the expected application behavior to the developer in language they can understand. The developer in turn must be able to articulate to you, in language *you* can understand, how he or she is going to create the required functionality to arrive at the desired behavior. Some developers are better at communicating technology to nontechnical people than others. It's your job to learn to interpret your developer's technospeak into language the client or producer can understand.

You also want to establish a high degree of trust that will allow you and the developer to be completely honest with each other. During the lifecycle of a project, everyone makes mistakes, and how you handle your own and other people's errors can have a dramatic impact on your project. You have to be comfortable telling the developer that you omitted a key bit of functionality from the specs or you misinterpreted the client's instructions. The developer in turn has to be comfortable telling you that an error he made could set the project back two weeks. Regardless of who erred, you have to be able to bypass the blame game and together strategize a solution and get on with the project. It's not easy for programmers to admit they screwed up. Create an atmosphere of trust and let them know you will back them up and not lay blame at their feet when the going gets tough.

The Tech Lead

The tech lead is your savior and friend. Cherish this person always and keep him or her close. Just as you are the bridge of communication between the technology staff and the stakeholder, the tech lead is the bridge between you and the high-voltage nether reaches of the developer's mind. Depending on the organization, the tech lead role can be a hands-on person, such as a senior developer, or a hands-off member of the technology department's managerial staff.

The tech lead is a great help during the technical design phase as you work out the backend specifications with the developer. The tech lead is also responsible for conducting code reviews and keeping developers on track during particulary thorny development projects. They are especially helpful when a junior or inexperienced developer is assigned to the project. The tech lead can also provide a buffer between yourself and a developer who is struggling and falling behind in the schedule or is not communicative.

The tech lead's deliverables and responsibilities can include the following.

- Technical specifications
- Code reviews
- Staff management
- Programming

If your company or department does not utilize a tech lead, it may be well worth your time to establish this role. Besides being a huge help for the project manager, the tech lead role can provide a career step for the development team. The role requires maturity and management skill and can provide a platform for acquiring both.

Working with the Tech Lead

As mentioned before, the tech lead can be your best friend in the technology department and your lifeline when things get hairy in the development phase. Keep the tech lead fully informed on the progress of the development as well as the performance of the developer. When the developer runs into trouble, give them a reasonable amount of time to work out the problem first, and then ask the tech lead to help out. This approach shows your confidence in the developer's ability to work out problems on their own and displays a healthy respect for the tech lead's time.

The Database Administrator

The database administrator (DBA) is one of the more specialized members of the team and is responsible for creating, advising, and controlling all aspects of the project that involve the database. The DBA is not typically a full-time member of the project team, but his or her contribution is invaluable to the project. The developer works closely with the DBA throughout the lifecycle of the build but more so at the outset of the project. Typically, a developer will create a database schema as one of the first steps in the technical design. The developer will then present the DBA with the schema, and the DBA will analyze it to be sure it meets the standards he enforces on the database. If the schema is not up to snuff, the DBA will consult with the developer on a more suitable schema for the project.

The DBA also writes code specific to the type of database being used for processes such as *stored procedures*. Once again, this work is done in collaboration with the developer assigned to the project. The bulk of the DBA's time is spent maintaining the database and optimizing its performance. The DBA's typical project deliverables and responsibilities can include

- Schema implementation
- Stored procedures and other database coding
- Staff management

Working with the DBA

During the course of the project your interaction with the DBA will more than likely be limited to providing milestones and following up on deliverables. However, if the DBA takes issue with a schema or database functionality request from the developer, hear her out and trust her opinion. The DBA knows the database better than the developer and will be looking to you to intervene if the developer does not want to cooperate.

G *Stored Procedure* A stored procedure is a group of database query statements that reside within the database and perform a certain task. The main advantage of creating stored procedures is that they prevent scripts from using tables directly. This keeps your database tables safe from poorly written query statements. Stored procedures are used to speed up the execution of commonly used queries and to keep the query syntax safely hidden from the business logic of an application. For example, the most commonly used operations on a product database (add a customer, delete a product, retrieve an invoice) could be coded as stored procedures.

The Quality Assurance Engineer

The QA tester is the final gateway between your project and life on the Web. Be kind to the QA department because the day will come when you will be negotiating with them for the release of your project and every advantage helps. Depending on the organization, QA testers can be very technical and troubleshoot bugs, or they may only test for poor user experience, design imperfections, and copy errors. Usually the QA tester is familiar enough with the technology to write up a coherent bug description but does not have the time or responsibility to get under the hood and investigate the cause of the bug. The QA tester should be involved early in the project and should be invited to all kickoff meetings. The QA department, like HTML, can be a bottleneck in the build process. Be sure to get your QA tester involved early in the process to ensure that your project is in his job queue and on his radar. Even though the bulk of their tasks begin during the second half of the project (depending on the development approach), getting QA involved early gives them a preview of the moving parts and an idea of where potential design and technical flaws may occur.

The QA tester's deliverables and responsibilities can include

- Bug reports
- Creation and maintenance of a QA methodology
- Creation or procurement of a bug reporting tool

Working with the QA Engineer

Similar to project managers, QA engineers have a great deal of responsibility but little, if any, authority. This can make for a frustrated QA tester. The QA tester will relentlessly work to expose bugs and flaws in the Web site and has a high set of standards to uphold, but the bottom line is, when it's time to go live, the stakeholder will brush aside QA's warnings and complaints and demand launch. Guess who gets to communicate this to the QA tester? Yup, *you* do. When the time comes for you to more or less tell the QA tester, "Thanks, but no thanks," and you are going to launch with a bug list full of open issues, it helps if you already have a good relationship in place.

KEY POINT

Get the QA department involved early in the development of the project. Be sure they have copies of or access to all relevant documentation such as specs, page mockups, page maps, and a project plan. Be sure they understand the scope of the project so they can plan accordingly for when the project moves into their department.

Common Team Problems

This section examines the symptoms of two common team problems and recommends solutions.

Missing in Action—Become Part of the Team

Even though your little square on the company org chart may reside just above that of the people performing the actual work, don't get a big head. The primary message you want to be sending to your teammates in both word and deed is "We are all in this together." And if this is not the message you are sending then nine times out of ten, the message you will be receiving from your team is "Get lost!"

Symptoms

- You notice a consistently cool, aloof reception from team members at meetings as well as one-on-one.

- Team members are always very quick to agree with everything you say or suggest but deliver the exact opposite.

- No one on the team speaks up at meetings or provides any suggestions or solutions to issues raised.

- The majority of the project milestones are being missed, and there is a consistent nonadherence to the specifications.

Solutions

- Check your ego. Your job is to guide, coach, and support the team—not do the actual work. The people on your team have specialized skill sets and are experts in their area of endeavor. You on the other hand tend to be more of a generalist with a good understanding of each player's tasks and deliverables. Therefore, while being able to speak to each disipline, you cannot deliver the level of quality the expert can.

- Demonstrate your commitment to the team by being willing and able to pitch in when the going gets tough. If you are asking your team to work on a Saturday, you'd better show up, too, and be willing to pitch in and help where you can: code HTML, copy edit, pick up lunch—whatever it takes.

- Empower each team member with the creative freedom to arrive at solutions to problems on his or her own. You may be able to sketch a reasonable depiction of the product, but the experts on your team will be performing the actual brushwork, which will result in the final, full-color rendering.

- Form a bond of trust and open communication with each member of the team. Good team dynamics can be arrived at quicker if you take the time to get to know each member of the team one-on-one. You don't have to become everyone's best friend, but you *do* need to understand each person's personality in order to better support them and give them the freedom they need to excel.

The Micromanaging Stakeholder

In the course of your career you will work with more than one project stakeholder who insists on managing every detail of the project, from concept to coding. While their heart may be in the right place, the message they send is one of mistrust and paranoia. It's very easy to recognize the micromanager—in fact, it's a frightening and annoying thing to behold. Stay cool. In just about every relationship there's always one partner who is more mature than the other. Guess which partner you are? To manage this problem correctly, you have to suck it up, take the high road, and call on those maturity genes to get you through.

Symptoms

♦ The stakeholder insists on attending EVERY meeting connected to the project.

♦ No task is too small for the stakeholder not to have an opinion on how to complete it.

♦ All tasks, milestones, and effort estimates in the project plan are suspect and open to question and change.

♦ All decisions are second guessed.

Solutions

♦ Instead of the stakeholder attending every meeting—which can stifle creativity, open discussion, and debate—suggest a weekly or even twice weekly status meeting where you can update them on every decision and bit of project minutiae. Providing this level of service will allow the stakeholder to maintain his sense of place in the hierarchy and involvement in the project.

♦ If necessary, frankly tell the stakeholder she is micromanaging. Ask her if her time might not be better spent on coordinating other business aspects of the project, like a marketing plan, instead of the nitty gritty of the build. This discussion obviously could turn into a potentially nasty confrontation, so it's important to be sure the topic can safely be raised. If you determine that a discussion like this must occur, be sure to maintain your sense of humor and calm regardless of how the stakeholder reacts.

♦ Remember that the stakeholder's heart is in the right place, and he wants the project to be successful as much as anybody. Unfortunately, he may also be a control freak who doesn't understand how to delegate or collaborate. Sometimes it's up to us to educate as well as manage.

Case Study: Startup Breakdown

This case study describes one project manager's experience as he attempts to unite a Web team made up of people from very different corporate cultures, who have little Web experience, are suspicious of each other, and are charged with a nearly impossible task—all the blood, guts, and glory the Web promises in 90 days.

Baby, You Can Drive My Car

Luxbaum, a multinational auto manufacturer, and Greenwood, a growing online marketing company, entered into a joint venture in 2000 with the goal of creating a Web site devoted to the various aspects of the car and driving culture. After much handwringing, soul-searching, and expensive brand consultant's input, it was decided the new site would be called iLikeToDrive.com. Luxbaum wanted to use the site as a vehicle (no pun intended) for collecting user demographic data to aid them in developing new models and ancillary brands and car-related products. The new online company would use office space, tech resources, and Web producers, all provided by Greenwood. An editorial staff was hired, and the auto company supplied the marketing team and part of the executive management.

From the outset the team never fully gelled. The auto people who were brought in from Detroit and other offices around the country had very little Web experience. The editorial people were straight from the magazine world, and this was their very first exposure to the Web environment. The Greenwood people who joined iLikeToDrive.com had been working together for at least three years and were a close-knit group and very Web-savvy. Consequently, the editorial and marketing people felt shut out. The venture was saddled with specific metrics goals it had to attain in its first year in order to get more funding from the parent companies. Time was quickly passing, and the team was having a hard time getting started. The situation was extremely volatile and highly political. Each group competed with the other for power and attention from the board of directors, and ownership of the vision for the Web site. All three factions came from extremely different corporate cultures, and a unifying direction or team mentality had yet to be established by the new management team.

After only four months there were shakeups at the top of the fledgling company. The CEO and technical director were both replaced in the same week. Neither had managed to bring the team together or create any type of unifying vision. Neither one liked the other, and both complained about the other behind his back. A new CEO was brought in from Luxbaum to straighten out the business side of the company, and a former Greenwood senior producer was rehired to help pull together the vision, voice, and design of the site. A member of the project management team from Greenwood was brought in to attempt to bring some focus and process to the project and get the development underway and keep it on track.

The iLikeToDrive.com board of directors told the new CEO they wanted the site launched in 90 days, and everyone's bonus (including his own) depended on meeting that deadline. Not only did the site have to launch within the 90-day timeframe, but the team had to develop a CRM solution that would capture the user data Luxbaum needed for marketing research purposes.

Broken and Bleeding

The iLikeToDrive.com team was approximately 30 people strong on the day Jim joined. The Greenwood offices where Jim normally worked were noisy and convivial places. By contrast, the iLikeToDrive.com wing was as quiet as a church. Everyone seemed very busy and quite serious as Jim moved into his new cubicle. Later that day he met with Karen, the new senior producer, to get the lay of the land. Jim considered her talented and very capable. He had worked with her in the past on large Greenwood initiatives, and they had always enjoyed an excellent rapport. She told him the team was in terrible shape and she could not imagine how they could meet the launch deadline with the team so fractured and non-communicative.

She described her first meeting with the editorial staff, in which she had tried to establish the voice and tone of iLikeToDrive.com. The meeting was a disaster. The editorial team was not used to collaborating with anyone on the content of their articles. They were confused and intimidated by the technical aspects of the Web and were not experienced enough to conceive of online tools or content that was interactive in nature. They had never been forced to think in interactive terms, and they had not been told this would be part of their job. Karen explained that her staff of producers (the production staff) were there to collaborate with the editors on the interactive aspects of the content, but the writers felt all aspects of the content creation should be their domain, even though they had no experience with creating Web content. Nothing was resolved in the meeting, and the division between the two groups grew deeper.

In addition to the tug-of-war between editorial and production, trouble was brewing with the marketing staff. Karen thought a lack of Web experience was again at the heart of the problem. The marketing staff wanted to know when a version of the home page would be ready so they could send the link to their ad agency. They wanted the home page finished within two weeks in order to fit into the marketing plan they were devising. It did not seem to matter that neither a final design direction nor a content plan had yet to be established—not to mention that there were no back-end systems in place to actually serve the Web site. To make matters worse, the marketing staff shut themselves off from the rest of the team and would only communicate through the CEO, a former Luxbaum colleague.

Karen did provide one ray of hope. The design company Luxbaum had hired was a good firm with which Jim was familiar. They were based in New York City and had a good project management team. At least that was one aspect of the build Jim felt he did not have to worry too much about.

To round out his first day, Jim payed a visit to the developers' cubicle to get their take on the state of the project to date. When Jim asked the developers to describe their experience over the last few months at iLikeToDrive.com, their thoughtful reply was "It's been like playing peewee golf on the recreation deck of the *Titanic*." They had yet to build anything for the new site because they had no direction or specs to work from. They had heard the site would require some sort of personalization functionality that would pass for a CRM system, and the site was supposed to provide the user with many "tools" and interactive features to use. The recently departed technology manager had never taken the time to work with them on conceiving any of this functionality, nor had he written a single spec to date. The technology manager had apparently spent the better part of each day arguing with the iLikeToDrive.com CEO and marketing department over issues such as who should create the organization chart for the company.

The developers verified Karen's summation that the team was badly divided and noncommunicative. In the months they had been with iLikeToDrive.com the developers said they had yet to have a conversation with the marketing or editorial team beyond "Good morning" and "Good night."

Jim's conversations on his first day on the job told him just how bad the situation was he had inherited. The board had mandated a launch in 90 days, the first round of design had not been completed, and there was no editorial plan for content or interactive tools and applications. The team was divided into three hostile camps that were not speaking to one another. It was going to be a big enough job working with the team on conceiving the interactive, architecture, navigation, and database requirements and then writing the resulting specifications, but he also had to somehow bring together the team for the necessary collaboration. Jim also had to establish his own credibility immediately if he hoped to have any sway over the team. Jim decided he would concentrate on accentuating the positive and avoiding any already existing turf wars. He would not be party to any form of gossip or complaining within the group, as this would be fatal to his neutrality, which was his primary strength in bringing together the team.

Creating a War Room

Even though some people on the team were already suspicious and wary of Jim simply because he had come from Greenwood, he knew he still had the advantage of being nearly completely neutral because he was so new. He had yet to form any obvious affiliations with any of the feuding groups. His first move would be to establish Monday morning status meetings, where a representative from each group would report what advancements or achievements that group had accomplished during the previous week and what they were hoping to achieve in the week ahead. He set up an e-mail alias in the iLikeToDrive.com e-mail system that he used to announce the meeting. His goal was to set up a war room–like atmosphere that would help to unite the team. He had found out from talking to people that not everyone was aware of the 90-day deadline, which was looming closer by the hour. He also found out that an early iteration of the design scheme had been completed by the agency, but only a few people had seen it. The agency could not proceed without an idea of the scope of the site and how the content would be organized.

Jim wanted to create a strong feeling of inclusion and open communication. He planned on sharing all the information about the build, design, deadline, and business goals he had learned over his first week. For whatever reason—culture clash, mistrust, paranoia—information had remained concealed in the various camps that comprised iLikeToDrive.com. If he could break down the walls and make everyone understand that hoarding information or keeping details secret would only serve to harm them rather than help, he thought he might have a chance at bringing the team together. There was no job security in keeping secrets when faced with a hard deadline of less than three months. On the first Monday morning meeting, after everyone had introduced themselves (or reintroduced themselves, as the case may be), Jim requested that a representative from each group share what the group was working on and provide a status report.

The first to speak was Karen. She described her vision for the Web site and the way users would interact with it. She spoke of how the Web site should be full of "sticky" content areas, tools, and quizzes that would allow car enthusiasts and nonenthusiasts alike to learn more about car and driving culture. Everyone listened quietly. When Karen finished, Jim asked her how her group would contribute to achieving this vision. He wanted Karen to state publicly the need for the editorial team to collaborate with her producers on conceiving the ideas for the site content. Karen did just that. She stated that even though her team had several ideas for content areas of the site as well as several interactive tools, they were bogged down by their lack of professional car knowledge as well as the manpower necessary to flesh out the content areas with articles, copy for tools, and other pieces of copy such as headlines and promotional blurbs. She said her team had tried to work with editorial on the content plan but had yet to make any progress. Karen stated her position matter-of-factly in a nonchallenging, nonaccusatory tone. She knew what she was doing and why Jim had asked her to speak first. She provided the setup Jim needed to break down the communication barriers between the production and editorial staffs.

Jim turned to the small group of editors and asked them to describe their status on content ideas and creation. Andy, the senior editor who had been brought in from the magazine world, spoke. He described his own vision for the Web site and told of content areas his team had conceived of to date. His vision and Karen's were nearly identical when layed out side by side. Jim asked Andy if he had thought about how the users would interact with the Web site, how they could navigate from place to place, and what types of quizzes or tools the users would find on the site. Andy responded that while his team had been able to envision the mission of the site with regard to content, they were having trouble translating their ideas into interactive applications. He explained how no one on his staff had ever worked for an Internet company, but they were all excited at the opportunity to create something vital and new in the online car culture space. Andy finished by stating in an even tone of voice, "We think we need more help from the producers to translate our ideas so they will work on a Web site."

Jim then asked the marketing people for a report on the status of the marketing plan for the site. The representative from the marketing group gave an enthusiastic account of a marketing plan for the launch of the site and described where they planned to advertise as well as the types of online and offline promotional campaigns that would soon begin. She also detailed some potential advertisers who were expressing interest in buying ad space on the site. "The only problem we have," she stated, "is we don't have any details on the site's design or content. So it's sort of hard to plan promotions when we don't know what we're selling." The assembled group broke into laughter at this statement. The tension that had filled the air up to that moment began to dissipate.

The two groups on the content side of the project had spoken and described their vision, and the business representatives had described how they planned to market the site and talked about potential for revenue. Jim believed an open dialogue, however slight, had been established. Jim then told the assembled group about the deadline they were all facing. He calculated they now had fewer than 90 days to launch the site that, to date, existed only in name. He asked the production, editorial, and tech groups to take the next few days to meet and flesh out the Web site. He asked that a representative from each group work with him on establishing the timetable and goals for this scoping exercise. "White-board the site," he told them. The editorial people didn't know what he was talking about. He explained to them how to diagram the framework of the Web site on a white board with a marker and how to draw the user experience as he or she interacted with a tool or quiz. "What the user puts in and what the user gets back in the form of results," he explained. "The developers will show you what I'm talking about." He asked the production team to give the editors the benefit of the doubt when they expressed an idea that may not seem immediately feasible. "Collaboration and cooperation are what we need right now if we want to meet the deadline." He told the group, "I'm not asking for a group hug but we have a long way to go and a short time to get there." The group chuckled at the "group hug" term, but Jim sensed his message was finally sinking in.

People began to return to their desks and cubicles in small groups of twos and threes. Everyone seemed excited, and a sense of purpose that was actually palpable filled the room. Karen and Andy disappeared into Karen's office to begin working on a new editorial and content plan for the site. They were both talking animatedly and laughing. Jim sat with the developers for a moment before returning to his desk. He thought the meeting had been a success and hoped it would be the catalyst needed for bringing the team together. "That was awesome, man," one of the developers told him. "I thought Andy was going to freak out when Karen said editorial wasn't helping her, but he seemed totally cool." Jim wasn't so sure Andy was totally cool. He thought he caught Andy mocking him by rolling his eyes more than once during the meeting. He also wasn't sure if the laughter Andy and Karen were now sharing was at his expense. Or was he just being paranoid?

Late Nights, Black Moods, and UNO

The next few weeks seemed to fly by. The team pulled together in a way no one thought possible. The editorial and production teams geled into a formidable content machine. The final design the agency created for the site was stunning and one of the best Jim had ever seen. The tech team conceived a brilliant plan for allowing the Web site user to view personalized content based on a few profile questions, the answers to which were stored in a database and later used for the marketing department to design promotions, for editorial to create content, and for Luxbaum to collect demographic data. Not every bit of corporate culture clash had fallen away, and there were still turf wars simmering under the surface. The Luxbaum people had still not entirely assimilated into the group, but they were at least more conversant. Whenever a particularly nasty battle flared up, the antagonists would turn to Jim to make a call one way or another. Jim didn't relish being in this position and would push back on the people fighting and tell them to work it out themselves but to keep the big picture in mind. He would remind them there would be time after launch to try out alternative ways of doing something, but under the current constraints, whatever was easiest to implement should be the way to go.

The biggest win of all was the incredible increase in productivity that was desperately needed to meet the deadline. The last 30 days of the build saw nearly every member of the team working seven days a week and at least ten hours a day. Jim kept his promise to the group and was on the job every day from early in the morning until late in the evening. Even if he had very little to do in the late hours of the evening, he remained with the developers or whoever else was working late to demonstrate his commitment to the project.

During the last third of the build the days seemed to drag on and on, and not much progress appeared to be made. The team would drift into collective black moods of despair as the odds of them making the deadline seemed incredibly small. Jim was carefully tracking the project and knew they were on target to make the deadline, and he would remind people of this. He knew people were suffering from extreme burnout and fatigue. The developers had started playing "UNO" every few hours to give their minds and eyes a rest from the computer. Jim began to join in the games and encouraged others to as well. Soon epic games of "UNO" with up to 12 people playing would break out just when the mood seemed especially black. Often problems of a technical, editorial, or business nature that were hampering progress on the site would be discussed and worked out around the "UNO" table. The game became another catalyst for solidarity among the iLikeToDrive.com team and a friendlier forum for releasing pent-up angst and working out petty squabbles among peers.

Champagne and High Fives

As with any large-scale Web development project, the last few hours are nail-biting time, and the launch of iLikeToDrive.com was no different. The team worked around the clock in the final 48 hours to fix all the bugs turned up by QA. Jim and the team were exhausted but full of adrenaline as the lead developer launched the Web site templates and iLikeToDrive.com was born. The team made the deadline and in the process overcame personal and professional obstacles that had threatened to undermine the enterprise from the beginning. Now the team would concentrate on growing and maintaining the Web site but without the sense of urgency that had so dominated the last three months and had contributed to the group bonding so tightly. Jim was not sure he would remain with iLikeToDrive.com and very well might be called back to Greenwood to work on another large-scale project.

On launch day, amidst the high fives and the champagne, several members of the team told Jim they never would have made it if he had not had the courage to step up and lead the group without any agenda other than making the date and helping them all learn how to work together as a team. They thanked him for the atmosphere he had created and how he had helped them to keep their eye on the ball throughout the build. Jim was exhausted but very proud of his accomplishment. He had managed to bring the team together by listening carefully to everyone's position early on when the team was fractured and allowing for an open forum for people to voice their opinions and dissents and then begin a dialogue to solve the problems and collaborate as a team. Without the ability to collaborate and share an open dialogue, Jim never could have asked or expected the team to work the long hours they put in. His success was also based on in his determination and willingness to lead by example. Without the personal commitment Jim demonstrated, he would not have succeeded to bring together a team with such substance.

Summary

The disparate yet dynamic nature of a Web development team is one of the most fantastic aspects of doing this work. On nearly every team there is an often unspoken but shared awareness that the work being conducted is specialized, cool, misunderstood, and totally revolutionary. Highly organized and functional Web teams are a product of the very late 20th century. There is still no standard for the Web team in terms of members, titles, or functions, since these elements change from organization to organization.

To successfully manage a Web development team, the project manager should be familiar with each team member's role and contribution. Although not an expert, the project manager is a generalist but must possess enough knowledge to be conversant with each resource. The following list of specialists is representative of a "standard" Web team.

- Project stakeholder/client
- Project manager
- Producer and/or content developer
- Information architect
- Graphic designer
- HTML developer
- Developer

- Tech lead
- Quality assurance engineer
- Project manager

All of these roles require a different interpersonal approach to manage effectively. Learn the quirks that tend to go along with each of these roles to better understand and communicate with the people who inhabit them.

To successfully manage your team, you must become a part of it both in deed and in spirit. Show your commitment to the team whenever you get the opportunity. Allow your people the freedom to arrive at their own solutions in their own way; don't micromanage or force a solution you might favor over one of their own devising. It's what they're paid to do, so let them be the heros and collect the kudos.

CHAPTER 3

Communication Cues

If there is only one skill you develop as a project manager, make it the ability to communicate effectively. Without good communication skills, all the other skills and techniques associated with your position will be rendered moot. Communication is the very essence of your position and is what you do better than anyone on the team. Web development teams tend to be articulate, if not downright verbose. However, most team members can only wax poetic about their own area of expertise. Ask a developer to describe how the search functionality works, and you could be treated to a solid half-hour of eye-glazing technospeak. Ask the same developer why a chosen color palette enhances a particular piece of content, and you'll be treated to a series of grunts, coughs, false starts, and finally an indifferent shrug.

This is not to suggest that all developers are tongue-tied or clueless about design: There are plenty of erudite philosophy majors on the loose who have parlayed their sense of logical syntax into programming jobs. The fact remains, however, that for the most part, the experts on your team are paid to do, not to explain.

Among the definitions for *communication* provided by Dictionary.com, this one seems most applicable to Web project work: "The exchange of thoughts, messages, or information, as by speech, signals, writing, or behavior." Simple and to the point. The definition contains the standard methods—speech and writing—but also mentions the more subtle methods of communication—signals and behavior. There is one important fact to grasp as early as possible: You communicate as much through your body language, countenance, and general behavior as you do with your voice and documentation. The truth is, no matter how much you talk, write, or draw, the message screaming loudest in the team's ears is the one you are silently sending through nonverbal channels. Scary, huh? Think about it: You are the leader of a group of people looking to you not only for direction but for cues on how to interact with you, the project, and each other. The same is true for clients with whom you are working, who will be acutely tuned in to your verbal and nonverbal messages.

Communication: What It Is

Put simply, communication is making yourself understood by others. Presentations, e-mail, meetings, one-on-one conversations, even lunch—these are all venues for communication. Making yourself understood implies clarity and consistency. Muddle the message with ambiguity or conflicting body language and you are not communicating but confusing. If your message is interpreted differently by each person on the team, your project will devolve into an expensive game of telephone.

Communication is also understanding the messages others are sending you. If you are not clear on what a coworker or client is telling you, ask for clarification. If you don't understand an e-mail, ask for clarification. Asking for an explanation is not admitting you are ignorant; it's part and parcel of your job to be certain you understand details so you can pass along the correct information. Do not let a stakeholder say to you, "It's a business issue. You don't need to know about it." If your gut is telling you that you should know more, then press the issue and get an explanation, because the odds are, this very detail will be what holds up a launch and will cause a great deal of anguish to you, the team, and the client.

The Unambiguous Information Society

Communicating your message unambiguously means it can only be understood one way. Whether speaking or writing, do your best to strive for clarity.

Before you speak or write, examine the message closely for any ambiguities or potential holes that could lead to a misread. Obviously, you will not always have the luxury of self-examination before you speak or write, and in these instances repetition is the way to distill or parse the message to its essence. Repeat yourself, or ask repeatedly for clarification, until both parties get the point.

Strive to communicate explicitly. Overcommunicate if necessary. Continue breaking down your message into simpler and simpler terms until your point gets across. Questions and answers are the tools we use to establish clarity. If no one asks any questions at a meeting or presentation or after reading a specification, consider this a red flag. Chances are the point is not getting across. Clients, stakeholders, and team members count on you to communicate all apects of the project clearly and explicitly.

Distilling technical minutiae into clear, unequivocal language is a challenge for everyone on the team. Look at the following.

PROJECT MANAGER: "Does the system only check user name and password for authentication?"

DEVELOPER: "E-mail is the unique identifier for authentication in the system."

PROJECT MANAGER: "What about user name and password?"

DEVELOPER: "Yes. Those, too."

PROJECT MANAGER: "So user name, password, and e-mail are all used for authentication?"

DEVELOPER: "No. Only e-mail."

PROJECT MANAGER: "So a user can put in the wrong user name and password but use an e-mail address the system recognizes and get in?"

DEVELOPER: "Yes and no. A user can have multiple identities but only one e-mail address."

PROJECT MANAGER: "So what you are saying is a user could enter any old user name and password along with an e-mail address the system will recognize and get in. Right?"

DEVELOPER: "Yes, the user can enter any login they want, but if the e-mail address is not in the database, they won't get in. If the e-mail addresses match but not the user name or password, they will get a message saying the login is incorrect."

PROJECT MANAGER: "So, then, they can't get in?"

DEVELOPER: "They could if they enter a user name and password that matches what is stored in their profile."

PROJECT MANAGER: "So, then, what you are saying is user name and password are not the only fields being checked for authentication?"

DEVELOPER: "Well, actually, yes, but technically, no."

PROJECT MANAGER: "I'm going to shoot myself now. Care to join me?"

DEVELOPER: "Not today, thanks."

Did this dialogue make your head hurt? These are the types of discussions you will have on a daily basis. The goal of the project manager is to get clear, unequivocal answers to questions in order to write accurate documentation and communicate details to the rest of the team. Ask repeatedly for an explanation until you understand. Your head may pound, but the pain will be worth the effort.

Translation Skills

The project manager is an information processing center. Information flows in from the functional experts on the team, is processed, interpreted, translated, and finally passed along in language that can be grasped by people who do not have an expert's grasp of the subject matter.

Before you can communicate complex business, technical, and design ideas or processes, you have to be able to understand them. To understand them you must have at least a passing familiarity with the components of the business. The preceding dialogue between the developer and project manager illustrates how a project manager attempts to gain clarity from the developer. The project manager has enough of an understanding of the technology to be able to ask the right questions and to know the developer is equivocating in his answers. Project managers are not required to be experts in every discipline associated with the project, but they are expected to be at least familiar with each. By definition you are a generalist, not a functional expert. But in order to be effective in your role as chief communicator, you have to constantly expand your breadth of knowledge about all the components of the project and business.

The goal of translating information is to keep clients, stakeholders, and team members on the same plane of comprehension regarding the project progress, problems, and many details along the way. The knowledge level of each team member and stakeholder will vary widely with regard to specific areas of expertise. Because you have a basic understanding of each expert's tasks and specialized language, you provide a bridge of communication between the client and the team.

Nonverbal Communication

Be aware that the nonverbal messages you send can speak much louder than what comes out of your mouth. By the same token, being tuned in to others' nonverbal messages and body language can help you better understand your clients and coworkers. People communicate nonverbally via facial expression, tone of voice, posture, hand movements, gaze, and even wardrobe. A complete study of nonverbal communication is beyond the scope of this book, but we do want to touch on the basic postures and potential translations you will regularly face on the job. Table 3.1 lists the most common body language postures and the associated signal.

Body Language at Work

If you are the type of person who uses a lot of animated gestures to get your point across, you may consider channeling some of that physicality into

TABLE 3.1 Body Language Translation Grid

Posture	Translation	Accompanying Internal Dialogue
Staring into space, slumped posture, foot tapping, doodling, legs crossed with foot swinging, eyes downcast, buttoning jacket, glancing around	Boredom, impatience, ready to flee	"Why is this guy talking about database triggers to designers? I wonder if I can sleep with my eyes open?"
Leaning forward, feet under chair, open arms, open body, open hands	Eager, engaged	"Wow, project managers are so smart! I never knew database triggers were so interesting."
Sucking pen or glasses, stroking chin, ankle on knee, hand to cheek	Evaluating	"I wonder if setting up a database trigger is the best solution here?"
Nodding, blinking a lot, tilted head, steady eye contact, smile, arms behind back, open feet	Listening, attentive	"Hmmm. Seems like database triggers have something to do with the database. This is sort of interesting."
Arms folded, head down, frowning, hands clenched, slightly rubbing nose, face turned away	Rejection, defensiveness, disbelief	"How could this guy assume I need a 15-minute lecture on database triggers?! I practically invented them!"
Finger tapping, foot tapping, staring, rubbing hands,	Combative	"Who annointed this guy the world's foremost authority on database triggers? What a showoff!"
Finger pointing, leaning forward, clenched fists, frowning, standing with hands on hips	Aggressive, defiant	"There is no way I'm going to sit here and listen to this guy talk about database triggers."
Pulling ear, eyes down, glances at you, touches face, hand over or near mouth, shifts in seat	Lying	"How can I fool the team into believing I know how to create database triggers?"

verbal dexterity. Animated gestures and hand motions, while fine in non-business settings, can set people on edge in a meeting and suggest you are taking a nonnegotiable position on an issue. This can hamper input and exposes you as an emotional rather than rational person. Keep the gesturing to a minimum and maintain an open posture.

➡ KEY POINT

People tend to believe nonverbal communication more than spoken words because nonverbal messages are considered to be more "truthful."

The tone of your voice can betray your true feelings when communicating with others. Do your best to maintain an even tone of voice at all times, even when things get hot in a meeting or in a one-on-one conversation. It's okay for others to get steamed and display their emotions, but as the leader of the project, your actions, tone, and demeanor speak louder than your words. Your tone of voice can convey many emotions and states of mind, including anger, boredom, apathy, and sarcasm.

If you suspect you may be sending the wrong messages with your body language or tone of voice, ask a trusted friend working on the project to observe you in action and offer feedback. Learning to master the nonverbal messages you send as well as being a good study of other people's nonverbal communication can provide you with an enormous advantage in the give-and-take world of project management.

Character Communicates

Effective communication skills are closely related to other interpersonal skills like empathy, rapport building, active listening, honesty, and truthfulness. These skills and attributes equal character, and character is the foundation of a successful project management career. A much larger percentage of your effectiveness and success will be based on your character rather than on your technical skills. In order to lead, you must gain the trust of your team and demonstrate the type of character people respect and wish to follow. Striving for good character should not be a new concept to you—this is straight out of Life 101—but in the occasionally high-strung and melodramatic office environment, maintaining your character and a positive outlook is an achievement in and of itself.

It is hard to fully appreciate what the various members of your team go through on a daily basis. After all, you are not the one who sits in front of a computer and writes code for 14 hours a day, struggles to come up with an idea for a crucial design element in an hour, or has to test and analyze the final

Web site before launch and notate every bug and imperfection. In a perfect world you may have had all of these experiences before moving into the project manager role, but the chance of anyone being that well rounded is slim. Strive to continue learning as much as you can about each production skill set by reading, searching the Web, and especially, speaking to your peers. The more you know about each person's tasks, the better you can empathize with that person. Developing empathy takes one-on-one interaction and good, active listening skills.

Knowing how to listen will help you build rapport and establish relationships with your coworkers and stakeholders. Meet with your team members individually at least once a week during the project. Let the person know you are not looking for a status report but simply stopping by to say hello and to answer any questions he or she might have about the project. Your goal is to listen without butting in, editorializing, or drawing conclusions. Show them you are grasping the essence of what they are saying, but keep your own comments few and as brief as possible. Summarize what you heard, and ask them if your summary is correct. Not everyone on the team will be interested or even appreciate informal one-on-one discussions with you. Don't be offended—some people would rather work than talk.

The Web Team as a Melting Pot

Chances are you have people on your team who come from a culture very different from your own. Cultural diversity on the job is commonplace today. It can be very helpful to be aware of your team's cultural backgrounds to avoid appearing insensitive or just plain clueless about the differences that may exist due to ethnicity, religious beliefs, and geography. Be cognizant of the fact that things you take for granted, such as hand gestures, personal space, tone of voice, touch, jokes, or figures of speech, can mean something entirely different to someone from a different culture than yours. Working on a team with people who have different customs and religious practices can be challenging and even frustrating if there is a communication issue, but getting past the differences and learning to accommodate everyone on your team will prove fruitful.

Sensitivity and a willingness to accept a person's religious or cultural differences are essential ingredients for creating a harmonious, culturally diverse team. For example, if one team member is a practicing Muslim, he might require a longer lunch break on Fridays to go to the mosque. Religious holidays vary, so be aware that some team members may be requesting time off at different times throughout the year for observation of their holidays. Be sure to notate these time-off requests in your project plan.

If you are working with team members who are not native speakers of your mother tongue, take the time to make sure they understand what you are saying. This does not mean yelling at them in a loud voice: They're not deaf, and doing so only makes you look insensitive and socially unskilled. Simply ask them if they understand what you are saying and if you need to repeat anything.

Communication: What It Isn't

Communication is not arriving at the office four hours late wearing only a raincoat, jumping on top of your desk, and loudly encouraging everyone to join you in a chorus of "I'm mad as hell, and I'm not going to take it anymore!" Effective communication does not need to be so demonstrative. Communication is a controlled activity. Losing your self-control in any business situation will serve only to undermine your credibility, not to mention scare people. Being in control of yourself also means you are in control of the message. Two things you want to avoid are not having a good understanding of your audience's knowledge level on the topic at hand and being rude. The first one takes a certain amount of prior understanding about whom you are talking to, and the second is just common sense. However, both of these gaffes are common among project managers and, to be fair, just about everyone at one time or another.

It Takes Tact

When was the last time someone treated you rudely? Remember how it felt—that sort of shocked and bewildered sensation? Did you feel like working, helping, or even speaking to that person afterwards? Probably not. Being rude, no matter how tempting or even seemingly appropriate (and we've all been there), will only harm your good standing among your peers and the company at large. Even unintentional rudeness is harmful. Although you may not know you are being perceived as offensive, the effects will still be the same. Learning good business etiquette skills will serve you far longer than being up on that latest highly complicated technical advancement in search engine results prioritization.

IT people can be blunt—not out of disrespect or rudeness, but simply because they occupy a very logical, concise intellectual space. Bluntness can easily be interpreted as rudeness. Be careful about going directly to the point, be tactful, and be aware of your audience. People will react to how you speak instead of what you say, and the message could be lost. Being abrupt and blunt is not the same as being candid, even if you are delivering bad news or giving a dissenting opinion. Be respectful, and use diplomacy in every interaction.

Tactfulness is a skill you will call on in many situations, especially those where you have to critique a resource or even—heaven forbid—the client. Beginning a performance review with the phrase "You stink!" as opposed to a more tactful critique will not inspire the resource to improve but will more than likely result in disciplinary action being taken against you or a more formal complaint being registered against the company. Remember: Employees who are the victims of rude or aggressive behavior do not complain to the instigator but to the company—or beyond if necessary. Here are two simple techniques for criticizing tactfully.

- *Praise in public; reprimand in private.* This classic technique is foolproof and always successful in demonstrating your sensitivity and ability to be discreet.

- *Use the "pat and slap" method to deliver criticism.* That is, "Here's what you do very well. That's what we're trying to achieve: Pat, pat. Now, here's where you don't measure up to your abilities: Slap."

The following are some rude behaviors you should avoid.

- *Not returning phone calls and e-mails.* Letting your calls go to voice mail and not immediately checking every single e-mail is okay, but be practical in your screening. Return all phone calls and e-mails as promptly as possible. You know your own frustration when your calls or e-mails are not returned, so why perpetuate the aggravation?

- *Side conversations during meetings.* This is distracting to others in the meeting and rude to the speaker.

- *Interrupting someone who is speaking.* Sometimes it's hard not to jump into a conversation and cut someone off, but don't do it. Let people finish speaking before you dive in and beat them to the point or show off your knowledge on the subject at hand. Speaking in turn shows that you are listening, and your point will be that much more appreciated.

Know Your Audience

Gone are the days when the designer can also backfill for the developer and bang out some HTML to help meet a deadline. Web teams are composed of functional experts who often have no idea how to perform another team member's tasks. The project manager provides the translation services across the team and also between resources and stakeholders. The knowledge level of any given Web development topic can be drastically different from person to person, so the same message may have to be told in a number of different ways. Avoid talking down to or over the head of the people you manage and support. Understand the knowledge level of your team with regard to their abilities outside their area of expertise. As you learn about each person's general Web knowledge you will discover how to tailor your messages.

Don't expect the HTML developer to understand what you mean when you tell him values will be passed from template to template via both the OID and the query string. He may sit in the tech department, but his programming knowledge more than likely is not that of a developer. Explain the situation in terms people can understand. Often people will not let on that they have no idea what you are talking about for fear of exposing a gap in their knowledge or appearing clueless. If you see their eyes glazing over, it's a safe assumption you are leaving your audience behind. Readjust the message either up or down, depending on how much or how little is getting through.

It can be a safe assumption that the client won't know squat about the table structure of the database or why the database performance would improve by implementing stored procedures. But before you lapse into baby talk and start grasping for interesting analogies to explain the topic, first ask them if they are familiar with the process so you can gauge how much you need to simplify the message, if at all. It is insulting to be spoken down to or have someone oversimplify information. Check first to see how much or how little your audience knows about the topic *before* you speak. This shows that you are considerate and want to communicate in the most effective manner possible.

Communication Best Practices

Putting all your communications skills into practice takes time and acute self-awareness. The secret to success is being patient, both with yourself and with others. Observation is the key to learning how well you communicate and will help you decipher verbal and nonverbal messages your team and stakeholder may be sending you. But there are also methods and steps you can take to help facilitate communication and keep the information flowing unencumbered and undiluted through the lifecycle of your projects.

Best Practice #1: Plan to Communicate

Wrapping a plan around when, where, what, and how you will be communicating with your team and stakeholders will greatly enhance the effectiveness of your process. Consider the myriad methods of communication you have in your arsenal: documentation, meetings, e-mail, telephone, instant messenger, and hallway conversations. Now think about your team and what methods you can match most effectively to each person. Once you know which method would work best per individual, think about the group as a whole and what methods would work best for communicating with the whole team. Creating a communication plan is simply organizing your methods with the team on an individual and group basis. The goal of creating the plan is to ensure that useful, targeted information is communicated to all involved in the project in a sensible, coordinated manner.

Some project management gurus recommend creating a complicated document or spreadsheet to house your communication plan. The document is then disseminated to the rest of the team. If you have the time or are working with a very large group, this can be a good idea. However, most Web development projects happen at an accelerated rate and are accomplished with small teams. A formal communication plan sent to the whole team may be overkill and would add yet another deliverable to your already heavy load. Create a document for yourself to help you organize your thoughts and plan of attack. Because you will be the primary driver of communication within the team, there is no need to send the document to the team: It exists to keep you on track and help you organize your plan.

Creating a communication plan is not an exercise you will have to repeat for every project either. Hopefully the pool of people you draw from will remain somewhat consistent, as will the methods you use to communicate. The communication plan is a reusable document and does not have to be considered a milestone or formal deliverable in the project but instead is something you can spend time on early in the project, store in notebook or in a Word document, and refer to as needed.

In your plan, list your resource groups and the methods you will use to reach them and how each will be communicating status and issues back to you. Keep in mind that all methods of communicating are two-way, so be sure

Table 3.2 Communication Methods per Resource Group

Resource Group	Method
Tech/Design: Designer, HTML, Developer, QA	E-mail, instant messenger, one-to-one status check, weekly team meeting, issue log, project plan, specs
Operations: DBA, System Administration	E-mail, instant messenger, specs, issue log
Content: Producer, editor, copy editor, production assistant	E-mail, instant messenger, one-to-one status check, weekly team meeting, specs, issue log, project plan
Client	E-mail, one-to-one status check, weekly or bi-weekly status meeting, conference call, issue log

that, for every method you intend to use, your resources are comfortable using them as well. Table 3.2 illustrates the best communication method for the resource groups you will be managing.

Not all the communication methods you implement during the course of the project will be readily adopted by the entire team. Namely, methods that require the maintenance of a document by the group are the hardest to initiate and keep alive if your company culture does not already include these methods. Examples of these documents, and the most useful and commonly used, are the issue log and the change request form. Because maintaining these documents involves time and effort, some resources on your team will simply not comply with the use of these documents but instead rely on you to maintain them and show their relevance to the project. This is an unfortunate but common situation. It will be up to you to show how these documents will help move the project along and keep details from slipping through the cracks.

KEY POINT

Part of your communication plan will be the creation of documents, some shared by the team, some not. For each project you should create a document management system that need be no more complicated than a set of folders and files on a public server. Be sure everyone has access to the necessary documents as well as permissions allowing them to change and save the documents. Having a public folder for all the project documents will enable everyone's participation in maintaining the documents and improve the success of these methods of project control.

Best Practice #2: The Issue Log and the Change Request Form: Communication Tools for Control

Once past the planning/kickoff stage of the project, you will move very quickly to the control stage. Here, all your communication skills, knowledge, and tools will come to the fore. Two highly customizable tools you can use that will enable a great deal of control and allow you a wider margin for success are the issue log and the change request form. These tools alone can be your keys to project control, but of course, there's a caveat: Both documents require input from the team and therefore a certain level of cooperation and collaboration, which is both a blessing and curse. If your process already includes these tools and your resources are familiar with using them, then cooperation should not be a problem when you roll them out for use. However, if you are introducing these tools into the process for the first time, you can expect a mixed reaction from your team and varied results until the tools have been universally adopted by the culture.

It takes repetition and dedication to facilitate cultural change. The first few times you use these tools on projects you will end up maintaining them by yourself. This goes with the territory. However, by using the tools yourself and demonstrating how you use them at meetings—one-on-one and with the stakeholder—people will eventually come around and support them as well. Like any other aspect of process change, it's imperative to get management buy-in and support when introducing new tools and process.

Got Issues? Manage Them and Thrive

Issue management may sound like a job for a psychiatrist, but it's really a big part of what you do on a daily basis. As the project progresses, issues small and large crop up at an alarming rate. Most new project managers record issues as they come up in their ever-present notebook, and the issues are then dealt with on an ad hoc basis and prioritized by severity or threat to the project or project phase. This method of issue management may work for a short time or for a simple project, but it is also a recipe for disaster. Because the project is moving so fast, there often is not time to thumb back through the pages of your notebook, and issues recorded there last week, if not addressed, are now buried and forgotten, only to resurface when it's least convenient.

Formalize your issue management process with an issue log. This simple document is easily maintained and keeps issues where they belong: in front of everyone's face. You can practically manage a project with this tool alone. It's the perfect meeting agenda creator, project plan checker, and performance reviewer—all rolled up into one simple sheet.

In its simplest form the issue log contains the following fields.

♦ Name/description

♦ Priority: can be recorded numerically—1 to 5—or linguistically—low, medium, high

♦ Opened by: who entered the issue into the log

♦ Assigned to: who the issue is assigned to for resolution

♦ Date assigned

♦ Status: usually "open" or "resolved"

♦ Resolution: description of the resolution

♦ Date resolved

This document can easily be created in MS Word or Excel (we've included an MS Word version on the CD that accompanies this book). There are also more elaborate issue logs available online that are tied to a database and provide a GUI for entering and maintaining issue records.

Regardless of how simple or elaborate your issue log may be, the measure of its success will be how much it was used by the team. Be sure to introduce the issue log early in the project. Explain how to use the log, the benefits of using it, and where it can be found. Bring the log to every status meeting and use it to help focus the agenda of these meetings. You may find it necessary to create a separate log for each resource group: design, tech, business. While this approach means more work on your part setting up the logs, it will be easier for the team to use the logs, and they won't have to waste a lot of time searching through the topical records or entries. You could also create the log in an MS Excel workbook and devote a worksheet to each resource group. If you are on the techie side, you could even create your issue log as part of a project intranet and give the tool as much functionality as you see fit.

Once you have your issue log created in whatever format is appropriate to your situation, you must put it into practice. Let's take a minute to think about issue management and tie the concepts to the different sections of the issue log. Issues, by definition, are elements that need to be addressed and resolved or, at the very least, acknowledged. On a Web development project, issues come and go quicker than a computer virus delivered by teenage hackers high on PlayStation II. Your job is to collect and record these issues in a suitable vessel, hence the creation of the issue log. In order to communicate effectively via your issue log, you must clearly describe the problem or issue. The Name/Description field is where you will do this. Keep it as brief and succinct as possible.

Now that you have your issue clearly articulated, you have to give it a ranking with regard to its severity in the Priority field. Will this issue halt your project if unattended? If so, then mark it "high" or give it a 5 on scale of 1 to 5, with 1 being analogous to "low." Be honest when you evaluate issues. Don't give every issue a high-priority rating: This tool is used to capture and hold information and issues until they can be addressed, not to create panic.

All team members who enter issues need to complete the Entered by field so that whoever happens to be named in the Assigned to field can contact them for answers to questions that are bound to come up. This is how the issue log facilitates two-way communication and collaboration.

Monitoring the log is a responsibility shared by all, but the project manager monitors it most closely to make sure issues are being addressed. Assigning a date in the Date Entered field helps the project manager and others on the team keep issues from getting too stale and can serve as a reference for judging how resources are paying attention to their tasks. Another field that helps the project manager monitor the log is the Status field, which usually is simply marked "open" for unresolved issued and "closed" or "resolved" for issues that have been addressed.

Once issues have been resolved, it's good practice for the resource who addressed or closed the issue to write a brief note in the Resolution field explaining what was done to close the issue. This bit of information can help to answer questions that others on the team may have had about the issue and hopefully help prevent the issue from recurring. Finally, when the issue is closed, a date should be entered in the Date Resolved field. This helps lend a sense of closure to the issue and can give the project manager a snapshot of the duration of the problem, which can be helpful at status and postmortem meetings.

Communicating Change

The Web was founded on the principle that changes both small and large to Web sites can happen at the drop of a hat. While it may be true to some degree that making minor changes to Web sites such as modifying copy, color, and images can be relatively easy, large-scale changes affecting the layout or functionality of the site are still wrongly considered "simple" by many clients and stakeholders who do not understand the complexity of a contemporary dynamic site. Change management is a fundamental skill that calls on your ability to clearly communicate sensitive and complicated information. In addition to rapid technology changes that can impact the technical architecture or behavior of a site, business priorities and goals for a Web initiative can change almost as quickly.

The process you apply to functionality and design change requests and the communication techniques associated with them will depend on several factors.

♦ Where the project is in the development cycle

♦ The scope of the change request

♦ The impact the change will have on the schedule, budget, and resource allocation

♦ Your working relationship with the client or stakeholder

Be sure the client or stakeholder understands that the very early phase of the project—usually before the front-end design is signed off and the technical build has begun—is the easiest time to make large-scale changes. Explain what type of sign-off procedure you will have and what exactly sign-off means. How formal a sign-off procedure you adopt will depend on the size of the project and what type of relationship you have with the stakeholder—a verbal "okay" or an e-mail may suffice. However, if you are working on a large-scale project with a large budget, it would be best to formalize the sign-off procedure with sign-off meetings and signed documents that record all approvals and approval dates.

Change management is analogous to managing client expectations. The client or stakeholder will think nothing of requesting a change that he or she considers basic but in reality involves major modifications to the site. Most of the time you will know what impact a change request will have and if the change is really in the client's best interest at this phase of the project, if it can be done within the current budget, if it is feasible, or if it even makes sense. Your tact and diplomacy will be put to the test repeatedly as you explain to the client why a requested change cannot be implemented without the schedule or budget taking a severe hit. The most common tactic at this point is to recommend that the change be added to a Phase 2 of the Web site. This tables the issue for the time being and allows you to start collecting requirements for a second leg of the project. It also encourages the client's thinking to shift away from trying to wedge in major changes during this phase and to start looking forward to a second phase of the site.

Not all change requests are bad or harmful. Some ideas for changes crop up only after the site is past a certain phase, like the HTML build, and the change will actually improve the project. Don't be too overprotective of your specs and the project timeline. You and your team will be able to gauge the impact of the change and communicate back to the stakeholder what the change entails for the schedule and budget. If you don't know what the impact of a change request will be on a project, ask the resource who will have to implement the change so you can properly communicate and understand the scope of the change. Minor changes can usually be handled on the fly and don't involve a lot of formal process. However, be sure to record the change either in the project schedule or issue log. Larger changes that impact the entire scope of the project require more process and documentation.

On large projects establish from the outset how you will be managing change requests. Explain that change is inevitable and that there must be a formal process in place with a sign-off procedure as well to ensure the change is properly communicated to both the stakeholder group and the development team. A change request form should be used for large-scale changes to the project, with signatures of the client, stakeholder, and project manager. In addition to a change request form, a log of changes can provide a good way to measure and monitor time spent on changes to the original plan. Regardless of who requests the change, if it is significant enough, a change request form should be filled out. The form should include the following fields.

- Name of person requesting change
- Request date
- Summary description of change
- Importance of change (high, medium, low)
- Justification of change
- Impact analysis of change (time and budget)
- Resource assigned to implement change
- Status of change request
- Stakeholder approval

If the change is initiating from the client or stakeholder, it is still a good idea to use the form. Obviously the approval is implicit, but the exercise of filling out the form will help them think through the changes they are requesting, especially the Justification field of the form. You in turn will be able to honestly and frankly assess the change in the Impact Analysis field, and together you can decide if the change is necessary. Once again, collaboration and communication are achieved via documentation.

Significant changes requested by those working on the project are subject to the same request process, with the added process of having to make a case for the change to both the project manager and the stakeholder. It is your responsibility to ensure that the form honestly assesses the requested change and to properly gauge the impact to the schedule and budget. Significant changes need to be communicated up or down the line as soon as possible to mitigate any major impact to the schedule and to get the scope adjusted quickly. Before you schedule a meeting to discuss the change, be sure the change request form is filled out and has been disseminated to all interested parties. This will ensure that everyone is prepared to debate the merits of the change.

Project Control Tools   In the Chapter 3 folder on this book's CD, there is a simple issue log that you can modify to suit your needs.

Case Study: Peeling the Corporate Onion

This case study describes a project manager's experience as he struggles to kick off an e-marketing project in an enormous multinational corporation. Layer upon layer of corporate bureaucracy and poor communication across the company threaten the success of his project.

The Kickoff Meeting

My first visit to World Globe Consumer Goods (WGCG) was impressive to say the least. The corporate offices were spread out over several acres of land and the parking lot was as big as an average shopping mall's. Inside Building 7, where my meeting was to take place, the aisles of cubicles seemed endless. We passed conference room after conference room until we finally arrived at the room where our kickoff meeting was going to be held. Oddly enough, the conference room reserved for the meeting was barely big enough to seat 5 people.

My company, Online Marketing and Development Associates (OMDA), had recently been contracted by WGCG to implement an e-mail list management system that was to be used for e-mail marketing blasts and e-mail newsletters. The list management system was part of WGCG's Customer Relationship Management (CRM) initiative and was to be managed by the CRM group. The CRM group was newly formed and not fully staffed. The person running the CRM effort at WGCG was Joe Reilly; he was also the project stakeholder. Joe and I had met briefly during a conference call some weeks before, and this was our first face-to-face meeting.

The meeting was attended by Joe, an engagement manager from the WGCG IT group, an account representative from a strategy consulting company, a freelancer working with the CRM group, and myself. The goal of the meeting was to establish the production workflow for a weekly newsletter that was to be targeted to the consumers of WGCG's home-care products.

Together we created a production schedule for the first three months of the project that included dates for materials handoffs and approvals. In order for the mailing to run smoothly, every milestone would have to be met each week. Joe assured me his team would make this a top priority and he would be sure all the approval and material handoff dates would be met.

After the meeting I felt confident that we were off to a good start with the project and things would fall quickly into place. When I returned to my office, I created a project plan that included the dates we had established in the meeting. The plan was set so that on Monday of each week I would receive the brand promotional material from the account rep of the consulting company. The newsletter content would be based on the product or brand being promoted. On Tuesday I would send the HTML version of the newsletter to the CRM freelancer, who would then get the piece approved. Any required changes would be done on Wednesday, and the mailing would occur on Thursday.

If It Sounds Too Good to Be True, It Probably Is

The first mailing of the newsletter was scheduled to go out on Thursday, October 31, which was still three weeks away. Two weeks before the mailing date, the engagement manager from the IT group was to provide me with a list of 50,000 opt-in e-mail addresses for the newsletter. The delivery date for the list passed without a word from the engagement manager. I e-mailed the engagement manager to find out when he would be sending over the list but received no reply. After a few more days passed without any word from the engagement manager, I called Joe to ask him whom I could follow up with at IT to get the list of names.

Joe said he would follow up internally with the IT group to find out what was going on with the list and he would call me back in an hour. By the end of the next day, I had not heard back from Joe or the engagement manager from IT. I called Joe again and left a voice mail reminding him that I needed the list. The next day was Friday, which came and went without any contact from Joe or the engagement manager.

When I arrived at work on the following Monday, I had a voice mail from Joe on my phone. He told me he was in Denver for the next few days and would not be reachable but would be checking e-mail. He told me to work with the account rep from the agency on any outstanding issues for the newsletter. He mentioned nothing about the newsletter list. "So much for 'top priority' status," I thought to myself. I e-mailed the account rep and explained the situation and asked if she could help me track down the mailing list at WGCG. She replied to my e-mail immediately, writing that she would be happy to follow up on my behalf but she didn't know anyone in the IT group except the engagement manager, whom she had just met at the kickoff meeting, and she didn't have his contact information. I had been trying for days to reach the engagement manager without success, so I had to wonder why she thought she would succeed where I had failed. I gave her the contact info for the engagement manager and wished her luck, never believing for a minute she would hear back from anyone at WGCG.

To my surprise my phone rang 30 minutes later. It was the engagement manager from IT. "Well, hello stranger," I said. He seemed to miss the point of the joke and got right down to business. He told me the list was not in his possession and that I would have to work with DRED, the Data Request Engagement Department, which was located in Atlanta. DRED was where all consumer data collected by WGCG was warehoused. I would also have to coordinate the data request with the WGCG legal department. This was the first time I was hearing about any of this. I asked him why hadn't someone told me this information sooner? The engagement manager replied it wasn't IT's place to tell vendors how to request data but was instead up to the project owner. "Why didn't you bring this up at the kickoff meeting?" I asked. He replied simply that he was under the impression Joe would explain this to me.

Peeling the Onion

The engagement manager gave me the contact information for a data manager at DRED. I called the account rep from the agency and asked if she had a contact person I could reach in WGCG legal who would be able to help me with the data request. She didn't have any contacts in the legal department but said she would work on it. I then called the data manager at DRED. I wasn't too surprised when the phone was not answered and my call was sent to voice mail. I wondered if anyone ever answered their phones at WGCG. I left a message for the data manager asking that he call me back as soon as possible. I also sent him an e-mail requesting he call me to discuss the newsletter data request.

Later that day I received an e-mail from the agency account rep with the name and contact information from someone in the WGCG legal department. Obviously, the agency people had a little more access within WGCG than I did. I called the legal contact but, again, was sent to voice mail. I left a message explaining the situation and asking that he get back to me immediately. I began to feel like Alice falling down the rabbit hole. I was worried that once I finally did reach the person at DRED or the WGCG legal contact they would tell me there was yet another layer to drill deeper still before I could receive the data.

The following day the data manager from DRED returned my call. His name was Hank Snow, and he told me he would be sending over a form that had to be completed and signed by the project owner, WGCG legal, WGCG IT, and finally by me. Once they got the form back, the request would be processed "as soon as there was time to cut the data." He also mentioned that it was highly unusual for someone from DRED to actually speak to a vendor and that vendor data requests were usually handled by the IT engagement manager. I was tempted to tell Hank that the engagement manager from IT was the person who told me to contact DRED directly; but I sensed there may be some political issues between IT and DRED, so I thought better of bringing it up.

While I had been on the phone with Hank, Joe had called me and left a voice mail. Joe's message was brief; he was only calling to find out if the mailing was on track. He had spent the last two days at an internal marketing conference and he had discussed the newsletter with executives and managers from all over the WGCG enterprise. He said he would be back in the office in the morning and to call him then if there were any problems.

The Black Hole

The next morning I called Joe at his office. Naturally I was only able to reach his voice mail, so I left a message telling him we had to speak immediately. I had been e-mailing Joe every day with a status update on my travails with the e-mail list quest, and I had also been cc'ing him on every e-mail I'd sent that was related to the project. I assumed he had to be aware of the problems I had been having, but when he finally called back at 6 p.m. from his cell phone as he drove home he professed total ignorance of my situation. I briefly recounted my experiences over the last 72 hours and finished by describing my conversation with Hank from DRED.

He said this was the first time he had heard about DRED's data request process. I asked him if he had seen any of my e-mails or any of Hank's e-mails on the subject, and he said he hadn't checked his e-mail in over a week. I told Joe getting the data from DRED was the most pressing issue at the moment and I would appreciate anything he could do to help. I explained that if there was a delay in getting the data from DRED we were in danger of missing the delivery date. He said he would make it a priority and he would also get the form signed by WGCG legal. He assured me I would receive the data in time.

After I got off the phone with Joe, I completed my portion of the form and faxed it to him. I tried to picture the fax machine on the other end of the line sitting unattended and forgotten in some random, dust-filled cubby hole in the massive WGCG complex. I wondered if the data request form would ever make it into Joe's hands.

The following day I sent an e-mail to Joe, Hank, and the WGCG legal contact to let them know I had faxed the data request form over the previous evening. A short time later I received an e-mail reply from the legal contact. Her reply was short and to the point: she did not handle data request forms. Unfortunately she neglected to mention who in the legal department did handle these requests. I replied to her e-mail and asked her to please provide me with the correct contact in her department. I was not very hopeful I would hear back from her, and true to WGCG form, I didn't.

I then called Joe and asked him to verify that he had received the fax. He said he had not retrieved the fax yet and was running off to a meeting but he would be sure to take care of the matter later and get back to me as soon as he had the form. Despite Joe's assurance, I doubted I would be hearing back from him anytime soon. The rest of the day passed, just as I had suspected, without hearing a word from Joe or anyone at WGCG.

A Plan Might Help

Over the weekend I thought about what I could do to improve the lines of communication with Joe and the team at WGCG. I needed to implement a communication plan that would help me navigate the many layers of WGCG more efficiently. It seemed that Joe was always on the go and not able (or willing) to check his e-mail very often. I decided to begin trying his cell phone first before I called his office or sent an e-mail. If I failed to reach him on his cell, I would then contact the account rep from the agency, who seemed to have a much easier time reaching Joe.

I also planned to build a project Web site that I could update regularly. The Web site would provide a centralized and easily accessible location for all important issues and project updates that needed to be disseminated to the team. On the Web site I would create an issue log where all outstanding issues would be listed and assigned an owner and a status. The Web site would also list the contact information for everyone on the team.

I decided to schedule a meeting for Monday and invite everyone on the team to discuss communication methods and escalation procedures for the duration of the project. This was something I should have done from the very beginning. I should have set up a communication plan at the kickoff meeting. The first mailing had not gone out yet and already the project was in danger. I was a little apprehensive, however, because if it was this difficult just to get someone at WGCG to pick up the phone or return an e-mail, then scheduling a meeting would be nearly impossible. I thought the best way to make this meeting happen would be to call Joe and explain the situation to him and get him to agree to the meeting first.

Implementing the Plan

Monday morning I called Joe on his cell phone before 9 a.m. When he answered he seemed a little surprised to hear my voice. I had reached him as he was driving to work. I told him the difficulties I was having reaching him and other people at WGCG was endangering the project and that we should meet to create a communication plan with contingency measures if someone on the team is not available or does not respond to urgent messages. He thought it was a good idea but said this was not a good week for him to have the meeting. I pushed him a bit and told him we had to resolve this as a team as soon as possible if we hoped to make the first mailing date, which was in four days.

He suggested we do a conference call with the team at 11 a.m. He said he had a regular Monday morning strategy meeting at 10 a.m. and all of the people who were working on the newsletter would be present. He said to call his secretary and she would give me the number of the conference room they would be in and to call the conference room at 11 a.m. and they would be assembled.

At 11, I called the conference room number I had received from Joe's secretary. The account rep from the agency answered the call and said everyone was present and ready for the call. I started off by explaining how important communication is on a project of this type. I explained that projects with so many regular milestones and that require so much coordination between departments need a sound communication plan. I used the DRED data request debacle to illustrate how poor communication could sabotage a project.

When I mentioned the data request issue, Joe spoke up. He said he had called DRED as soon as he got into his office and told them to send me the data immediately and to do so without all the paperwork. He assured me I would have the data today. I was impressed with Joe's ability to get things moving at his company, but why did he have to wait until the situation was nearly out of hand?

I continued with my explanation of the communication plan. I first described how I thought I should be communicating with Joe. I told him about my idea to contact him on his cell phone before I tried his office phone or e-mail. Failing that, I would try to reach him through the agency account rep. Joe and the account rep both thought that was a good plan. The account rep suggested following up all important calls with an e-mail to her to provide a message trail. I agreed.

I then explained the project Web site. I had come into the office early and was able to build a simple Web site that included a project update section, an issue log, and a contact list. I gave them the URL of the site, and they were able to access it on a computer in the conference room. Everyone thought the project site was a good idea and would help tremendously with keeping people on track. I then asked each person in the group to tell me the best time to call them during the day should I need to reach them immediately, and I also asked for everyone's cell phone. I told them this information would be added to the project Web site.

We then spent some time creating an escalation procedure for issues that may arise during the life of the project—mainly missing deliverables or missed approval. Everyone contributed to the plan and seemed eager to cooperate, which made me feel like there was hope after all. I think it was the first time someone had tried to actually create a process around communicating through the various layers in the giant WGCG enterprise.

Lessons Learned

The communication plan we put together that day sounded great in theory but ended up being difficult to put into practice. As it turned out, the DRED data never arrived as promised and the first mailing went out a week behind schedule. Missing the first mailing was the necessary catalyst to cause Joe to send off an angry e-mail to the team in which he demanded everyone stick to the communication and project plan. What made things seem somewhat futile was the fact that Joe himself was the weak link. With his job pulling him in so many directions and the newsletter project being only one project of many he was responsible for, it seemed hopeless that things would ever improve.

Finally, after only two months, during which three more mailings were missed due to a lack of coordination and communication, Joe had had enough. He pulled the plug on the project. During the short life of the project, I had generated hundreds of e-mails and phone calls and only a handful had been replied to or returned.

The biggest lesson I learned on this project was just how important it was to establish a communication plan from the very beginning of a project. Also, I realized how important it is to meet with the project owner, face to face, to communicate how critical it is for resources in the client organization to be dedicated to the project. Without total buy-in across the organization and communication at every level, projects of this type have little chance to succeed.

Summary

Communication gets to the very core of what you do on a day-to-day basis. It's great to know a lot about building Web sites and the attendant technology and design, but if you cannot speak about the details in any kind of coherent and easily understandable manner, you are in trouble. Communication is composed of much more than just speech. The effective communicator will use all the available communication tools at his disposal to get his message across. These include writing, body language, listening, tone of voice, and even dress.

Because you are at the very center of the project and the majority of the information will be flowing through you, you need to know how to translate and relay messages effectively. For instance, the technical knowledge level will vary greatly from person to person on your team. However, each person on the team has to grasp how certain types of technology work and how it will impact her piece of the project. It's your job to explain this technology to each person in language that is appropriate to his or her level of understanding.

Clarity is your goal in all your communication tasks and responsibilities. Write clear, concise specifications; give clear, well-articulated status reports at meetings; clearly explain to the client why the project is three weeks behind schedule. Do not equivocate. Say what you mean and mean what you say. It won't be so much what you say as how you say it that will determine how people judge you—even when you tell them something they do not want to hear—like the project is not really only three but six weeks behind schedule.

Besides meetings and e-mail there are other tools you can use to communicate with your team, such as the issue log and the change request form. While these tools are integral parts of the project workflow and process, they are also important vehicles for communicating details. When embraced by the team and managed correctly, they can help keep a project on track and the lines of communication wide open.

The act of communicating during the lifecycle of a project is ultimately what you will spend the bulk of your time doing. It can be trying and difficult, but remember: Communicating is your most vital skill as you manage a Web project through to its completion.

THE VOICE OF EXPERIENCE

Tracy Brown is the former Director of Production at Red Sky Interactive and a veteran New Media producer who has worked on many large-scale development projects including altoids.com and sony.com. While at Red Sky, Tracy won the prestigious "Visionary Award," which distinguished her among her peers as a thought leader. Here she describes how crucial effective communication is to a project and offers some tips for being a better communicator.

How do you manage the communication aspects of a Web development project?

The key for me is, how much communication? You don't want to communicate too much, and yet you want to communicate enough. That's the biggest beef I've found in break-out sessions where people were either communicating too much or not enough. If a project manager sends everyone a 300-word e-mail every day about the status of the project, half your team at least are just going to delete it without reading it. People do not want really long e-mails, and people do not want really long meetings. People want short e-mails and short meetings. E-mail is not a replacement for meetings, and anyone who believes that is headed for trouble. E-mail is good for things that people need at their desks like lists of tasks or reminders: Remember to do this; remember to do that.

People need two-way communication in a group. It's not just a hub-and-spokes system with the project manager at the middle dispersing information to the other teammates. The project manager needs to get everyone on the team in the room at least once a week, I think, but maybe even more often, depending on how quickly the project is moving. And maybe it's subgroups and not the whole group, depending on how big the team is. But they need to have people get together in a room so they can communicate with each other and misconceptions that different people have about deliverables, roles, and so forth, can be aired. The project manager needs to be a facilitator of the meetings. It shouldn't just be the project manager talking the entire time. You know, it's important to get everyone to speak so people can hear what others are saying and thinking and assuming about the project. And brevity—cover all the high points. People are going to tune you out if you are going on and on or if they have to listen too much in too much detail about what the other people are doing.

Can you break down that idea a bit further, say, to the individual level?

I think individually you can't communicate too much. I think the producer or project manager needs to have a sense of each person individually on the team and how they can be communicated with. I don't think it should be "I am the producer, and this is how I communicate." They have to adapt to the needs and the style of each person on their team. So individual communication should vary greatly. I think the group communication should be brief and clear but with enough detail that all the issues are brought up. So the person who isn't inclined to speak unless spoken to or unless she has to speak has a forum to speak and to hear other people saying things. And the people who want to go over everything ad nauseum, which usually is the project manager—often that personality type—they have to be respectful that not everyone in the room needs to understand the depth of knowledge they have about every part of the project. I think status meetings are an important opportunity for project managers to also have a moment where they get to demonstrate their authority. They are running a meeting—it's an event, and they are running it. And they should have an agenda ready, and they should tell people how long the meeting is going to take. They should always start on time. They should always stick to how long it's going to be, unless there is some really good reason why not. And it's a chance for them to lead with the people getting to see them in that role but without being totally dominant—to be leading but in a facilitating way.

In these instances a lot of nonverbal communication is occurring.

I'd say nonverbal communication is a very positive thing. And one of the things that gets really compromised when people just use e-mail is you lose all that nonverbal stuff that makes people so human and more friendly. Actually working on a lot of projects where there are team members in different offices, I've found that the difference between having a team meeting and doing phone conferencing versus having a team meeting and doing videoconferencing is huge. Just to be able to really see people. And see their body language and get a sense of who they are as people just makes the other people on the team so much more inclined to be open to them and be flexible and feel like a team. If you just hear a disembodied voice, the people come off much more as "others," even when they are on your own team. And it's just so much easier to look around your table and say, "Well, this is us, I see us, and we don't see them, so they're not a part of us." So I think videoconferencing is really where it's at in terms of time and money if people are working remotely.

CHAPTER 4

Defining the Project

A *Web project* is a temporary endeavor that employs Internet technologies to achieve a specific objective by creating or enhancing a unique product. To qualify as a project, it must do the following.

- Produce a unique outcome or deliverable
- Be finite in duration, having a clearly defined beginning, middle, and end

- ♦ Require work
- ♦ Seek to fulfill a measurable objective

Your Web project may be the result of a corporate initiative originating from within your company or a proposal that has been accepted by a client. In either case, your immediate task during this embryonic stage is to define the project by assessing the needs of stakeholders and working with your team to draft requirements documentation. There are several key documents that will serve as a road map for your team as you set off to deliver Web development services.

The Creative Brief

Project definition begins with the creative brief. A creative brief is a work request containing a high-level description of the business objectives and functional requirements, drafted by a project stakeholder and used to initiate the project. The creative brief may consist of an accepted proposal or a form that project stakeholders inside your company are required to complete.

The purpose of the creative brief is to communicate the objectives and describe the major deliverables of the project, including significant features and deadlines. The brief should include business objectives, desired launch date, user profile, budget, project description, success metrics, a list of model Web sites, and a feature summary. Using the creative brief as a springboard, you are ready to leap into the murky waters of project definition.

Getting Started with Internal Initiatives

Internal corporate initiatives are particularly susceptible to the phenomenon of runaway requirements. This is due to the fact that true costs are often difficult to measure in the absence of rigorous employee time-tracking and profit-center accounting. Since the real costs are unclear, project stakeholders have little incentive to limit the scope of their ambitions. New project managers who are struggling to establish a process for handling Web initiatives within their organization usually begin by creating templates for project stakeholders. The creative brief is the most common of these documents. While the introduction of a creative brief template is a crucial step in gaining control over the project, it can provide a false sense of security. The creative brief is only the first of a series of documents that must be created in collaboration with project stakeholders.

Are you doing enough to manage requirements in the early phases of a project? What are the early symptoms of incomplete project definition? The

♦ Sample Creative Brief

A sample creative brief is in the Chapter 4 folder of the CD-ROM and on this book's Web site at *http://www.realwebprojects.com*.

This sample presents a thorough and concise description of a promotional book club Web site. Submitted by the marketing VP of a large publishing company, this brief shows the level of detail that can be expected after a project stakeholder has received some assistance from the project team.

Creative Brief

PROJECT NAME: Writer's Club Web Site
PROJECT STAKEHOLDER: Annie LePlume, VP Marketing, Book Publishing Company Inc.
DESIRED LAUNCH DATE: April 2002
DEVELOPMENT BUDGET: $500,000 plus $3,000/ month hosting

Business Objectives

This new Web site will provide visitors with the opportunity to achieve a very special goal: getting published in paperback. We expect this promotional site to do the following.

♦ Attract new visitors to our site through promotions with writers' clubs. For example, the XYZ Writers Club of America has 8,000 members who are specifically committed to getting their novels published.
♦ Increase traffic and retention on our corporate Web site through direct participation (visitors submit entries, read, rate, and review other members' stories) and due to the nature of the contest (new stories/ winners posted monthly)
♦ Increase minutes per pages
♦ Promote our brand as a leading publisher of fiction
♦ Attract high-level stakeholders and generate revenue in the $1 million-plus range
♦ Increase online book sales by driving traffic to our online bookstore
♦ Obtain newsletter sign-ups and add these users to our marketing database

Project Description

♦ The Book Club Web site will allow visitors to submit works of short fiction, rate and review one another's submissions, sign up for an e-mail newsletter, and share content with friends.
♦ Visitors will be encouraged to submit short stories (length 5,000–7,500 words), of which two per month will be chosen as a winner by a celebrity author judge or panel of judges provided by Book Publishing Company.
♦ At the end of six months, winning stories will be published in paperback as a collection of short fiction by Book Publishing Company.
♦ Each monthly winner will have the option to submit a completed novel manuscript for review; one of 12 complete novel submissions will also be published in paperback form.

Model Web Sites

The following sites have some examples of similar features with desirable look and feel.

http://www.ivillage.com/books/
http://www.amazon.com
http://www.writersdigest.com/

User Profile

The typical user will be female, college-educated, age 25 to 50, who is a frequent buyer of popular fiction. She will probably access the site from home. Her motivations for visiting the site include the desire to connect with women of similar interests, the possibility of being published, and curiosity about fiction created by women like herself. Detailed demographic data to follow.

Feature Summary

The Book Club site will consist of the following major features.

♦ Home Page
♦ Registration
♦ E-mail Newsletter
♦ Submit a Story

(Continued)

◆ **Sample Creative Brief (*Continued*)**

- Journaling Tool
- Editors' Publishing Tool
- Story Archive
- Read and Review
- Send to a Friend

Home Page

- When users arrive at this page, they will find a welcome message and a description of the contest with an introduction to the celebrity judge(s). The bottom of this page will also house a brief profile and photo of the last month's winner. We may also want to include a small photo of the judge(s), as well as audiorecorded messages.
- The rest of the page will be dedicated to related links.
- At the bottom of the page users will be invited to sign in if they'd like to submit an entry or read other stories.
- Clicking "sign-in" will bring the user to a registration page.

Registration Page

Before they can either submit or read a story, visitors will have to sign up and submit their e-mail, which provides them with a membership in the contest.

Monthly E-mail Newsletter

Visitors receive a monthly newsletter that does the following.

- Announces the monthly winner
- Introduces new books
- Presents book discounts and promotions
- Links to the writing center on our Web site
- Highlights the monthly deadline

Submit a Story

When members select "submit," they arrive at a Submit home page. This page will feature How to Submit, Official Rules, FAQs (with links to separate article pages where relevant), and a "Submit Your Story Now" button.

- Clicking the "Submit Your Story Now" button will allow the user to submit a story of 5,000–7,500 words via a Journaling Tool.

- After entering the story in the tool, they will arrive at a Thank You page. This page will offer links to read and review other stories and go back to the Book Club. Also, auto-reply e-mails will be sent to the submitter.
- Each submission will need to be monitored before being published on the site to confirm that there is no inappropriate content. Each submission should enter a queue, which can then be reviewed and either "accepted" (published) or "denied" (perhaps a form e-mail should be sent informing the party that their story could not be posted on the site). Submissions will all be read a second time by judges to determine the monthly winner.
- When the submitter is notified that the story has been posted, there will be the option to send to friends and family e-mail inviting them to come and read the submission.
- Winners will be notified via e-mail of their success.

Read and Review

- When members click "Read and Review," they arrive at a "Read and Review" home page.
- This page provides links to directories of this month's stories organized either by title or by author.
- Visitors will be invited to be a "Peer Judge" and rate and review the stories.
- There will also be a self-updating list of the Top Ten peer-rated stories here. Each story title will be a direct link to the story. These stories could be identified with a "Top Ten" icon at the top; this icon would serve as a link back to the Top Ten list page so members can opt to read all 10 of the Top Ten stories.
- Each story will have a Rate and Review option.
- Each story will have a Send to a Friend feature.

following scenario illustrates a recurring nightmare that may be familiar to you if your organization is new to the process of Web site development.

> The creative brief arrives as an "urgent" e-mail, addressed from an important project stakeholder. The message contains an awkward subject line: "Okay, I filled out your form. Let's get the ball rolling." The attached brief announces broad business objectives, includes a rough sketch of a home page, and displays a list of model Web sites with notes like "We love their color choices" or "We can do better than this, right?"

> You quickly find that your inbox is choking under a deluge of mysterious messages originating from remote divisions of the company. Each of these e-mails features a massive block of text in the "cc" line. With each successive reply, the names on the "cc" list grow like an alphabetic bacterium. The guerrilla lobbying effort of another inspired project stakeholder has begun.

> In an effort to drum up support for the project idea, the creative brief has been circulated to potential allies across the company. With each thread of the electronic brainstorming session, feedback blurbs are introduced by "my comments in CAPS" or "see responses below." Random feature suggestions appear, perhaps including a "peer-to-peer networking for sharing pet photos." People stop you in the hallway and ask, "When is the launch date?" The list of requirements is already out of control, and you haven't even announced a kickoff meeting yet! "Feature creep" begins to resemble an avalanche, and you're at the receiving end.

The next section introduces the project documentation that will help you seize the reins of runaway projects.

Project Documentation

Now that the project stakeholders have communicated the project concept and are asking your team to commit resources, it is time to roll up your sleeves and draft the requirements documents. The purpose of this extremely labor-intensive activity is to work with your team to describe the project. Table 4.1 summarizes the main documents that are used to define a Web project, as well as the chief collaborators who will be instrumental in their creation.

Several key documents are used to describe the characteristics of a Web site. Guided by a thorough needs assessment, *use-case scenarios,* and other requirements-gathering techniques, these documents capture the business objectives and functionality at the genesis of the project.

- ◆ Project charter
- ◆ Statement of work
- ◆ Wireframe mockups

♦ Content map

♦ Application flow diagrams

♦ Technical specifications

G   *Use-Case Scenarios*   Use-case scenarios are narratives that describe all the possible ways in which users interact with a Web site as they seek information or make a transaction. Use-case scenarios are explained in detail later in this chapter.

Needs Assessment

Needs assessment is an ongoing process that usually takes place in a series of formal meetings with project stakeholders. Regardless of whether these stakeholders are coworkers (in the case of an internal project) or external customers who are paying consulting fees, the goals are the same. The initial objectives of the needs assessment process are to address gray areas or omissions in the creative brief and to gather information that will be used to create the project charter. If the business objectives are unclear, address these first by distributing the creative brief to project stakeholders and compiling their feedback, while placing a time limit on the response. Allow dissenting opinions to be heard and evaluated before the features are set down on paper. Work with the project stakeholder to refine the business objectives. If your team includes a business or marketing strategist, their consultations will be crucial at this

TABLE 4.1 Project Definition Activities and Deliverables

Task	Collaborators	Deliverable
Assess Needs		
Define business objectives	Project Stakeholder Business/Marketing Strategist	Project Charter
Describe user profiles	Project Stakeholder Business/Marketing Strategist Information Architect	
List assumptions	Project Stakeholder	
Identify success metrics	Business/Marketing Strategist	
Conduct competitive review	Producer/Product Manager	
Identify model sites		
Draft project charter		

(Continued)

TABLE 4.1 (Continued)

Task	Collaborators	Deliverable
Define Requirements		
Create client wish list	Project Stakeholder Account Manager Producer/Product Manager	Statement of Work
Review technical feasibility	Tech Lead	
Prioritize deliverables	Project Stakeholder Account Manager Producer/Product Manager	
Draft statement of work	Producer/Product Manager	
Create use-case scenarios	Information Architect Producer/Product Manager Tech Lead Developer	Use-Case Scenarios
Draft wireframe mockups	Information Architect Tech Lead Developer	Wireframe Mockups
Draft content map	Information Architect Editor/Content Producer Project Stakeholder Producer/Product Manager	Content Map
Hold tech requirements meeting	Tech Lead Developer Information Architect Producer/Product Manager	Application Flow Diagrams Technical Specifications
Draft application flow diagrams	Information Architect Tech Lead Developer	
Draft technical specifications	Tech Lead Developer Information Architect	
Evaluate Risk		
List constraints and dependencies	Project Stakeholder Tech Lead	Risk Assessment
Identify technical risk	Tech Lead	
Plan contingencies	Project Stakeholder Tech Lead	Contingency Plans

stage. These specialists have expertise in applying Web-based solutions to the business problems of a particular industry.

Once the business goals are clear, hold a series of feature brainstorming sessions, but insist that each idea must relate to the business objectives and provide a clear success metric. You may feel that you are exposing the product to a cycle of endless revisions, but it is important to address feature suggestions early so that everyone will be on board. This will lessen the impact of the inevitable second-guessing that occurs at later stages and hopefully prevent radical changes in direction.

The desire to put the brakes on open-ended feature discussions or resort to the easiest solution can be irresistible for deadline-driven project managers. However, creative problem solving plays a crucial role in this new medium. Given the blistering speed at which new features and technologies appear on the Web, the "right solution" to your business objectives will rarely be obvious. This is the case even if your project team includes top business strategists. If you are fortunate enough to retain business strategists, keep an open mind. The record of business initiatives on the Web is littered with pompous whitepapers expounding on the virtues of debunked technologies and business models that were rendered embarrassingly obsolete in six months.

Top Web project managers make it their business to stay informed about recent developments and serve as a valuable resource for stakeholders. Be courageous by opening up the debate in these early stages and presenting creative suggestions. Do your homework, take a deep breath, and then take the lead by initiating a creative, open-ended needs assessment.

Here are some tips for conducting a needs assessment.

- ♦ Provide a questionnaire for project stakeholders that will help them to clarify their thinking about their new initiative.
- ♦ Solicit examples of existing projects that are similar, and then define the similarities and differences between existing projects and the proposed initiative.
- ♦ Define your terms as you go along (for example, "What do you mean by 'category' versus 'section'?").
- ♦ Communicate ideas visually with diagrams and sketches.
- ♦ Paraphrase/repeat back each important concept to demonstrate understanding of the issue, to clarify a point, and to reassure.
- ♦ Explore the project objectives at a greater level of detail than what was brought up in the creative brief.
- ♦ Find out what determines a successful outcome for the project and how this outcome can be measured.

♦ Ask the client to envision how the Web site will change over time.

♦ Solicit suggestions for future enhancements.

Needs Assessment Questionnaire   Open the Chapter 4 folder of this book's CD-ROM to find specific examples of the questions that you'll need to ask. The book Web site contains an updated version at *http://www.realwebprojects.com*.

The purpose of the needs assessment questionnaire is to assist project stakeholders in defining the initial scope and objectives of the project from a business perspective. Based on these core business needs, the Web development team, led by the project manager, can suggest appropriate Web-based solutions.

These types of questions are also used by account managers during the sales process to uncover the customer's problems and open the door to a solutions proposal. Rather than duplicating their efforts, you should try to fill any remaining gaps in the creative brief or accepted proposal.

The Project Charter

The purpose of the project charter is to obtain consensus on the mission of the project and establish the high-level expectations of the project stakeholders in terms of schedule and resources. Putting the objectives into writing helps expose any hidden agendas, misunderstandings, or confusion on the part of project stakeholders. Eventually, project owners will have to resolve priority conflicts by making difficult choices about which features to include in the initial launch. The project charter sets forth the guiding principles that will inform these choices, and it will keep the project from becoming easily sidetracked by one of the random suggestions that your client makes late in the game. When drafting the charter, try to avoid delving too deeply into specific features. The objective here is to justify the project. The project charter is usually divided into several sections covering objectives, scope, success measures, resources, and risks from a strategic or "executive" level.

Strategic Objectives

While it's okay to strike a high-level corporate tone in this "made-for-CEOs" section, do try to be specific. Avoid vague cop-outs like "The purpose of this project is to increase the value of our brand by enhancing our customer's experience on the site." You can do better by taking some time to ask probing questions of your stakeholders while you explore the following.

♦ The mission, which conveys the general purpose of the project

♦ The business objectives, which justify the project in terms of the overall company strategy

♦ The main deliverables, which define the primary outcomes of the project. These outcomes should present a solution to a strategic business problem, described in terms of what benefits the customer or end-user will derive from the successful completion of the project.

Scope Overview

A project must be finite in duration and produce a measurable outcome. While it is not necessary to anticipate each activity that will appear in the project plan, a summary of the top-level project phases should be presented in outline form. This section should answer the question "How will we know when the project is over?" It is also extremely useful to list major deliverables that are related to the project but fall outside the scope.

Success Metrics

The primary concern of project stakeholders is the expected return on investment (ROI). By showing sensitivity to this issue and presenting a plan for measuring results, you can manage expectations and be sure that clients appreciate the benefits they will receive from the project. Each major deliverable identified in the strategic objectives section should have a corresponding measure of success. Statistical measures of success are more meaningful if they are expressed over time (for example, will there be a sudden spike in Web site traffic followed by a gradual leveling off, or will traffic slowly build?). It may be necessary to include additional activities in the project plan to implement measurement technology like Web server log analysis tools.

Resources

This section addresses the overall expectations of project stakeholders regarding the budget, final deadline, and personnel. Although the project plan will provide specific details later, it is important to set the general parameters now. This section may include the following.

♦ Core project team roster with a brief description of roles and responsibilities

♦ Approval procedure for major deliverables

♦ Timing and format for periodic status reports

♦ Deadline for the final project deliverables

♦ Spending limit or burn rate, in terms of staff manpower and cash

♦ Project constraints and tradeoffs—for example, is the deadline a more crucial factor than the cost?

Project: Acquisition of JustAcquired Inc., a Health Content Publisher

Mission: To integrate the JustAcquired.com Web site into its new parent company by rebranding JustAcquired.com's content and integrating its major features into the parent company's Web site.

Business Objective: This integration of the JustAcquired.com Web site will remove a potential competitor from the market. Successful completion of this project will allow the parent company to enhance its market position by rebranding the content of JustAcquired.com and redirecting its Web site traffic to the parent company site. We will also achieve significant cost savings by the elimination of redundant or obsolete hardware and software as the hosting infrastructure is assimilated.

Main Deliverable: In order to provide for a seamless user experience after the merger, customer data and content from JustAcquired.com will be imported into the current database. This will create a single source of customer data for all of our marketing initiatives. The content database of health articles will also be consolidated in order to provide visitors with a single point of access to the content and product offerings of both companies.

Project Scope: The JustAcquired.com integration project will proceed in three phases. During Phase 1, some important content assets will be rebranded and migrated into the new hosting environment. Phase 2 will involve consolidation of the membership database and the relaunch of some interactive tools that will be salvaged from JustAcquired.com. During Phase 3, redundant hardware from JustAcquired.com will be decommissioned.

Phase 1 Summary
- Change logos on all content areas.
- Migrate message boards and chat system into the new hosting environment.

Phase 2 Summary
- Merge membership and content databases.
- Relaunch health care products shopping area with access to consolidated database.
- Migrate selected interactive tools from JustAcquired.com to parent company's Web site.

Phase 3 Summary
- Decommission JustAcquired.com Web servers.

Out of Scope: The scope of this project does not include the integration of JustAcquired.com's cobranded sponsors' Web sites. Each of these sites will be dealt with as a separate project, depending on how the sponsor contracts are renegotiated by the new parent company.

Success Metrics

1. After the integration project is complete and hosting redundancies have been eliminated, hosting costs for the enterprise should decrease by 30 percent when compared with combined, premerger expenditures.
2. We hope to increase subscriptions to premium health content areas by 30 percent.
3. We expect to increase our market share by retaining 50 percent of JustAcquired.com's customers as measured by increased unique visitors.
4. Total Web site traffic should see a spike of .5 million page views per month in the first three weeks after the JustAcquired.com message boards are migrated. Traffic should then settle down to a steady .25 million page views per month.

Resources: This effort will probably require a five-month coordinated effort among editorial, design, production, operations, and application development. The total cost estimate based on man-hours is $300K to $500K. An additional $100K in consulting costs may be incurred for the database integration tasks.

The Statement of Work

This document describes each of the project deliverables. In many cases, this is an expanded version of the original proposal that was presented to the client. Eventually you will ask the client to prioritize this list and narrow it down. For now, you can be generous by pulling a comprehensive list of deliverables from several sources, including the following.

- The original proposal or creative brief
- The client wish list that was obtained during needs assessment
- Additional features that have been recommended by strategy consultants or other experts

The format is contractual, containing a laundry list of items that the client will receive when the project is concluded. The statement of work (SOW) does not provide the implementation team with a blueprint or specification. Its primary purpose is to list deliverables, rather than describe the means by which they will be produced.

As the outline of deliverables takes shape, it is important to call upon a senior tech representative to conduct a brief feasibility review. The tech lead should draft a memo listing the major deliverables and providing a few comments on the level of technical difficulty that each entails. This memo should also include a brief discussion of the technologies and resources that might be

---

◆ Statement of Work (Excerpt) for a Streaming Media Player System

The contractor will design and develop a media player system (MPS), which is a system for entering, publishing, and playing multimedia across the client's Web site.

The MPS will consist of the following.

- *Media Database:* This database will hold all pertinent information to be associated with every audio and video asset that is published to the client Web site.

- *Media Pop-up Player:* The pop-up player is the interface through which the user will watch multimedia assets. It will display streamed media content.

- *User Media Preferences:* This feature will accommodate broadband users. The MPS will capture a user's streaming and bandwidth preferences and serve up the appropriate media based on those preferences.

- *Media Promotion Box:* The MPS will allow site administrators to easily add boxes to various pages throughout the client's site and permit content producers to publish content to these boxes using a publishing tool. The Promotion Box contains a link to the media clip that launches the pop-up player and promotional copy.

◆ Feasibility Review Memo

```
-----Original Message-----
From:    Tech Guru
Sent:    Thursday, November 08, 3:34 PM
To:      Anxiety Girl Project Manager
Subject: Feasibility Review
```

Hey:

Thanks for asking me to stop by yesterday's meeting with the client—I do think it's important for the tech team to get involved as early as possible in the process. Here are a few thoughts on the project.

So far, the features that were mentioned in the preliminary Statement of Work could all be handled by making some minor adjustments to the content management system that we built for the last job. No worries there.

One issue, however, was the client's request for an interactive trivia quiz that could be "syndicated" to third parties. At first I wasn't sure how to export dynamically generated results without requiring each partner to clone the trivia quiz and host a version of it themselves. We also talked about simply using HTML frames, but this isn't cool because with a framed solution the quiz would have our logo and other branding, etc.

However, I've taken a look at the latest Web Services XML technology, which provides a solution that could allow us to "export" dynamic results data in a platform-independent fashion to any affiliate. By building a standard XML interface to the trivia quiz, the client could license it on demand without altering the underlying code base.

The XML interface would sit on top of the quiz engine and extract the quiz results, transforming them into XML and delivering them to the affiliate. The affiliate would apply their own style transformation and display the results in their own hosting environment.

Although this will probably be a significant cost item, we can definitely do it since our developers have been learning XML. Also, we could develop it in a Win2K /.NET environment, which has pretty good support for Web Services and SOAP if we decide to go that route. Otherwise, we already have some great Java packages for dealing with XML.

Okay, so anyway tell the client it's cool and we can move forward. Let me know when we're ready to start writing the specs.

Joe Guru

brought to bear and identify any serious challenges that could derail the project. These challenges should also be reflected in the risk assessment that you will be drafting. Since this review is based on incomplete information, the memo is not to be shared with external clients. A simple e-mail will do.

Use-Case Scenarios

While detailed site blueprints and page mockups are a helpful starting point for designers and developers, the dynamic environment of the Web requires specifications that focus on functional goals from the user's perspective. A detailed inventory of buttons and widgets presented to a client for sign-off will not ensure success. As you begin to gather detailed requirements, use-case scenarios are a crucial tool.

➡️ KEY POINT

Web project managers should work with stakeholders to draft detailed require-ments, but a laundry list of specific features won't hold up for long. In addition to taking inventory of every checkbox and radio button on the page, project man-agers should focus on describing the "stories" or use-case scenarios by which suc-cess will be measured.

Use-case scenarios are step-by-step narratives describing how a user progresses through the application as he or she attempts to solve a problem. If your project team does not include an information architect, you may be called upon to drive this process. Seek advice from any experienced graphic designers on your team, many of whom will have developed a knack for information architecture as part of their design education and as a natural result of the page layout process. Once the process is underway, a tech lead should be brought in to provide early feedback on the technical feasibility of supporting the scenarios that are being tossed around during the meeting.

Begin constructing scenarios by referring to the original business problem that the project is trying to solve, rather than starting with the list of deliver-ables. By doing this, you may find that many features are actually secondary or even irrelevant to your users' needs. Design the site around core activities (searching for information, making a purchase, updating account informa-tion) and build outward to accommodate secondary needs (editing a shipping address, modifying a search). In your design, be sure to accommodate multi-ple browsing styles. For example, some users prefer keyword searching, whereas others prefer to "drill down" topic trees.

> *Effective Information Architecture*   If Frank Lloyd Wright had used Visio instead of canti-levered cement blocks, he might have been featured on the Argus Center for Infor-mation Architecture: *http://www.argus-acia.com/*.

Wireframe Mockups

Once your team has developed use-case scenarios and a corresponding fea-ture list, the next step is to draft functional mockups for the major pages of the site. These mockups are rough sketches—usually created in MS Word, Adobe Illustrator, or Visio Professional—which show the major interactive features and content on each page. Each major feature on the page is enclosed in a box that includes descriptive information. Once again, the information architect can play a crucial role here.

It is better to begin drafting the requirements around the user scenarios, rather than beginning with a high-level site map. This is because your visitors will experience the site one page at a time, encountering a slender cross section of the Web site depending on the scenario. As they follow the path of a particluar scenario, your users will be interacting with individual pages, not the "site architecture" as a whole.

If you are creating the wireframe mockups, resist the temptation to "design" the page. Produce bare-bones functional skeletons, not graphic design proposals. Keep your hands off Adobe PhotoShop, Dreamweaver, or FrontPage because you will inevitably spend time fussing over visual appearance rather than thinking about functionality. Any time you spend on layout will be wasted when stakeholders reshuffle features during the second round of meetings.

A far greater danger lurks in the likelihood that your amateur attempt to beautify the page ignites a passionate debate over aesthetics before the design team has even looked at the proposal. At this stage, the conversation must focus on function, not form. The discussions should revolve around "inputs and outputs," not color choices or layout. By keeping the mockups rough, no one will mistake them for first-round design treatments, and your designer won't be raising her eyebrows over the goofy stock icons you decided to plop into the page.

Don't Mock It 'Til You Try It   The Chapter 4 folder of this book's CD-ROM contains examples of wireframe mockups, application flow diagrams, and other scope documents for several different types of projects. These documents are updated on the Web site at *http://www.realwebprojects.com*.

Content Map

The content map (also called the "site map") is used to identify the major content areas of the site and define their relationship to each other. Start by sitting down with the content producers and taking a general inventory. Create index cards for each content area, listing the following.

- ◆ Name or descriptive label, as well as suggested alternate labels that will be meaningful to users—for example, "This Week" is more specific than "Features."

- Purpose of the content—for example, "An archive of articles organized by topic and listed in date order."

- Subject category or topics that are addressed.

- Related content areas and topical overlaps (for example, divorce law and personal finance).

- Related interactive features and tools (for example, a calorie counter tool should accompany diet articles).

- Parent and child categories.

Once this content inventory is complete, place the cards on a large table and arrange them in groups. Organize the content areas by priority (how well does each area support the business objectives?) and by content category or topic. Design a content category "tree" that illustrates the parent and child topics. As you document this process, be sure that the site structure will be compatible with the user scenarios that were established earlier. The final content map will be a collection of diagrams and descriptive notes, including the following.

- A flowchart diagram showing the "content tree"

- A detailed description of each content area, based on the index card exercise just mentioned

- Diagrams that follow the visitor through the typical user scenarios, showing which content the visitor encounters

Tech Requirements Meeting

The technical specifications provide a road map for the technical team to follow when designing the software that will meet the stakeholder's requirements. Technical specifications may be written by the project manager in collaboration with the tech lead or by a technical writer under the supervision of the project manager. The project manager is ultimately responsible for the quality of project documenation, so exercise care in delegating this task. The specs will provide the basis for the development team's blueprint, and they are the centerpiece of your overall contract with the project stakeholders.

The effort of drafting the specifications begins at a "tech requirements meeting," wherein the tech team reviews the full project documentation to date (creative brief or proposal, project charter, user scenarios, and wireframe page mockups). The purpose of this meeting is to identify ambiguities in the requirements and gather the information that will be needed to draft the specs. By the end of this process, you should do the following.

- Determine who will be drafting the application flow diagrams and technical specifications.

- Ensure that you have a suffcient conceptual understanding of the technical issues impacting the project.

- Identify the major components of the system (for example, "There needs to be a content database, a streaming media server, and a credit card processing system"). It is not necessary to come up with a specific solution (such as "We will use an Oracle database").

- Walk through the project charter, user scenarios, and wireframe mockups. Identify areas of ambiguity in the requirements and make note of them in an issue log.

- Reach consensus on a rough application flow diagram.

During this process, the wireframe mockups are used to guide the discussion and keep it focused on solutions to a user's problem. As the technical team walks through the various use-case scenarios, developers will ask for clarification and go off on tangents about the various platforms and software solutions they will use to solve the problem. Keep in mind that this is not intended to be a full "technical design" or "tech brainstorming meeting." The purpose of this meeting is to gather information in order to write the final technical specifications and deliver them to the client for approval.

Application Flow Diagrams

The page-by-page experience of the user has been established, and now it's time to take a bird's-eye view of the application as a whole. The application flow diagram helps the tech team envision how each individual page is linked together and what behind-the-scenes components will come into play from the middle tier and back end. These system components might include login authentication, a third-party payment processing system, or a product database. The application flow diagram should display each page in a flowchart format and address the architecture of the system as a whole. The point of this exercise is to produce a list of all the major system components and a schematic diagram showing how the parts relate to each other.

Application flow diagrams can follow a "decision tree" layout, where the reader follows arrows through the path of a scenario. Figure 4.1 illustrates a simple application flow diagram for displaying content, stored in XML format, that is pulled from a database and published to a Web page. This diagram uses a three-tier format, with each system component appearing in its respective column.

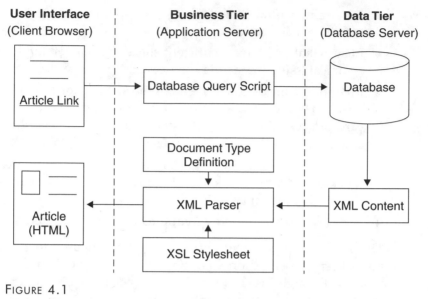

FIGURE 4.1
Application Flow Diagram for a Dynamic News Article

Technical Specification

The technical specification is the glue that holds together the flowcharts, functional mockups, and other evidence of the frustrated draftsman inside you. Since you didn't follow your dad's advice to become an architect, instead taking a job with an interactive agency, you'll need another document to explain all of those lines, boxes, and mysterious Visio icons. The purpose of the technical summary is to provide the tech team (and the client) with a detailed description of what each technical requirement is and how it will be addressed. The technical summary may include the following.

♦ Hyperlinks to all project documentation, on an intranet or other project Web site

♦ The current state of the system

♦ A summary of the major technical requirements, "stories," or user scenarios

♦ A summary of any feasibility studies or discussions

♦ A site overview listing of all the important technical components with a brief description of each

♦ A taxonomy, or definition of terms—for example, "Parent Category refers to the content category node that resides one level up in the tree from the category in question—for example, 'respiratory problems' is the parent category for asthma."

♦ Performance requirements for databases and Web servers (such as how much data will be stored in the database, estimated Web site traffic)

♦ A description of the hosting environment

♦ A detailed description of each important feature within the application

♦ An outline of plans for future technical enhancements

Technical Specifications—Let's Get Visual   As graphic designs are created, use PhotoShop to include cropped selections from these designs in your specifications. By accompanying your text explanations with selections from actual screenshots, you will avoid a great deal of confusion ("Uh, which search box are you talking about? There are three of them on the page!"). A fine example of this technique awaits you in the Technical Specifications folder under Chapter 4 of the CD-ROM. (An updated version is maintained on the book Web site: *http://www.realwebprojects.com*.) These specifications, created for a content portal, showcase highly detailed descriptions with accompanying snapshots from the design.

Project Risk Assessment

Most Web projects don't come with insurance policies other than general contractor "errors and omissions," so you'll have to roll your own. Project risk may be addressed within the project charter or in a separate evaluation. Risk assessment documents for Web projects usually touch on three points.

♦ Dependencies

♦ Technical risks

♦ Contingencies

The first step in risk management is to identify the potential dangers that lie ahead. When drafting this part of the document with your project team, summarize the risk areas at the project level. Start with dependencies, identifying any other initiatives that might impact this project. Find out if there are any other projects that must be completed before this project can begin. For technical risk areas, focus on the final deliverables and any uncertainties that surround them. The tech lead can assist you in determining whether the requirements fit within your project teams' core competencies. Contingency plans propose an alternative course of action should problems arise. They

♦ Sample Risk Assessment and Contingency Plan

Dependencies: The following dependencies will affect the migration of editorial content from JustAcquired.com to the parent company's Web site.

1. For the next three months most editorial staff will be working on the content archiving project, which will reduce the amount of time that they can spend on reviewing and editing the new content.

2. Technology consultants must finish the database upgrade before editorial staff can begin entering new content into the publishing system.

The following technical and other risk areas may impact the deadline for content migration from JustAcquired.com.

1. There may be database integration issues that may delay the data port from Informix into Oracle.

2. The amount of content that will be migrated is uncertain until the audit of JustAcquired.com is completed.

3. The legal department must approve some content migration due to content syndication licensing.

4. There has been a high turnover in the editorial group due to staff cuts.

Contingency Plan

1. Freelance editorial assistants may be brought in to perform copyediting and content entry tasks.

2. Database administrators can be pulled from certain lower-priority projects to assist in the data migration.

3. A short list of must-have content areas is being prepared.

usually contain provisions for outsourcing and a list of "B-list" requirements that can be pushed back to later phases if necessary.

Case Study: Defining the Project with HTML "Shells"

In the winter of 2001, SeaState Internet Solutions was commissioned to develop an online testing system for Adkins Matchett & Toy Ltd., which trains investment banking professionals. This educational software would allow the firm to administer assessment examinations for Wall Street financial analysts, whom the firm trains in accounting, math, and other financial topics. The online system would be used by the course administrators to set up student accounts and run reports on student scores by company, class, and exam. Students would use the system to log in and take the exams, which were delivered in various formats ranging from multiple choice to free-form numeric answers. Student exams were automatically scored and linked to study materials, depending on their answers. The exam reports used graphical bar charts that indicated what topics students had difficulty with, as well as their individual performance. Corporations whose employees were participating in the seminars could log on to the system to track the performance of their trainees. The entire system, including the student exams and the instructor administration, would be accessible on the Web.

Road Map for a Virtual Team

Since SeaState Internet Solutions is a small development shop, it employed virtual teams of freelance consultants. The necessity of outsourcing portions of the job to remote staff made the written specifications absolutely crucial to success. These remote developers required a crystal-clear blueprint as they worked from their offices in Dallas and Washington, D.C. An additional challenge was that the three project stakeholders were busy professionals who split their time between New York and London providing hands-on seminars to investment bankers.

Ponderous Plans

Anxious to meet the financial industry's high standards, the project manager at SeaState spent a great deal of time drafting detailed descriptions of every feature. While the reams of documentation were valuable for the offsite developers, they did little to address the concerns of the busy project stakeholders. Once the basic feature set had been agreed upon, the client's primary consideration was usability: Would students, corporate training managers, and course administrators find the system intuitive and easy to use?

Flat design mockups and storyboards didn't provide the answer. The system was being built in a Microsoft Windows 2000 environment, with a high-end SQL Server 2000 database. Consequently, the budget did not allow for the creation of working prototypes, which would have required an upfront investment in the exam database, which was the most expensive deliverable. The clients were finance instructors whose time was scarce. They certainly didn't have the leisure time or the inclination to sift through the technical specifications and "imagine" how the application would feel to its demanding end-users. Since most online learning tools were proprietary licensed products, there were few publicly accessible examples that could serve as a model.

Seeing It in "Shells"

The solution required a demo format that was a cut above wireframe mockups and a step below a real working prototype. In response, the information architect revisited his HTML skills, converting the page designs for the exam administrator's area into a static simulation (see Figure 4.2). This demo was built entirely in HTML and populated with "dummy" data. The demo was simply a dressed-up facade, or "shell," of the original. This approach is analogous to the construction of a fake Hollywood movie set that simulates the real "look and feel" experience without the construction costs. By using an HTML skeleton, the clients could quickly walk through the application, playing with the drop-down menus and running fake exam reports. The shell was a big hit with the client, who was able to suggest a variety of feature and usability improvements that would have been difficult to make later in the project.

FIGURE 4.2
Administrator's Bar Chart Report, DirectTesting.com
Source: Screen capture copyright © Adkins Matchett & Toy, Ossining, NY. Used with permission.

The technique of using HTML mockups to demo a feature was not new to the project team. However, HTML mockups were not normally shown to the client until well after the production phase was underway. In this instance, the shell was not simply showcasing a feature in the specs. Indeed, after several iterations the shell had become the cornerstone of the specification.

In many ways this highly realistic simulation was superior to the written documentation, in that it was closer to the code and visually communicated all of the features. Since it was built in HTML, it was easy to change and didn't require a staging server or other technical development environment. The project manager decided to use the final version of the shell as the authoritative specification, with the written documentation provided as a supplement for the use of the developers. The URL of the HTML simulation was referenced in the contract for the development phase. The clients felt reassured as the cloud of mystery surrounding the 18-page specification evaporated to reveal something that they could see and touch.

Summary

Depending on your role, background, and expertise, you may be called upon to shape the product by providing creative input into the requirements documentation. While this can be a satisfying part of the job, you will be most effective if you can act as a humble facilitator. Use your active listening skills to draw the project requirements out of stakeholders and encourage the experts on your team to describe their vision of the solution. If you are fortunate, your organization may employ a technical writer to do the heavy lifting, but ultimately the project documentation is your best safeguard against the risks that lie ahead. Consequently, you should undertake an intense, personal involvement in their creation and dissemination. The production and stewardship of requirements documentation is one of your core responsibilities.

Defining the project is the first important step toward a successful launch. However, as soon as you have enshrined the project requirements on paper, the forces of change will begin to act against your fixed set of features. Changing technology, business objectives, client demands, and other factors can easily render your blueprints obsolete. In the next chapter, we will explore innovative techniques for navigating your way through the inevitable sea of changes.

CHAPTER 5

Managing Change

The *scope* of a project is the set of affordable systems and software that the project team has agreed to deliver.

Defining and managing scope is one of your most important responsibilities. By the end of this chapter, you will have the answers to these three important questions about scope:

1. What are the standard techniques for defining and controlling scope?
2. Why do the standard techniques seem to fail for most Web projects?
3. What are the latest best practices that seem to work for the Web?

A New Perspective on Scope

Most standard models for software development assume a fixed scope that can be clearly defined at the outset of a project before any work begins. This presents a problem, since Web sites constantly evolve in a changing technological and business environment. In this chapter you'll learn to look at scope organically, as a collection of requirements that need to be described, documented, and managed as they grow. We'll also examine processes that embrace change through the use of *iteration*. These newer approaches allow the requirements to evolve through a series of small releases, showing early results and incorporating client feedback during production.

G   *Iteration*   The process of making incremental refinements to software. The product gradu-ally evolves in a series of working prototypes. These prototypes incorporate client feed-back into each release cycle.

During its initial stages, scope definition is analogous to a legal agreement between two parties. As you draft the first round of requirements documents, your goal is to create a "contract" between yourself and the project stake-holders, in which you agree on the features of the site you are about to build. The key to success is defining what you intend to deliver and how you plan to deliver it while obtaining the client's consent before implementation begins. Once work has begun, the project documentation will grow and change with each iteration of the product. Project management theorists have come up with a standard methodology to guide you through this process.

Classic Scope Control

Standard software development models are requirements-driven: They as-sume that the project team will be delivering a final product with characteris-tics that can be clearly defined up front. These methodologies provide a disciplined, sequential process for defining the schedule, budget, resources, risks, and scope. For the sake of simplicity, let's assume a representative process with four stages: Define, Implement, Control, and End (DICE). The hypothetical "DICE" approach has a few distinguishing characteristics.

- ♦ *Define.* All project requirements should be captured in the Define stage. The output of the Define stage is the project plan. The ap-proved plan includes the scope, budget, and schedule. Project work is broken down into a hierarchy of phases, activities, and tasks. The plan serves as a contract between the project manager and the project sponsor. The purpose of this contract is to commit the project team to the terms of the plan. The plan should capture as much detail as pos-sible, and it must be complete before implementation begins.

- ♦ *Implement.* Once the schedule of deliverables has been set, Imple-mentation begins. During Implementation, the project manager assembles and deploys the resources (people, hardware, and software) that are needed to deliver what was agreed on during the Define stage.

♦ *Control.* During the Control stage, the project manager monitors and reviews the project team's progress against the schedule of deliverables. The project manager also resists the introduction of changes into the plan.

♦ *End.* At the End, the product is released. Project success is measured by comparing the final results to the original set of requirements. If the project team delivered against the original specifiations on time and within budget, the project is deemed a success. Project failure is usually attributed to scope changes on the part of the client or inaccurate effort estimates up front. This analysis is used to make more accurate effort estimates in the future.

Figure 5.1 illustrates this generic software development process. This diagram is a simplified representation of the "classic" approach, which has been adapted to the Web.

Classic software development processes were designed to hit a fixed target. Unfortunately, the Web presents a moving target, as business models

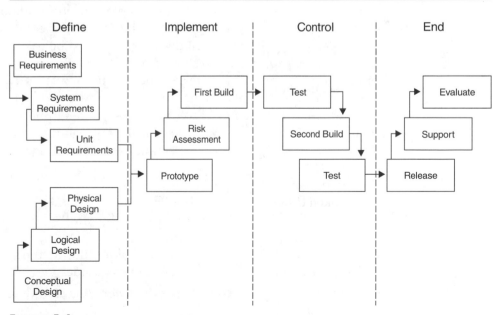

FIGURE 5.1
DICE Software Development Lifecycle

♦ **The Standard**

It is difficult to identify a "canon" of software development methodology, but a few heavy hitters set the bar for industry standards:

Guide to the Project Management Body of Knowledge (PMBOK®), 2000 Edition. Newtown Square, PA: Project Management Institute, 2000.

McConnell, Steve. *Software Project Survival Guide: How to Be Sure Your First Important Project Isn't Your Last.* Redmond, WA: Microsoft Press, 1997.

Rational Unified Process®: The RUP is a Web-enabled set of software engineering best practices. RUP is used today by many organizations that develop e-business applications. See *http://www.rational.com.*

and implementation technologies are reinvented at an exhausting pace. In spite of this mismatch, the majority of current best practices in use by Web project managers today are inherited from this classic model.

The Project Web Site—Getting Everyone on the Same (Home) Page

Document and version control is essential to scope management. If your team can't easily access the latest project documentation, they cannot know the scope of your project. Once your requirements documentation has been created, it needs a home. Important documents should be easily accessible to all members of the project team. As the scope of the project evolves, "Who has the latest version?" becomes a very popular question! A project Web site should contain links to all of the latest project documentation, upcoming milestones, and the date of the most recent updates. As the project manager, you should maintain the project Web site, which will solidify your role as the "chief librarian" for all project documentation. Here are a few tips.

- ♦ Use a file-naming convention that includes author, version, and date.
- ♦ Only one person should be responsible for maintaining the most recent copy of a document and uploading it to the site. (That means *you!*)
- ♦ Do not be lazy by simply overwriting older files with new ones. Be disciplined about keeping backup copies of older versions.
- ♦ Provide links to an archive of previous versions as well as the most recent version.

◆ Project Web Sites Made Easy

Maintaining and updating the content on your project Web site can turn you into an HTML slave. Avoid the headache by using Web logs. "Blogs" are free, easy-to-use, customizable publishing tools that can be placed directly on your own Web server or used as a third-party service (*http://www.blogger.com*).

Several service providers offer customizable project extranets at low cost or even free of charge! Two of them are:

◆ eProject Express (*http://www.eproject.com*)
◆ Intranets.com (*http://www.intranets.com*)

- ◆ Provide multiple file formats for project team members who do not have Visio, MS Project, or other software. For example, export Visio diagrams as .GIF files. Export MS Project documents in Excel. Specify the file format and file size alongside the hyperlink.

- ◆ Upload meeting notes and status reports in addition to the usual project documentation.

- ◆ Include a project team roster with contact information (including instant messenger handles), titles, and a brief description of each person's roles and responsibilities on the team.

- ◆ Use a Web log system like Blogger (*www.blogger.com*) to make the job of updating content on the site easier.

- ◆ Include links to the various rounds of graphic design mockups, prototypes, and demos in addition to technical documentation.

Managing Scope Change

There are several change management techniques you can employ to avoid an adversarial relationship with the project sponsor.

The Project Triangle—Scope, Schedule, Resources

A cornerstone of the project manager's role is to ensure that stakeholders understand the tradeoff between scope, schedule, and resources. Tact, diplomacy, and good negotiating skills will go to waste if the client does not understand where their project sits along these three axes. The customer must be able to articulate which legs of the constraint triangle she is willing to change

◆ **Point–Counterpoint: Stakeholder Tradeoffs**

When confronting the unforgiving tradeoffs of the project Triangle, always be a polite problem solver. You should be assisting stakeholders to navigate through difficult choices. Compare these two reactions to a change order that was issued late in the project.

"As the project manager it is my duty to inform you that we just can't cram this feature in and still make the deadline. It's entirely your choice, but if we issue this change order, there is no way my team can hit the deadline. We can't commit to the date if you really want to have this new feature. I must be frank and up front about this so your expectations will be in line with reality. The other option is to add this feature to Phase 2, which I strongly recommend. We can also hire additonal consultants, but you must decide that you're willing to waste

$20,000. We'll need a decision within two days so we can revise the project plan."

"Yes, we certainly can build this feature! I've read the description, and I think I understand what you're asking for. In order to build it we'll all have to make some tough decisions. The work that this new feature requires would push us over the deadline, given our current staffing. One solution is to bring additional consultants on board. I ran this scenario on the project plan, and this option adds about $20,000 to the development fees. Optionally, we can move this feature into Phase 2. I suggest that we all sit down and make a list of the consequences that might result from pushing back the deadline. Then we'll measure these against the benefits of having this feature in Phase 1 and consider the budgetary impact of the $20,000."

and understand their interdependence. This is a communication challenge that must be met with careful education and reinforced at every opportunity. Rather than being the "project policeman," a more effective approach is to assume a helpful "consulting" role that lasts throughout the duration of the project. As the helpful consultant, you assist the project stakeholders in navigating all sides of the project triangle.

Getting Project Documents Approved by the Client

As you collaborate with the project team to draft all of the requirements, you will also have to get those documents approved by your client, who will try to squeeze as much work as possible out of your team. The tug-of-war begins as soon as you post the first page mockups to the project Web site. Your new client may drag your team toward defeat by adding features while the deadline remains fixed. Other clients try to cut costs by haggling over every detail as they try to wring a few extra hours out of your overworked developers, or perhaps the first draft page mockups have launched the client into a brainstorming hurricane that spins aimlessly with no end in sight. Threatening to quit seems like a good option, but you'll have better luck scheduling a priorities meeting and applying a few time-tested techniques.

The Chinese Take-Out Menu Approach

A common approach to obtaining sign-off is to help the project stakeholders prioritize features. Once you have all of the decision makers in the room, pull out a complete "wish list" summarizing all of the features that have been suggested. Ask everyone to prioritize the list. If the room explodes into a frenzied debate, add structure by having each stakeholder work independently. After everyone has ordered his or her own list, ask them to present their list to the group with the reasons for their selections. As the group moves toward consensus, priority conflicts will emerge. The debate over some features will become deadlocked, and stakeholders will ask for more information about cost. When you hear "I can't decide—it depends which one is cheaper," then it's time to add the price column to your Chinese take-out menu.

Now that you have the prioritized list and you've taken note of the deadlocked or "tied" combinations, you can bring on the implementation team. Use a flip chart or white board and create two columns, one for time and the other for money. Don't provide actual figures in terms of days or dollars, since this information could compromise your negotiations with the client. Simply assign a scale of 1 to 5, from low cost to high cost. Determine which lower-priority features may be bundled with higher-priority features—for example, "If we decide to provide online music samples, then we can also include the film clips at minimal extra cost because they both use the same streaming media server."

During this discussion, be careful to recognize the intrinsic value of software that you may be repurposing, as well as the "sunk costs," R&D, and other up-front investments that were poured into your technology infrastruture. Just because you've built a highly scalable solution that only takes an hour to adapt, it does not mean that the software is only "worth" an hour of a developer's time.

As you make progress, take a moment to introduce the concept of "Phase 2." Some of the riskier features may require a proof-of-concept or prototype. Consider developing "pilots" to test the business validity of a feature. Take baby steps. Create an e-mail newsletter campaign as a one-off, and send it to a small target list of customers before investing in the million-dollar publishing interface. Build a long-term relationship with your client through a series of small successes, and avoid the disastrously expensive "white elephant" or "Maginot Line" projects that become legendary failures.

The "Surgeon" Analogy

Cost is naturally a major roadblock to getting a client to approve a set of features. The "surgeon" analogy is a technique for helping the project stakeholder understand the hidden costs of software development ("Why are you billing him so much for tasks that appear to be no big deal?"). When discussing cost tradeoffs, some project stakeholders may try to reduce the terms of the discussion into pure man-hours. They will assume that the faster an application can be built, the less expensive it should be. These clients are computing the value of your work based on man-hours alone. Remind the client that graphic design and software development are not like automobile repair, factory production, or bricklaying. A better analogy is the complicated surgical procedure. In the case of laser eye surgery, the procedure takes only a few minutes, but the doctor is being paid for years of knowledge and expertise. The cost of a medical procedure reflects the thousands of hours of training and preparation that qualify the surgeon to provide a service that is both technologically complex and customized to the patient's needs.

Furthermore, rapid deployment and decreased time-to-market provide significant competitive advantages. The scalability of your team's software is a valuable asset. Your team should be rewarded for developing its expertise and infrastructure to the point that you can produce a quality product in a short amount of time.

Playing Defense

Project managers seek to define the project and then build a protective wall around the initial set of features. Scope "creep" usually manifests as a gradual erosion of this wall. Most project stakeholders are sensible enough to quell major changes, but the cumulative effect of tiny incremental changes takes its toll. How do you prevent new requests from coming in over the wall? Formalize the process. Establish a change committee and a formalized change procedure so that you will not find yourself desperately plugging leaks as small requests pour in from all directions.

Change Orders

Use a written change request document whenever there is a change in scope or requirements. The change request form should include mention of the relative priority of the change and the importance of the change in terms of time and resources. Be consistent about requiring the use of change orders, or the client may assume that a change has no cost impact. The purpose of this protocol is to manage expectations and costs, not to discourage change or to appear inflexible in the face of a dynamic business environment.

Problems with Classic Approaches

When your project feels like it is spinning out of control from scope "creep," you may be tempted into a destructive battle with stakeholders. From your standpoint, the objective of this tug-of-war is to aggressively limit the scope of deliverables. After the scope has been "set" and the project is underway, you will be called upon to battle the client to prevent changes. "Scope management" becomes a reaction to changes initiated by the project stakeholders, who are laying siege to the integrity of the original plan. Caught in a destructive dynamic, your team will begin to feel like a defensive garrison as you fend off salvoes of change requests that threaten to erode the fixed set of features. The traditional "siege mentality" creates an adversarial climate that quickly infects the entire project team. The fallout from this power struggle between the project manager and project sponsors sets a tone of conflict that can last for the duration of the project.

In this hostile environment, traditional project managers focus on the plan, tracking inputs, deliverables, and milestones against a fixed set of requirements. Unfortunately, the attempt to specify every feature ahead of time and draft a static plan has proved to be unrealistic for Web projects. During the lifetime of your project, stakeholders will learn about the technology as well as their own business needs. The overall business climate may change if the project lasts several months. In response to this reality, innovative approaches like Rapid Application Development (RAD) and Extreme Programming (XP) have taken the spotlight. These methodologies share an "iterative approach" to scope management.

Iterative Approaches

Given the limitations of the standard model when applied to the Web, you will be called upon to find creative ways of controlling requirements throughout the lifetime of the project. The details of implementation will cause the specifications to be modified on the fly. Several new methodologies have formalized this iterative process. RAD is one of the most commonly accepted iterative approaches.

The Rapid Application Development methodology was designed to build software with speed as the most important success criterion. The RAD approach is not appropriate for every Web project. RAD is best suited for projects that have a limited, well-defined scope and a measurable outcome. RAD works best with a small, tightly knit project team and an on-site stakeholder who is empowered to make quick decisons about functionality. The ideal team size is under ten people. RAD also requires a stable technical architecture: It is not well suited for creating large, complex systems on top of a completely new or untested infrastructure.

The cornerstone of RAD is rapid prototyping, wherein developers try to create a small working product as soon as possible. The working prototype is then refined based on direct feedback from the client. Each refinement, or "iteration," is a step closer to the finished product. RAD project managers use a technique called "timeboxing," in which scope is allowed to change but the delivery date remains fixed for each iteration. The main advantages of RAD are that the client is able to see results right away and frequent scope changes are allowed. With conventional methods, there is often nothing delivered to the client until 100 percent of the process is finished and the completed software is unveiled.

Extreme programming represents one of the most notable applications of RAD techniques to the Web. This client-centric approach aims to deliver just enough software to meet the customers' needs, incorporating the immediate feedback of clients during the development of a series of rapid prototypes. In fact, there is no distinction between the "prototypes" and the finished product. XP utilizes several innovative techniques like "pair programming" to encourage teamwork, creativity, and collaboration among developers. The interview section of this chapter describes how XP works in the real world.

Extreme Programming (XP) Resources   See *http://www.extremeprogramming.org/ http://groups.yahoo.com/group/extremeprogramming/links.*

Common Scope Headaches

Most day-to-day problems with scope are caused by weaknesses in the project definition process. While you work to create a methodology for managing scope that is high on concept, keep an eye out for these nuts-and-bolts breakdowns. This section describes the most common headaches, along with the cures.

Problem #1: I Sketched the Site Out on a Napkin— Is that Okay?

It's difficult to draft project specifications if the initial requirements were poorly defined by the customer in the first place. The "cocktail napkin blueprint" can be used to memorialize a moment of inspiration, but it is not a valid input for your specification. Sure, you can "wing it" and attempt to fill in the blanks for your client, but this guessing game usually ends in dissatisfaction with an end product that doesn't match your customer's expectations.

Symptoms

- There is no creative brief or written document signed off by the client that states the scope of the project and its features.
- There is a creative brief, but it is vague or poorly written.
- The project stakeholders are new to the Web or inexperienced with user interface design.
- The developer has numerous questions about the specifications.

Solutions

- Build a feature inventory by asking the client to list all the items that appear on each page.
- Build out a use-case scenario by walking a hypothetical user through the application and asking the following questions.

  What are the user inputs?
  What sort of output should users receive?
  What are all the possible actions a user might take?

- Find an example of a similar site that can be used as a model. Ask the customer how her vision differs from the example or how the model should be modified.
- When all else fails, take a stab at designing the application yourself. E-mail the specifications to the project owner with the alternate features and design choices presented as a series of questions highlighted in red. As the client answers the list of questions, he effectively builds the specifications.
- Circulate early versions of the spec to a tech lead for a brief review and obtain a list of questions for clarification.

Problem #2: It's Nice, But It's Not What We Had in Mind.

So you did a great job writing a 20-page specification, using plenty of technical jargon to impress the developers. Unfortunately, your project is in trouble because your nontechnical client didn't "get it" until round one of the design popped up on her monitor. The fateful words "We didn't know it was going to work like *this*" spell disaster for your deadline. In order to prevent drastic revisions late in the game, steps need to be taken right now during scope definition.

Symptoms

- The client signed off on a feature summary but never reviewed the detailed specifications.
- The client has very few questions about the specifications.
- The client makes radical scope change requests late in the design phase.

Solutions

- Conduct a face-to-face review of the spec where each feature is discussed in detail. Many project stakeholders do not read through e-mail attachments.
- Be aware of different comprehension styles when you present the final specifications to your client for sign-off. Convey your concepts visually, orally, and in writing.
- Include visual mockups in your specs in addition to text explanations.
- Identify all the project stakeholders and have them sign off on the specifications.
- If your project owners are inexperienced, do not sign off on the specs until there is a demo/front-end prototype or finished design mock-ups. Build an HTML skeleton or "shell" of the application and walk stakeholders through the demo. Many inexperienced stakeholders don't understand what they are getting until they see it on their monitors.

Problem #3: Just One More Tiny Little Change . . .

The cost of changes tends to increase as the launch date approaches. However, your client may not realize that creative brainstorming and "tweaking" just isn't appropriate during system testing!

Symptoms

- The project deadline is repeatedly pushed back.
- The client can submit feature changes without incurring any cost.

Solutions

- Draft a detailed scope document or specification and require a formal sign-off before any work begins.

- Break payment schedules into a series of installments for each itemized deliverable rather than a single payment for the finished product.

- Create a formal change order procedure and assign a cost to change orders by making arrangements for additional fees or deadline extensions. Require change orders to be authorized by the ultimate project sponsor.

- When drafting your documentation, include features that are *not* required. Ask stakeholders to identify categories of requirements that will not be included, like credit card transactions or personalization features.

- Circulate updates to the project plan and specifications after each change order.

- Try an approach that employs rapid prototyping techniques. Shorten the release cycle. Establish an open-ended "burn rate" fee structure, and invite the client to provide continuous creative input.

Summary

Your job as a project manager is not to prevent change but to help your stakeholders navigate through the inevitable tradeoffs between scope, schedule, and resources. Avoid assuming the role of the "scope police" and become your client's trusted partner, educating stakeholders so that they can make intelligent choices. The inevitability of change may cause you to throw up your hands in despair, but keep in mind that you are managing a creative process in a dynamic communication medium, not building a suspension bridge. Attitudes and methodologies inherited from civil engineering, the military, and other project management cultures may not fit the open-ended, creative world of Web site design.

Although they represent an exciting development, iterative models are not a panacea to the problem of scope change. Many prototype-centric methodologies require unique conditions for success. For example, rapid prototyping requires a client who is knowledgeable about the Web, responsive, creative, and willing to participate actively in the ongoing design process. Such clients are a very rare breed! The techniques of pair programming advocated by XP enthusiasts often require significant changes in organizational culture and work habits, as well as a suitable personality! While it is true that many new appraoches promise to be better suited to the Web, it is advisable to first acquire a firm foundation in commonly accepted practices. Once you have mastered the fundamentals of scope management, don't be afraid to experiment on small projects. As you work toward mastery of the basics, stay abreast of novel approaches that offer a treasure trove of techniques that will assist you in confronting change.

In the end, change can make your project better. Often the best ideas emerge in the late stages of the graphic design phase, originating as an unwelcome "suggestion" from a client that threatens your stranglehold on the scope. As you prepare to embrace change, be forewarned that its inevitability is not an excuse for vague or shabby specifications. A clear and well-defined set of requirements will go a long way toward managing the client's expectations. Solid specifications will provide a baseline against which you can measure the costs of future enhancements and a valuable addition to your company's knowledge base. If you've done a thorough job of defining the product, you will enjoy a smooth transition into the next phase—creating the plan.

EXTREME PROGRAMMING

Alex Cone, CEO of CodeFab Enterprise Development (http://www.codefab.com), *talks about using Extreme Programming to move beyond the traditional methods for managing scope.*

This interview was conducted in October 2001 over a few margaritas at Tortilla Flats restaurant in New York City's West Village. The restaurant served up a spicy mix of retro 1950s paraphernalia and Mexican home cooking to local patrons. The booths were packed with art gallery owners, bikers staggering in from meat packing district bars, and Silicon Alley computer geeks taking a break from their labors in the raw industrial loft spaces that litter the neighborhood.

After a distinguished career developing back-end applications for Wall Street trading systems, Alex teamed up with some of the top developers in town and set up shop in a warehouse space in 1997. Since then, his team has abandoned traditional software development methodologies to produce innovative applications for clients like Apple Computer and Standard & Poor's.

So we're writing a book about how to get Web projects done. Any advice?

When we started CodeFab, the first thing we did was look back at most of the software development projects that we'd done over the last 10, 15 years, and conclude that most of them had failed.

You mean failed from a process point of view?

They failed from the point of view that they didn't get finished in the timeframe or within the budget, and we generally weren't happy with the end results. We wanted to know why. We wanted to actually finish projects and do them the right way. By and large we've been successful over the last four and a half years that we've had this company. At the two-year point, I had already finished more software projects than I had in the previous 15 years. I actually finished them and delivered them to a satisfied client: They were a success.

In most of my experiences on Wall Street, you started some grandiose project, people worked on it for a while, and then all the significant players left. It was never finished, things got changed along the way, and you never saw a completed piece of software that matched what you set out to do.

We started examining the current wisdom on software development and why software projects failed. At that time the point person was Steve McConnell, who had written a number of good books, including *Code Complete, Rapid Development,* and *The Software Project Survival Guide.* There was some really good thinking in there, but much of it focused around the cost of introducing changes into your specifications and controlling the scope of your project over time, as well as management issues in terms of keeping on track with what you're doing and the importance of having more or less complete requirements up front. This works very well if your focus is to be able to do fixed-scope projects.

The traditional approach was to do a whole bunch of work against a set of specifications and deliver what was in the specs before moving onward. It seemed like a good way to go, and it certainly provided good backup in terms of a contract with the client. When you're two weeks into the project and the client wants to change something significant, you can say, "Look at the cost associated with making a change at this point."

However, by and large this didn't really work for us. We had some notable failures, and part of it was our fault and some of it was the fact that this development model really didn't fit with the Web. One of the primary tenets of the standard process was that you can know at the start of your project what it is that you want to do, what you'll need over the next 6 or 12 months, and that those needs will remain consistent over that time period. And this has turned out to be completely unrealistic. It was also founded on the idea that you could induce a client to actually describe in sufficient depth and detail exactly what they wanted you to do up front, before any work had been done yet. And that also turned out to be impossible. You go out of your way to discourage the client to change the project in midstream. You needed a change control committee, you billed them extra fees for changes, and so on. That tended to foster a very bad working relationship with the client.

In fact, this adversarial relationship was the source of our biggest problems. Bascially, it forces you to have a huge fight up front with the client, wherein you wrestle over the features and the specs and the cost and so on and so forth. The client is trying to get the cost down as far as possible, while you're trying to limit the features. You're trying to get detail out of them when they don't want to be detailed, and then you have this huge fight before you even start the project.

Once the project gets going, you have another big crisis every time the client has a brilliant idea about how they would like to do something. This is because the client wants you to accommodate the change at no cost. Naturally, you show the client your documentation, which proves that the new feature is going to cost a lot of time, energy, and money—so you think you should be paid for it. The brawling continues.

Finally, when you finish the project, you have a big fight at the end. "We're done." "No, you're not." "Yes, we are—see, here are the specifications showing that we did exactly what we said we were going to do." The client is only trying to be financially prudent. This is their opportunity to get you to do more work for free by saying, "Finish this, change this slightly, try and do this," but you're trying to be financially prudent by saying, "Look, if we do another development hour, that is costing me money, and you're not paying me anymore for doing that, so we have to draw the line." So after you wrestle each other to a total standstill, you're probably not in a good head for doing the next project with this client, and he's not psyched to work with you, either.

So the main problem you've identified with the standard methodology is that the customer does not really know what they want, and, to make matters worse, you're working with a new technology that is changing rapidly along with the business environment.

Right, and you're starting off with some assumptions that are fundamentally unreasonable. You can't know exactly where you want to land. This isn't some kind of a ballistic missile. This is like trying to drive to Boston by pointing the front wheels of your car exactly in the direction of your destination address in Cambridge. Then you take your hands off the wheel and just press on the accelerator and hope that you'll get there. That isn't how you really drive to Cambridge. Making such complicated journeys is about midcourse corrections and about being adaptable. The traditional process fundamentally rejects change rather than embracing change.

The only advantage of the standard methodology is that it fits well within the corporate consulting mindset. The corporate client says, "We want to have this e-commerce Web site up by June. I've got to go back to the budget people and get a check for this piece of development. How much will it cost me?" The only people who really succeeded at this were the overpriced consulting agencies who would say, "Okay, then, I'll pull a number out of my butt and completely pad it with a $2 million markup." For a while, clients actually said okay to this, but now we're back to square one.

So if the situation is unworkable unless you pad your estimates by some ridiculous amount, then what do we do?

We really needed to start this whole process off on a completely different foot. One of my developers came to me with this new methodology, started by this guy Kent Beck, who was one of the original developers of Perl. It's called extreme programming, or XP. We started working with this, and we basically came up with a CodeFab version of XP. We worked on a couple of projects with this and found that it addresses pretty much all of our concerns.

The basic idea is—to continue my driving analogy—you agree that we're heading toward Boston, but all we work out initially is how to get to I-95. We'll take the next step once we're on I-95. The client comes in, and you put together a "story" rather than trying to do functional specifications. By trying to write these highly detailed specs, you are struggling to do technological implementation during the wrong phase. You're focusing on the details instead of the goal.

My emphasis on stories is that we want a good customer experience. For example, one story says, "We want to build the application so that the next time the visitor comes to the site we should know what they wanted the last time they came to the site." As you start programming, you come back to this one-paragraph story that describes the idea behind the user experience. You're not focusing on the features. You don't care about specifying the details like "there should be buttons on the left side instead of the right side, and the user should be able to turn on one-click buying with a checkbox."

So the specifications are experience-driven rather than widget-driven. The specifications are just stories about what the user gets out of the experience.

True, but there are a couple of restrictions on the client. The client has to be willing to put somebody on site. The client has to be part of the development team because you are doing short iterations. I can never get more than two weeks away from a working version, but the client has to be able to fine-tune things all the time. For example, there may be two different solutions to a problem, so we have to ask the customer, "Which one do you like?" Or we say, "We're at this point, and we could do any one of these three stories next—which one is the most important?" It really requires close interaction on the client, and that person has to be somebody with authority to make a decision. It can't just be somebody who makes a phone call, because we can make a phone call ourselves. This system requires some serious participation and accountability on the part of the client.

The actual process involves a series of prototypes, developed rapidly with immediate feedback from the client.

You're doing just enough to get the story to work. And then you move on to the next story and get that to work. You build this stuff up. You don't think to yourself, "Okay, we need a grand shopping cart infrastructure before we start anything else. We need a network communications layer before we start anything else." You just do a little bit and then get back to work and do a little bit more. Everything is based on making the stories come true. You iterate in the direction that you want to go. When the client comes in on Monday and says, "I had a great idea over the weekend," you can say, "Okay, great, let's do that now."

How do you get scalability into your software design if you are doing a series of one-offs?

They are not one-offs. You are just adding more features to the baseline. They are not prototypes. They are the real thing. You just make the specs into a story, like "We should be able to handle a thousand users shopping at the same time." The trick is to make it work, make it work right, make it work fast.

The major tenet of the whole XP thing is this refactoring. As you get a new requirement, you are not afraid to rewrite the code to accomplish a new goal. It steers you away from a tendency to design some vast infrastructure that you may not need. You avoid maintaining all of this useless code just because you might need it. You use just enough. You refactor and optimize the stuff that isn't good enough. You don't work on any part that isn't actually a problem.

This is a classic problem with all software development. People tend to optimize too early and optimize the wrong thing. If you find out that one spot is 80 percent of your problem, then you put your efforts there. Don't try and solve a problem if it isn't a problem yet. The client is right there, saying "It's fast enough to go live with now." If it's not fast enough to go live with, let's change this one piece. Let's stop adding new features and make this one thing faster.

If the product evolves on the fly, how do you handle billing?

Basically the client hires a team on a burn rate—say, for $150,000 you get these four guys and their project manager for a month. And we just continue iterating, executing stories, testing, rolling out a version for as long as the client wants. When are we done testing? When the client says we're done testing. When have we got enough features built into the product? When the client says we have enough features.

So the client has to manage their own scope!

Absolutely. But they get lots of short-term feedback. They can take shortcuts if they want to. They can say, "We need to go live with this feature, so we'll just iterate in that direction until we get something that is good enough." They can say, "Now I want to work on the user interface. Now I want to work on the communication with the CRM software." The client can really drive the process.

Since the development team has been doing a series of short-term iterations, they are never more than two weeks away from a working version. The client always has something to play with. The client can always refer to a working version, which allows them to base their ideas and suggestions on a realistic model. Plus, we do other things. We integrate unit tests into everything right up front. You cope with the story, write your first test and run it, and it fails because you haven't written any software. You write the software until it passes the test. If you want to make some changes, you re-run all the tests. If the code passes the tests, then you have a piece of software that does all the stories you've defined so far. You get much higher quality software that way.

We also do a lot pair programming, which is very nice. One person types, and the other person navigates, and we keep rotating people around. This way everyone sort of takes ownership of all of the code. Everyone has a piece of developing the product. It's no longer "This is the JavaScript guy; this is the guy who does all of the database stuff." Everybody gets a piece of everything, and you don't have to study a bunch of documentation to figure out what the other guy did because you worked on developing it. You have the developers volunteer to take on certain tasks. You write them up on 3 × 5 cards like you saw on the wall, and people volunteer to do them. This way the client isn't paying for twice as many programmers as they need, and generally after a month or two they are completely sold on the process.

The client feels like part of a team is their team and that they've come up with an idea and have seen it turned into reality very quickly, as opposed to fighting through some change control committee and then six months later finding out whether the feature was useful or not. My experience is that clients change what they wanted, or even what they thought they wanted, all the time. The changes don't necessarily have anything to do with what they were originally thinking.

How do these clients manage the overall budget?

They basically have to accept a degree of uncertainty. It usually takes them a month or two or three to realize that we've got such velocity on this project that it's worth the ambiguity.

In the traditional model, the guy who is writing the check never looked over a set of detailed requirements anyway. The budget guys are just trusting the client manager to pick the right features and do the right implementation, so we don't need to be that much more specific. Either they trust him or they don't. And if there are specific requirements that can be conveyed to us up front, so much the better.

Nonetheless, that person continues to be responsible all the way. And it eliminates the classic "It's the consultant's fault," which generally was just a smokescreen for a person who could never make up his mind about what he wanted.

I guess the client sells this model to their manager by virtue of its flexibility.

Right. Basically the client adds features until they are happy with the feature set or until they can't add more features within the budget. They're deciding what the next feature will be and what features do not make the cut because they will take too long to develop.

We want to shift the burden of expectations and prioritization back to the client and make someone a proactive participant in the process rather than having a project manager who is placed in an adversarial relationship with the client. The client gets a lot more responsibility out of this process, and they also feel tremendously empowered.

How does the project manager's role shift in this relationship? They are not necessarily managing deliverables because deliverables are being established by the client in concert with the developer.

The project manager sort of glues everything together. They are responsible for getting the stories and the tasks written up and estimated, coordinating who is doing what where, and also overseeing interaction with the QA people. Since you start with unit testing right away, QA people get very involved. And there is still the matter of putting together project documentation that has to go through the client's approval process, so the project manager does all that. Plus the project manager is still the primary point of contact for the client. They make sure we have the right documentation and document status reports on what was actually accomplished. Yes, there is a board with a bunch of 3×5 cards on it, but there needs to be more formal status reports conveyed.

I love this process because I know I am getting paid fair value for the developer. They work as long as the client wants them to work, and they are being paid for it. If the client wants more developers or less developers, we can adjust. I avoid the typical scenario wherein we're working like mad for the last three months, for the final one-sixth of the overall project payment. And what's more, you are in such a perfect state to go on to phase two.

Also, you're in a perpetual brainstorming mode, a creative process as opposed to being on an assembly line process. Developers often feel like they are on the receiving end of a directive, and if you're on the assembly line, you've got to churn out whatever the directive tells them to churn out. There is no creativity.

With this system the developers are empowered to volunteer to take on this or that story and estimate tasks. Then you reiterate, compare the estimates to the actual time, and calculate your velocity or your fudge factor and estimate accordingly. You get more and more accurate about estimating over the course of the project.

Alex, what's your definition of a story, and how do you measure it?

You're trying not to describe technological implementation so much as what the user does and what outputs he receives. No longer than a paragraph. Something that can be easily communicated so that we can say, "Can we make this come true? Do these features make this true?" There is a strong emphasis on using metaphors. You want to be able to give people a good sound bite so they really get a feeling for what this is supposed to do.

Give me an example of a story from one of the cards that would appear up on the wall.

We're doing this distributed publishing product for these Japanese guys. It's basically a Japanese car magazine, but they have thousands of distributors and editors who are on the road all over the place. They want to put a contributor on the road with his laptop. He should be able to upload an article, upload the images that go with the article, and do it all remotely from a laptop over a wireless connection. The users should be able to search for an article by title in English or in Japanese, and the user should be able to find articles pertaining to cars by the model year. That's not saying anything about what their search algorithm is or what the tool is that allows them to upload pictures pertaining to the article.

    The stories can change over time. We started out with a Web-based solution. Then we came up with a solution that integrates directly into Microsoft Word, but the story continues to be true. The developer might break the story down into tasks and provide a broad effort estimate for the story. And, of course, everything continues to be recorded on 3 × 5 cards, and you work on things until they are done. Then you mark them down and put them up on the board. The project manager is measuring the velocity by saying, "You did that in half a week instead of two weeks."

What makes a good project manager really great?

Good people skills, good organizational skills, willingness to be perceptive about the client and the client's mindset, good ability to digest fairly complex technological issues and translate them into something that the client can really inhale, good ability to work with the employees and balance all the egos. There is still a lot of developer ego management. Making sure that two people don't pair with each other all the time or that nobody leaves anybody out in the cold, making sure that developers are not spinning their wheels for too long on a problem and that they are respecting decisions that were laid down about how we are going to do this or that or the other thing. You are still doing client management. You are still doing status reports. All the clients are different, and they all want weird stuff.

    One of our top project managers is a nationally ranked pinball champion and often competes in championships. One of my developers brought us XP and insisted that we use it and is fanatical about it. He keeps sending e-mail messages with sound bites about why this is good or bad or evil or whatever else. But I am actually trying to encourage developers to be in this mode. Part of this is like trying to be a housing coordinator at a college, trying to match roommates.

CHAPTER 6

The Art of Planning

Planning is the process of identifying what work must be completed and how it will be finished within the approved time and resource constraints.

The Project Schedule

A key outcome of the planning process is the *project schedule,* which specifies the duration of activities and when they will begin.

As you follow the steps required to draft a project schedule, keep it flexible, and work to create a document that can withstand change. From the perspective of your project team, the schedule provides answers to a few key questions.

What work is required of me?

What needs to be done before I can start working?

When does it have to be done?

What work happens next?

Infatuation with Planning Software

As project managers, we are often guilty of falling in love with planning software. After toiling away on Microsoft Project or Excel, we can't wait to show off the elaborate fruits of our labors: cascading *GANTT charts* drawn in confident colors selected just for this project. We imagine ourselves in starched, short-sleeve, button-down shirts with skinny black ties, crew cuts, and Buddy Holly eyeglasses, striding confidently into Mission Control Houston to announce the launch sequence. Nervous executives mutter to themselves, "How much will it cost? How long will it take?," and we provide the answers in cool monotones. Four weeks into the project, our NASA fantasies implode as the original plan becomes a Maginot Line defense against the forces of change, a monument to the weekend we spent plugging man-hours into planning software.

G   *GANTT Chart*   The GANTT chart shows task information about your project as a series of bars along a timescale. The bars graphically display task durations with start and finish dates as they progress through time. The relative position of the GANTT bars shows the sequence in which your project tasks are scheduled to occur. GANTT charts are discussed in detail later in the chapter.

We know that the plan will quickly become obsolete as the client issues change orders. Stakeholders will change business priorities throughout the course of the project as they progress along their own learning curve and their vision of the end product crystallizes. Given these realities, how can we avoid feeling like planning is a doomed enterprise? The first step is to realize that planning is an art disguised as a science.

The project schedule should be a dynamic, living document, designed to be highly flexible. Its purpose is to identify major deliverables and dependencies. As a perpetual "work in progress," it should be customized to fit the unique characteristics of the project. Don't waste time attempting to force-fit a simple project plan into a Byzantine, all-encompassing "uber-template" that attempts to capture and quantify every minute detail. Production and design specialists already know how to do their jobs and how to schedule their own time. They are not robots on an assembly line. Members of your team need the plan to tell them what's expected of them and how they are affected by what other people are doing—not how to budget their next 15 minutes.

Planning by the Numbers

Planning requires the following steps that you must undertake as part of your core responsibilities.

1. Develop a work breakdown structure (WBS) by identifying the project phases and activities. Consult with your team to break down the activities into tasks.

2. Identify the dependencies between activities and highlight these in your schedule by using color or special notations. Major dependencies are a risk, so be sure to "raise a red flag" and identify them to project stakeholders.

3. Identify activities that can be run simultaneously or in parallel (for example, data modeling and graphic design).

4. Estimate the effort and duration of each activity in consultation with your team. If the project timeline allows, pad your time estimates by 15 percent. Be sure to clarify whether the estimates you receive from your project team are based on sheer man-hours or total duration of effort. Try to ask for both: You will need duration for creating your schedule and man-hours for billing your client! Most scheduling software allows you to enter both.

5. Determine the costs for each activity in terms of staff man-hours, subcontractors, hardware, and software licenses.

6. Draft the project schedule and analyze the results.

7. Obtain approval, assign resources, and schedule work assignments.

The Work Breakdown Structure

The work breakdown structure is a hierarchical listing of the work that must be completed in order to meet all of the project deliverables. The Statement of Work, technical specifications, and other scope documents provide the raw material from which the WBS is created. The WBS is created through a process of "decomposition," which simply entails breaking each component of the project into progressively smaller pieces until it becomes a collection of tasks or work packages. By using this process, a monstrously large and intimidating project is transformed into a series of small, manageable subprojects.

The WBS contains phases, activities, and tasks in outline form. The outline can be broken down along functional lines (search engines and shopping carts) or by physical components (page templates, content database, mail server).

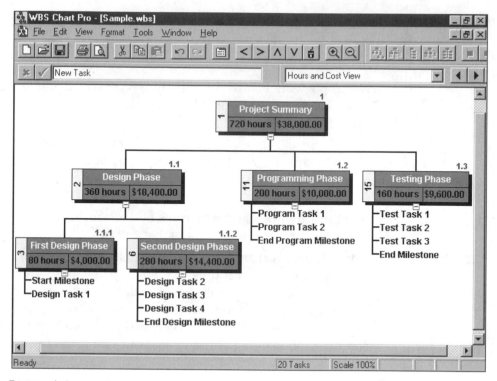

FIGURE 6.1
Sample Work Breakdown Structure Chart

Source: Screen capture from the WBS Chart Pro™ software. Copyright © 2002 by Critical Tools, Inc., a Texas corporation. Used with permission.

Creating WBS Charts   Work breakdown structures are usually expressed as hierarchical flowcharts, with each item assigned a number (see Figure 6.1). In Microsoft Project, this structure is created by "indenting" tasks in the GANTT chart to show the different levels of detail in a project.

Software tools, such as WBS Chart Pro™ from Critical Tools, Inc., are available for use in conjunction with Microsoft Project, allowing you to easily generate WBS charts (see *http://www.criticaltools.com*).

Drafting the Schedule

Regardless of whether you are using MS Project, Excel spreadsheets, or other software, the final document should contain the following items.

♦ A descriptive name for each activity, defining a specific deliverable. For example, "Create product info tables" is a better name than

♦ Tip: Scheduling Meetings

Include all of the important project meetings (especially client deliverable reviews and inter- view sessions) in the project schedule. Have clients sign off on the timing of these meetings and confirm it with all attendees up front. Client review meetings that are pushed back or de- layed can contribute significantly to "slippage" in the project schedule.

"Database coding" because it specifies the deliverable that signals the successful completion of the activity.

♦ The resources that are assigned to each activity. This can be generic until work assignments are finalized. For example, "Designer 1" and "Designer 2" can be replaced with the names of actual people later. Nonpersonnel resources like servers and other hardware that need to be purchased can be mentioned in a "notes" column.

♦ The start and end dates of the activity.

♦ Overall cost estimates in terms of man-hours, subcontractors, and fixed costs like hardware and software licenses.

The essence of project planning is the art of knowing what to leave out. Focus on the *critical path*, the activities that must be finished on time, or else the whole project will fall behind. Lump together routine tasks that represent standard operating procedures (for example, installing and configuring oper- ating system software on a Web server). Focus on deliverables that are unique to the project. A bloated schedule will add unnecessary administrative over- head and confuse the people who need to use it as a road map. In addition to being a cost estimating tool, the schedule is an important communication medium and should be designed with a few key principles in mind.

♦ Major milestones and high-risk work efforts should feature promi- nently.

♦ The sequence should follow the natural timeline of events as closely as possible.

♦ Task ownership should be clear. Avoid grouping unrelated tasks or tasks that overlap across several resources. For example, if you are outsourcing a portion of the development to contractors, consolidate their work into a self-contained, separate activity.

♦ The plan should be comprehensible to people who are not project managers.

G *Critical Path*   The sequence of activities that determines the completion date of the project is the "critical path." The critical path can be seen by tracing the longest duration path through your GANNT chart or other schedule diagram.

The standard format for conveying schedule information is the GANTT or "waterfall" chart. (See the sample GANTT chart display in Figure 6.2 and the sample project plan on the CD-ROM for examples.) A GANTT chart conveys the project schedule as a series of cascading task bars arrayed across a calendar. The chart is a visual expression of the WBS, the projected dates each task is to be started and completed, and the resources assigned. Since the GANTT chart is a crucial tool for conveying schedule information to project stakeholders, it should be thoughtfully designed. Many project disasters can be traced back to a project schedule that was difficult to understand or just poorly communicated. When creating the plan, think of yourself as an information designer whose job it is to communicate complex data clearly and succinctly. The bottom line: It's worth taking the time to customize the appearance, layout, and labeling of the task bars.

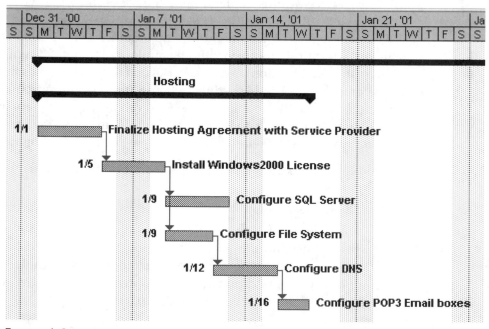

FIGURE 6.2
Sample GANTT Chart Display in MS Project

Sample Project Plan   Open the Chapter 6 folder on this book's CD-ROM and you'll find a sample project plan for a simple subscription-based content Web site. An updated version of this document is maintained on *http://www.realwebprojects.com*.

Assigning Resources

During resource scheduling meetings, your task is to identify and assign the specific resources that will be required to complete the project. With their historical perspective and managerial expertise, project managers play an important role in advising senior managers as they make resource assignments. The most interesting and challenging aspect of this process is the discussions (in other words, corporate politics) that surround personnel assignments. You'll be asked to state your opinion during these debates, and you should do so using objective criteria that take into account the interests of the organization in addition to the interests of the project.

Besides the obvious technical and professional expertise, the criteria include the following.

- ◆ Role definitions and requirements. For example, on smaller projects a programmer may also be required to interact with the client as a senior architect or tech lead.
- ◆ Availability and scheduling conflicts. Identify any political minefields with respect to company priorities and competing demands on resources.
- ◆ Experience with the project development process. A designer with a big ego might not be the right fit for a collaborative design model. A Java guru who is an infamous *prima donna* might not want to participate in an experimental "pair programming" methodology.
- ◆ Knowledge of proprietary systems.
- ◆ Industry knowledge. For example, a Java developer who has worked with online trading systems will be better suited for a financial project than a colleague who has spent his career working on content publishing sites.
- ◆ Knowledge of previous, related projects.
- ◆ Professional development. For example, a simple interactive pop-up advertisement may provide an opportunity for a designer to get her feet wet with the latest version of Flash.

Don't forget to account for mundane project resources like workspace, office supplies, videoconference facilities, and so forth. An appendix depicting miscellaneous costs may be included with the plan.

Obtaining Approval and Scheduling Work

Once the plan has been approved by the client and your senior management, don't rely on anyone to "delegate" the work assignments for you. Call a scheduling meeting and present the final plan to the entire team. Be sure to include department heads and other resource managers who may be aware of concurrent projects that might cause scheduling conflicts. The purpose of this meeting is to clarify roles and ensure that your schedule is accurately reflected in the work assignment calendars. Present the plan to your client as a work in progress that will be revisited at each milestone. Communicate confidence in the initial estimates. Remind them that while change is inevitable, you will help them to make the necessary tradeoffs between scope, schedule, and resources that will keep the project on time and within their budget.

Plan (and Pay) as You Go

Exactly how can the rigid structure of the planning process be applied to the ever-changing realities of the Web? Many innovative project managers have learned to break their project deliverables into a series of "installments." The installments do not necessarily correspond to classic project "phases" like design, production, testing, and launch. Instead, they are defined to include whatever set of deliverables the team is comfortable with estimating. At the end of each installment, the client receives something of value, the project team gets paid, and the plan for the next round is drawn up. This model is similar to a housing construction project, wherein a building contractor takes a disbursement from the bank at the completion of each phase of the project. For example, he is paid 10 percent of the total cost to lay the concrete foundation. Once the foundation is inspected, the bank wires him another 15 percent to build the frame, and so on. A layer of complexity is added for Web projects, since the final cost is a moving target, depending on scope changes initiated by the client.

Under the "Plan as You Go" approach, the client is provided with a rough estimate of the overall project duration and cost. However, the project team is only required to commit to the deadlines and budget for the current installment. The team does not commit to future installments until all the current deliverables have been met. While it might appear that the project team is "copping out," this tentative approach actually decreases the risk for the client, since the client can back out of the project at the end of each installment. Assuming that the project deliverables are to be built using standard Web technologies, the client will not be left high and dry if he needs to walk away and find another team to finish the project. By the same token, the risk and delay involved in finding a new project team encourage the client to go the distance.

The project team gains several advantages as well, since it is able to insulate itself from the risk of scope creep by reassessing the requirements and creating a new plan at the close of each phase. This "Plan as You Go" approach allows the project team to avoid "betting the store" on the initial time/ cost estimates, since it would otherwise end up "eating" the inevitable cost overruns.

The key to selling your client on this approach is to communicate that he will be receiving something of real value at the end of each install-ment. It is also helpful to have a solid track record of success on similar projects so that the client will be more comfortable with the fact that your team has not committed to an overall budget. A simplified set of installments for a small project might contain six separate project plans, one for each of the installments.

1. *First installment: scope documentation.* The client pays 20 percent of the total estimated development fees and in return receives a detailed "blueprint" of the site based on a thorough needs assessment. The blueprint consists of the complete scope documentation (techncial specifications, content map, and so on).

2. *Second installment: design mockups.* Based on the scope documentation, a new estimate for the overall project and the design concept is provided. The client typically pays fees amounting to 15 percent of the revised total and receives the final page mockups as PhotoShop files in layers for all of the major site templates.

3. *Third installment: final design.* The client pays another 15 percent and receives the finished HTML code along with optimized images. This production-ready design is tested for browser compatibility and may also include client-side coding (JavaScript, applets, and so on).

4. *Fourth installment: working prototype.* The client pays 30 percent upon receipt of a functioning back-end prototype. The system may or may not be "married" to the front end. If additional iterations of the proto-type are required, a new estimate is provided for each iteration.

5. *Fifth installment: pretesting.* The client pays approximately 10 percent for the integrated system.

6. *Sixth installment: launch.* The Web site is tested and launched. The client pays the balance of the fees.

Using Your Judgment

If project planning is really an art, where does the creativity come into play? Find out by asking yourself a few questions before you tie up the network printer with 53 pages of diagrams.

♦ What tasks should I group together and why?

♦ What deliverables are most likely to change or be discarded by the client? How should the plan reflect this possibility?

♦ What is the minimum amount of detail that needs to show up in the documentation? Can I use this data set to create a summary or "brief" for the client?

♦ What is the core product, and how can I schedule tasks so that the core features will be ready as soon as possible, with optional or enhanced features coming in at the end?

♦ What tasks can be folded into one supertask because they are standard or routine?

♦ What activities can be run in parallel?

♦ What is the most important fact or idea that the plan should communicate to the project stakeholders?

♦ What will clients learn from the plan that they didn't know before, and does that lesson come across clearly in the documentation?

♦ Do my charts and graphs communicate the milestones, timeline, and dependencies in a clear and simple format, or do my diagrams of overlapping arrows and boxes resemble a bowl of spaghetti?

♦ Should the project plan be shared with the client, or will a list of project milestones and client deliverables suffice? Many clients cannot resist the temptation to micromanage your project team, so don't arm them with excessive details.

♦ What are the client's deliverables, and does the client have the resources to produce? Has the client signed off on their deadlines? What happens if the client misses the deadline?

Planning Pitfalls

Project schedules run into trouble for two major reasons: inaccurate effort estimates and "hidden" tasks that were overlooked when the WBS was created. This section will address several activities that consistently run amuck and examine why it happens.

A telling rule of thumb has emerged in the industry, suggesting that effort estimates should be doubled, since they are usually off by 100 percent. This is not due to the fact that developers can't figure out how long it takes to do a job but rather that they are forced to make hidden assumptions about features that were poorly defined up front. For example, the development of your Web site's search engine takes twice as long because the client "assumed" that search results would show percent relevance matching, while the developer assumed an unsorted results set. Simply put, the requirements were not understood when the effort estimates were given. Padding the project plan by an arbitrary "fudge factor" is not the best solution. Take a step back and review your specifications for thoroughness, completeness, and level of detail before you calculate a launch date.

"Hidden" tasks are an even more insidious culprit. These little thieves rob your project of resources and strangle your deadline with the cumulative effect of unseen delays. They are commonly referred to as "slippage." This attitude implies that we are powerless against an invisible force that is almost mechanical in nature and often attributed to organizational inertia. In reality, many of these hidden tasks have a name and can be identified. They simply slip through the cracks of the WBS because they are "organizational" or "process" tasks that do not relate directly to a feature that appears in the final product, or their deliverable is subjectively defined (for example, client satisfaction with a color scheme). Since they are not associated with a physical deliverable, they are often overlooked in the plan.

Approvals and Revisions

Approval tasks often appear in project plans as a "check-off" line item, with minimal time allocated to them. In fact, the outcome of a review session with the client is usually a series of new feature requests and modifications. To account for this, each approval step should be assigned a duration of approximately 30 percent of the total activity to include the inevitable revisions and corrections. This is especially true during the graphic design stage. For example, if the first round of design took 20 days, schedule 6 days to implement any tweaks and modifications requested by the client.

Copy Editing for Design

Most project plans for Web sites include steps for writing and editing the copy that will eventually appear on the site. The deliverable for this activity is usually defined as a collection of Word documents stored in an "approved" folder on the development server or network. Once copy has been approved and delivered, most editors are happy to report that their work is "done." This is a false deliverable, however, because the copy rarely gels perfectly with the design and layout once it has been published to the live pages of the site.

Immediately after the content is published to the site (either during the HTML phase or during the database content entry phase), designers will begin complaining. During these "emergency meetings" called by the creative director, you'll learn that the text is too long to fit within the layout or too short to fill out a block of space next to a photo. The use of multiple font sizes, Flash animation windows, fixed table widths, and other technical parameters will put demands on the copy. Also, the copy that was initially provided to the design team during the mockup stage will have changed significantly. The inevitable rewrites constitute a "hidden activity" that causes significant slippage immediately after the content entry stage. Unfortunately, this review of copy "on the monitor" occurs late in the project, since content entry is usually one of the last steps before launch. Experienced project managers will insert an additional activity in the plan to account for this review of content after it has been published to the pages of the Web site.

QA Testing

Estimating the duration of the testing phase presents a unique challenge, since there is no way to predict the number of bugs that will appear. Each bug represents a "hidden" or unexpected new task. Naturally, the expertise of your tech team will impact your assessment of the likelihood of serious bugs. A general rule of thumb is that the duration of the QA testing phase should be about 30 percent of the total development time, but this can vary widely. Hedge your bets by including an HTML testing step and several code review or prototype testing stages throughout the entire development process.

Prelaunch Review

Senior executives can throw a wrench into your project plan at the worst possible time. After having been absent from the process since the original deal was signed, the CEO of your client's company loves to swoop in on the eve of launch and drop the opinion of his wife, dog, or 15-year-old nephew who "knows how to make a Web site." He might not have figured out how to open e-mail attachments, but the CEO is definitely willing to delay his Friday morning tee time to check out the site just in time to derail your Monday launch.

When you first drafted your WBS, you probably envisioned the "launch" task as a two-day event involving a cranky systems administrator who has

◆ Getting Started with Microsoft Project

Microsoft Project is one of the most widely used software applications for creating a schedule, estimating resource requirements, analyzing task dependencies, and tracking costs. It is used to create a graphical presentation of the schedule, which is very useful for project stakeholders. Project 2000 features Project Central, which allows team members to enter their own schedules directly into a master plan through a Web browser. MS Project has a huge number of features that can easily intimidate the novice user. Here are a few tips on getting started.

1. Assign a start date to the project: The project start date that you enter in the "Project Information" setting is used as the default start date for all tasks unless overridden by a dependency. It is recommended that you enter only the project start date and let Microsoft Project calculate the finish date after you have entered and scheduled tasks.

2. Create a task list: Copy your WBS outline into the left-hand column of the GANTT view. Use the toolbar indent (arrow) buttons to properly indent tasks under activities and phases. Do this until the outline structure reflects the organization and sequence of your WBS.

3. Input resources, using generic names that can be replaced with actual people later.

4. Input duration. Do not use end dates to set task duration! The end dates will be calculated automatically. If you force an end date, MS Project will create a "finish no earlier than" constraint. If you want to capture actual work effort rather than duration, you have to insert an extra column. If you do not want Project to automatically calculate duration, create a "fixed duration" task by double-clicking the task line and unchecking "Effort Driven." Adjust the resource allocation if the durations are calculated to yield an unrealistic result. You can also change the "working time" to reflect the working days and hours for everyone on your project.

5. Set the dependencies in the "Predecessors" column.

6. Estimate costs by using the "View/Resource Usage" option, which can be exported to Excel.

7. Make your schedule easier to read and review by using the "Bar Styles" option (right-click on the GANTT chart calendar display). Use the Bar Styles dialog box to customize the appearance of the task bars and add useful labels like start dates, task names, and resource names.

8. Get the plan approved and save the initial version as a baseline. This will allow you to use the tracking GANTT features that show which tasks are on schedule as you input actual work.

9. Save an HTML version of the plan by selecting the "Export to HTML using standard template" option. This can be easily disseminated and uploaded to your project Web site.

pulled an all-nighter waiting for the new domain name to propagate to your mirror site in Japan. This will be the least of your worries when hidden stakeholders from offices you never heard of materialize at the last minute to deliver their opinion on the home page copy. Identify these influential but silent players early, and include them in "rubber stamp" sign-offs during the graphic design phase. If your client representative is elusive about getting senior management involved for fear of losing control of the approval process, then add a "prelaunch review" step. Allocate at least 48 hours for the "annoucement" e-mail to circulate and another 72 hours to sort through (and deflect) the gratuitous responses. If you're lucky, someone might even catch a typo that your editors missed.

Case Study: Planning Software Overload

In an attempt to create enterprisewide planning standards, many interactive agencies have adopted unified project, process, and resource management software. These complex software packages offer the combined benefits of managing projects, building and using standard methodologies, and efficiently leveraging resources to help minimize project lifecycles. With the rapid growth of Web consulting agencies in the late 1990s, many small firms rushed to mandate centralized resource planning systems and "graft" them onto their current workflow. Sometimes these ambitious attempts yielded disastrous results for companies whose culture and workflow were a poor fit for monolithic planning systems.

This case study presents the story of Agency X, a fictional Web design shop whose experiences are representative of a wider phenomenon in the industry. Agency X's oldest office, based in New York, began as a design-oriented New Media agency, which grew rapidly as its client base exploded between 1998 and 2000. As Agency X strove to provide a full range of solutions, it acquired other interactive agencies in an attempt to round out its service offerings. The rapid pace of acquisitions led to cultural and role conflicts as the new entities were assimilated. In an attempt to integrate the various business units, the company tried to create a single, all-encompassing project development methodology. This centralized process was implemented in an enterprise planning software package. The attempt to force-fit a broad range of project types into a single mold added massive administrative costs to smaller projects. Eventually this complex model was discarded in favor of a staged, "plan-as-you-go" approach within a looser framework.

The Problem

The company started its explosive growth when the New York office merged with a California-based technology shop, which filled a gap by providing back-end programming. The respective organizational cultures were at odds, however, and conflicts emerged as the first joint projects got underway. Since the New York office was front-end oriented, it produced a creative culture with open and dynamic team roles. Experimentation was encouraged, and creative contributions were accepted from various members of the team. Producers were expected to provide a great deal of creative input and were involved in brainstorming sessions during conception. The project planning methodology was loosely defined, since the company relied on experienced team members to adapt an open process to the particular needs of the situation.

In contrast, the technical people in California used the joint application development (JAD) process. JAD uses structured, faciliated sessions to gather requirements, model the business logic, and design the functional details. These detailed specifications drove the entire process. The project managers in California had no direct relationship with the client, which was managed exclusively by the sales team. Project managers assumed a "back office" role, administering the plan by obtaining resource estimates from the tech leads who actually designed the applications.

As a result of these differences, the two offices had completely divergent ideas regarding the roles of project managers and producers, especially with respect to who had the client's ear. This aspect of the role was crucial because it determined who had power and authority on the team. In New York, the producer was also the account manager. Since the producer was not responsible for specific deliverables, their authority was based on the fact that they controlled the client relationship. This presented a huge cultural chasm as New York producers desperately avoided being assigned to California projects where they would be doomed to obscurity and discouraged from providing creative input.

In order to get everyone on the same page, management hired an expert who was based in the California office to develop a production process for the whole company. While this effort got underway, Agency X was busy acquiring more firms. At its apex, the company had offices in five cities. Each acquisition brought its own unique culture to the mix, based on its specific competencies. Management forged ahead in the race to create the "one-stop shop" solution for clients.

The Solution

The process consultant hired a team and set about devising a universal planning model that could accommodate any kind of Web development project. The model consisted of standard documentation and checklists for each phase. Thousands of man-hours were devoted to the design of the ultimate "uber-plan." By designing the most complex hypothetical project imaginable, the consultants attempted to capture the characteristics of all the possible smaller projects.

The model was implemented and enforced by the universal adoption of a centralized resource tracking, planning, and accounting tool. The software was extremely robust and contained an all-encompassing variety of features, including timesheet tracking, workflow, and reusable project templates. It displayed role-specific features tailored to each of the team member's needs, responsibilities, and skills. It delivered comprehensive information on all of the projects in development, from executive-level summaries to detailed work assignments for each team member.

Management found the tool appealing for a variety of reasons. The company wanted to copyright its new process, which would make an attractive point on the annual report and provide rich fodder for sales pitches and press releases. The tactical objective was to create a knowledge management system so that managers could collect historical baseline information about costs and deliverables. In the long run, this was supposed to enable project managers to quickly build schedules and budgets.

The Problem with the Solution

As the tool was rolled out, project managers logged on to create their schedule, budget, and resource "buckets" for time tracking. Everyone entered his or her time in the tool, which tracked effort estimates versus actual work in real-time. Problems began to arise when project managers attempted to create a schedule for simple marketing Web sites, consisting of five to ten basic pages. These sites were relatively easy to create and provided a high-profit, "quick-hit" revenue boost for the company with their low overhead. Ready to make a quick $100,000 for the team, project managers were stumped by a system that pummeled them with a two-year-long development schedule for a generic CRM/e-commerce site. The creative brief alone featured several dozen line items, with a multitude of fixed tasks delegated to each person on the team. For each of the 30+ task line items, employees were required to input their activities for each hour of the day.

The producer's job was transformed into a monotonous data entry nightmare. Hired to be creative, flexible, able to think on their feet, and to bring a team together, these producers now spent their day sitting in front of a machine, plugging away at the schedules and tweaking their time sheets. Hundreds of hours were spent simply learning the tool and the dictionary of acronyms required to navigate its multitude of fill-in forms.

There was significant cultural resistance to the tool, and soon enough people began to find ways to "cheat" the system. Graphic designers took a great deal of pride in their creations and wanted to work overtime on their cutting-edge assignments. Often the more interesting work was found with smaller, low-budget clients who couldn't afford the extra man-hours. With its fixed resource allocations and comprehensive time tracking, the system discouraged this work. Designers began to hide the extra hours they were spending on these fun, portfolio-building projects. Hours were "stolen" from easier projects that took a short time to complete. The surplus time would be spent honing Flash skills on fun projects. Crushed by the data entry workload, project managers devised shortcuts that allowed them to lump tasks together into aggregate categories. These activities diluted the value of the reporting features.

The extended planning and design phase had other repercussions. Clients began to complain, saying, "The design phase is taking too long—we need a prototype *now!*" The team would build a prototype, and inevitably the client would ask to "just launch it." When pressed, the development team would give the prototype a facelift, launch it, and then deal with a barrage of bugs.

The Harsh Reality

As resistance to the scheduling system mounted, the process consultant was shuffled around and reported to several different people. Finally, she was replaced by a VP of Production with real Web production experience, who adopted a simpler process. The new head of production concluded that the best process is a skeletal guideline that provides the most flexibility and allows talented project managers to think on their feet, take ownership of the process, and innovate. The consensus was that given the multitude of ways to cut corners based on the unique needs of every project, there is no "universal" process.

The new process was phase-based rather than project-based. Project managers created a new budget and a new schedule at the end of every phase. There were four basic phases. The process began with a ballpark estimate for the entire project. This estimate was revised as the project progressed through each stage. The first phase included the analysis, requirements, concept, and the creative. The client signed the new budget and a new schedule at the end of each phase. By breaking the project into four budgets, project managers enlisted the client in controlling scope. The end of each phase provided a reality check and an opportunity to cut back on scope. This avoided the impossibility of adhering to a fixed schedule from the beginning and empowered project managers to "evolve" the plan.

Summary

There is little correlation between the effectiveness of a schedule and the number of tasks you were able to identify and list in Microsoft Project. The schedule is a communication tool that must express key concepts like task dependencies and next steps. Good plans are designed with moving parts that respond to change and can shift into new configurations without crashing to the ground. In practice, this means discarding monolithic schedules and resisting the utopian impulse to force-fit a project into a preordained mold. Web projects require creative solutions that move beyond the traditional approach, which calls for a centralized "master plan" that must be set in stone before work can begin. Today's innovators are taking a "plan-as-you-go" approach, breaking the planning phase apart and allowing the documentation to evolve naturally along with the rest of the project. Within this staged structure, client sign-off becomes an ongoing dialogue rather than an item on a checklist.

A flexible planning framework is your best companion as you enter the uncertain waters of the graphic design phase. With its subjectively defined deliverables, this stage of the project is the source of considerable uncertainty. The majority of scope changes will occur during this phase as the client is able to visualize the end product for the first time. It is common practice to roll the graphic design phase into the planning process, since many clients consider page mockups to be the "final blueprint" for the site. As you deliver the "final" plan and enter the graphic design phase, be sure to let the client know that it is a baseline "best guess," a rough sketch of the landscape that will need to be redrawn with their assistance.

CHAPTER 7

Learning to Love Meetings

Just about everyone involved in the Web development industry will tell you the same thing: They have spent too much time in pointless, badly managed, and needless meetings. Spending time in a hot conference room talking about nothing in particular is a mind-numbing experience, but the mismanaged meeting syndrome perseveres. Project managers need to know how to run good meetings that do not waste the team's time and the client's money. There are some very simple rules you can use to run effective meetings where the attendees leave feeling like progress was made and action items were created. It's a good feeling to run a successful meeting that engenders confidence from the team and client. It's an awful feeling to be faced with a hostile group of people or an angry client because you called yet another needless meeting.

Besides being one of the major communication tools at the project manager's disposal, meetings are a chance for project managers to spread their wings and demonstrate authority. If you can run effective meetings that move along quickly, get things accomplished, and allow for constructive communication, you will be doing your part to improve the project manage-ment culture in your company and to establish your reputation as a leader.

Why Are We Here?

Why do people call meetings when they really have nothing to talk about? Calling agenda-less meetings is a common management blunder. As project manager you will be responsible for scheduling many meetings, so try not to abuse this responsibility. You don't need to call a meeting for every little issue that pops up. Always strive to use alternative communication methods to solve problems other than calling a meeting. When faced with an unexpected issue or challenge, such as a sudden change request from the client, curb the urge to call a meeting. Use the method prescribed for people with anger man-agement problems: Take a deep breath and count to ten. Do you really need to assemble the team to solve the issue, or can the issue be handled via e-mail or just visiting someone's cubicle? The surest way to expose yourself as a novice or as an overreactive manager is to call too many meetings or call meetings without a focused agenda.

➡ KEY POINT

The number one rule for meeting facilitation is to *have an agenda*. Without a clear, focused agenda you will be wasting people's time and eroding your cred-ibility.

Keep in mind that your peers must attend other meetings throughout the day, such as department meetings, performance reviews, and strategy sessions. Remember, your job is to enable productivity for your team. Sched-uling them into too many meetings is a surefire way to kill productivity, not enhance it.

Table 7.1 shows some common situations that crop up and which require a meeting and which do not. Try to liken these examples to circumstances you currently face.

The Agenda Is Your Road Map

Remember the Boy Scout motto and "be prepared." Your Scouting days may be over, but that doesn't mean you can go into meetings unprepared, and in this case, unprepared means no agenda. Even if the agenda has only one item on it, taking the time to write this down shows you are thinking of the group's time. The purpose of an agenda is to focus the meeting and keep everyone on

TABLE 7.1 Recognizing When a Meeting Is Required

Circumstance	Meeting Required: Y/N	Alternative Solution
The directory path and resulting URL for the Web site must be established. The system administrator, developer, and business owner all must agree on the URL structure so the path can be created.	No	While this seems like it may require a meeting because of the various groups involved, it doesn't. Common tasks such as this one can be handled via e-mail.
The client just called and wants to change the background color on the home page.	No	Speak to the designer or creative director working on the project and get a mockup made with the new background color. Send the mockup to the client for approval and move on.
Unsubscribing users from your fantastic new Web subscription service requires three separate procedures performed on two databases. Customer service, the application development team, and the business owner are arguing over who owns this responsibility from start to finish.	Yes	In a case like this where process is in question and competing factions are taking up positions, call a meeting, establish the process, and settle the dispute.
The e-commerce portion of your Web site is going to be outsourced. The business development team has three deals on the table and has asked you to evaluate the three candidates from a tech perspective. You have prepared a brief on each candidate and would like to make your recommendation.	Yes	This situation could be handled by simply e-mailing your briefs to the business development people with your recommendation. However, there are bound to be questions about your findings, which could result in a slew of e-mails between yourself and the business folks. It would be best to call a meeting to settle the issue.

track. It's the road map for the meeting and will keep the conversation from going astray. Your agenda will be derived from whatever issue you want the team to discuss, clear up, or resolve. Know what you want to accomplish ahead of time instead of calling the meeting with a vague idea in mind and hoping your team will pick up your slack.

The scope of the meeting will dictate the scope of your agenda. If the meeting is to brainstorm a solution for a particular problem, the agenda may have only one item. If the meeting requires input from every group involved in the project, such as a postmortem, the agenda could be complex.

Stating the agenda is the most effective way to begin meetings. Be sure everyone understands the topics on the agenda and how the meeting will be conducted. By stating the agenda at the outset, you can set the tone for the meeting and focus everyone's attention.

At the very least your agenda should include the following items.

♦ The primary purpose of the meeting

♦ The meeting topics and in what order they will be addressed

♦ Who will be addressing each topic or at least speaking first on the matter

♦ How much time will be spent covering the various topics

♦ What deliverables and action items should come from the meeting

If there are many items on your agenda, make copies of it for all attendees. This is a good practice even if there are only a few agenda items. It demonstrates your professionalism and will provide everyone with a road map for the meeting. It's also a good practice to send your agenda out to all attendees ahead of time. If you are using MS Outlook to schedule your meetings, you can write up the agenda in the invite e-mail, but it's better to attach it as a Word document.

Participation Is Key

Not everyone who attends your meeting is going to be relishing the opportunity to participate. It can be frustrating for the person conducting the meeting or speaking to feel like not everyone assembled is interested in being there or is engaged in the discussion. It is fair to assume that if a person has been invited, they will be expected to participate. However, this is not always the case. Here are some reasons why people are reluctant to participate in meetings.

♦ There is not a clear agenda for the meeting, or it was not stated from the outset.

♦ Some people do not feel comfortable speaking in groups.

♦ They may not have "bought in" to the meeting topic or project.

♦ Some people feel like their contribution will be ignored by their peers or management.

♦ The group has not worked together before, and a sense of trust has not been established.

A skill you will quickly develop is how to elicit participation from everyone (or nearly everyone) in the group. There are some simple things you can do to draw reluctant participants out of their shell. The first and most important thing you can do is to be sure everyone understands and is interested in the agenda. Once you state the agenda out loud and describe what you hope the "takeaways" or action items will be, ask the group if they agree. Look around the table and make eye contact with everyone assembled to be sure they heard and understood the question. By making eye contact with everyone there you are signaling to them that you are expecting their participation.

After you have agreement from the group as to why you are all assembled, thank the group for giving up some of their time to attend. Rarely are people thanked or acknowledged for attending meetings and giving up an hour that could have been used on completing tasks. Finally, before the meeting begins, you can mention to the group how important everyone's participation and input will be to solving the issue at hand. People like to be acknowledged for their expertise and talent, especially publicly. A simple statement like "You were invited to this meeting because you are the experts in this area, and I know we can come up with an excellent solution for . . ." will go a long way toward setting the right tone for the meeting.

Some people recommend breaking the ice before diving into the meeting topics. Taking time to perform an ice-breaking activity like introducing yourself to the people sitting to your left and right can get the conversational juices flowing, but they can also be risky. Side conversations could develop that do not stop when it's time to begin working through the agenda. You should use your best judgment with regard to what ice-breaking activities you choose to perform and how much time you devote to them. If the meeting is a kickoff meeting or is attended by a group of people who have never met, ask everyone to introduce themselves and describe their role in the project.

What to Do When the Fur Starts to Fly

When the pressure is on and critical decisions have to be made quickly by a disparate group of experts, there are bound to be conflicting points of view. It's natural and expected and, most importantly, healthy. Everyone wants to contribute and do a good job, but in tense situations some people believe their idea or solution is the only correct one. Usually a debate ensues that is also important and healthy. How else can the best decision be made if the issues involved cannot be debated? Opposing views are a good thing, and it's the group's job to choose the best one. However, as the person conducting the meeting you have to be on the lookout for a healthy debate becoming an unhealthy argument. It happens. People in this business are passionate about what they do and can be very turf conscience. Be on the lookout for behaviors such as these.

- An overly aggressive tone
- Personal attacks
- Withdrawn and silent behavior
- Speaking over someone else; not letting others finish their sentences
- Aggressive body language
- Assigning blame

When conflict arises in a meeting, you must remain neutral. Your credibility is founded on your resistance to taking sides. You also need to stay calm when the fur starts to fly. If you also lose your cool, the chances of reeling in the meeting and calming hostile emotions are greatly diminished. Try to get people to focus on the facts, not on each other. Remember: You are all there to solve a problem, and doing so will benefit everyone.

Here are some steps you can take when your meeting begins to resemble a battle scene from *Planet of the Apes*.

- *Be assertive.* This does not mean join in the fray, but change your tone of voice to get people's attention and rein in the situation. Only allow one person to speak at a time, and remind the group to stay on the topic. Tell them emphatically that getting personal will not be tolerated.

- *Slow the pace of the discussion.* If the situation is heating up and opinions are flying fast and furious, ask the group to pause for a moment so you can catch up on the discussion and ask the person speaking to summarize her point.

- *Do not tolerate rudeness.* As soon as someone in the group makes an off-color or rude remark, do not hesitate to call them on it. It's your job to keep the group on track, and insulting remarks only serve to derail people's attention. Tell the person who made the remark to please refrain from inappropriate comments no matter how much they think they are warranted.

- *Call off the meeting.* When things get out of control or are well on their way to becoming out of control and any hope of productivity is out the window, halt the meeting. Tell the group it's time to stop until everyone calms down and clearer heads can prevail.

When meetings begin to spin out of control and emotions are raw, it's very easy to dive into the mix and kick up a little dust of your own. Don't do it. This moment will pass, and you and your team still have a long way to go before you finish the project. You need to maintain everyone's respect throughout, and nothing helps your credibility and position like effectively managing a dicey meeting where the chips are down and emotions are high.

Meeting Pitfalls

Your peers on the job are professionals just as you are, and it's probably safe to say they have a good grasp of basic social skills. However, everyone forgets their manners occasionally, and not everyone is socially adept in all situations. Here are a few meeting pitfalls you may encounter.

- ◆ *Mismanaging the clock.* If you have a lot to cover and one hour to do so, keep a close eye on the clock. If the meeting becomes snagged on a single topic, halt the conversation and suggest a new meeting be scheduled to cover that topic. Remind the group there are a lot of other topics to get through on the agenda.

- ◆ *The hijacked meeting.* Often two or three people in the group will latch onto a topic and run with it. This will leave the rest of the group doodling, staring at their hands, or glaring at you. When this occurs, ask the people hogging the conversation to "take it offline" so the meeting can continue. Use an assertive tone; they'll get the message.

- ◆ *The personal agenda.* Similar to the hijacked meeting is the attendee who chooses to ignore the stated meeting agenda but instead insists on changing the topic of discussion to something they want to talk about. Don't let this person get away with this side-tracking technique. Politely cut them off with a comment like "That's an excellent point, and we should schedule some time to talk about that issue. However, today we have to cover the agenda items we discussed at the beginning of the meeting."

- ◆ *The expensive meeting.* Does the HTML intern really need to be sitting in a design meeting? Meetings can get very expensive for your client when you invite people who are not absolutely required. As project manager you should be on top of all the details and able to answer questions and cover for a resource who may not be in attendance. Giving good service means watching out for your client's well-being. Save them money when you can, and they'll have that much more to spend on future projects.

- ◆ *The insidious side conversation.* It's often tempting when stuck in a boring meeting to begin a conversation with the person sitting next to you. If you are facilitating a meeting and observe a side conversation, shut it down by clearing your throat or catching the eye of one of the side-conversationalists. You don't have to be obnoxious about it; you're not the meeting police, but there should only be one conversation going at a time.

♦ *Bad scheduling.* Scheduling meetings around everyone's busy day is always a challenge. However, there are some times it's best to avoid, like early Monday mornings, late Friday afternoons, and during the lunch hour. Lunch meetings tend to become more about the food than the topic, and not much work gets done. Who can concentrate on the marketing plan for a Web site when you're eating egg salad?

Being aware of these common meeting pitfalls and how to deal with them will make you a star meeting facilitator in your organization and enable your team to maximize their time.

Common Project Meetings

The following sections describe several types of standard meetings you will call regularly during the life of a project.

Kickoff Meetings

Kickoff meetings should be lively affairs. The average project has at least three kickoff meetings: the project kickoff, the design kickoff, and the tech kickoff. Kickoff meetings are a chance to get the team pumped up about the project and share their enthusiasm with the client. Kickoff meetings set the tone for the project, so be sure to keep them focused and upbeat.

Before the project kickoff meeting, you should already have a first draft specification and timeline. These materials will be handed out at the meeting. The project kickoff meeting is a chance to cover the goals of the project, the expectations, the communication plan, and the larger milestones in the project. Review the spec with the group and ask if there are any questions or comments. This exercise is more about saying to the team, client, and yourself, "We are committing ourselves to building this Web site with this feature set in this amount of time, and nothing is going to deter us from our mission!" Be sure to touch on the project risk areas, and talk about any contingency plans you may be working on.

The design and tech kickoff meetings serve the same purpose as the project kickoff meeting. The purpose of the meeting is to review deliverables, milestones, expectations, and risk. At the design kickoff meeting be sure to have the information architect, tech lead, or lead developer present. Having a tech person present at the design kickoff meeting will allow the designer's feasibility questions to get answered before they get too far along in the design process.

Kickoff meetings are also an opportunity for the project manager to demonstrate his or her authority (or impression thereof) to the assembled team.

Status Meetings

Status meetings can be the lifeblood of a project. You will generally be attending at least two regular status meetings per project: one with your team and another with your client. Schedule your status meetings with the team late in the week and with your client early. The goal of these meetings is to check in on the project milestones with your team and to keep your client informed on progress, problems, and any issues that may have arisen during the previous week. Keep these meetings as brief as possible, but don't skip them altogether. Even if there has not been a great deal of progress made on the milestones (in a Web site build this is rarely the case), gather the team and get a report from all the leads.

Use your judgment with regard to how many people are required to attend the team status meeting. Generally the team leads are sufficient, but you may want the people performing the tasks to give the report. These meetings are a good opportunity to foster a feeling of solidarity among the team because they are those rare instances when the business, marketing, tech, and design resources all gather to talk about their particular part of the project. One would think that people would naturally be interested in their teammates' tasks, but unless someone is contemplating a move to another department, people generally are not interested in this level of detail.

Status meetings with your client should also be kept as short as possible, and once again, use your best judgment with regard to the invite list. This meeting is on the client's dime, and they do not want to be paying for resources to attend a meeting when they could (should) be working on knocking off the project milestones.

Postmortems

By far the most intense meeting you will preside over, the postmortem is an opportunity to generate valid, documented lessons from your projects and move your company, the process, and, potentially, your career forward. Postmortems are meetings designed to review the project that just ended (or phase of the project completed) and allow the team to share their views on what and who made the project simple, difficult, pleasurable, or miserable. The focus of the discussion is on the process—what more could a project manager ask for?

Many people confuse postmortems with gripe sessions and come to the meeting ready to point their finger at anything that moves. It's your job to be sure everyone understands that the postmortem is conducted not to blame individuals but to expose the flaws as well as the strong points in the process. The idea is to improve the process, not punish individuals for perceived poor performance or settle a feud.

Postmortems require all of your people and meeting facilitation skills. You may not necessarily need to wear a striped jersey and carry a whistle, but you should be ready to dive in should the discussion turn into an argument or, worse, a full-scale brawl.

If there was ever a meeting where you want to send out a meeting prep kit, it's this one. The kit should contain at the minimum an agenda, a list of attendees, and a guideline for behavior during the meeting.

In order for the postmortem to be successful, you have to create the right environment and set the stage properly for uninhibited participation. This doesn't mean dim lights, soft music, and a clothing optional policy (although you never know). Setting the stage properly means communicating to the team that open, honest, *constructive* participation is expected, and there will be no retaliation from management or other team members for comments or viewpoints that are critical of the process. Stress to the team both in the rules you send out ahead of time and in how you facilitate the meeting that blaming individuals is not helpful in improving the process and will only serve to divide the team and potentially alienate people. If someone has a personal issue with you or another member of the team, this meeting is not the place to air it.

Because you will be deeply engaged in facilitating the meeting discussion, you may not want to keep notes. Assign a note taker before the meeting so you can be free to stay engaged in the discussion. You should, however, be sure to capture the points made, lessons uncovered, and process improvements suggested on a white board or flip chart as the meeting progresses. Successfully facilitating a postmortem where the team leaves feeling good about their input is one of the biggest challenges you will face. Successfully conducted postmortems are the sign of a mature and experienced project manager.

Postmortem on the Web   An excellent postmortem questionnaire template is available on Gantthead.com at *http://www.gantthead.com/Gantthead/content/templates/Project_Post-mortem_Survey.doc.*

Case Study: The Exploding Meeting

This case study describes a project manager's experience as a meeting he is trying to facilitate devolves into a full-blown rumble.

Background

I had been dreading the meeting all day. I was working on a project to build a new, highly complex Web-based interface for the recently purchased list management system. The new system was state of the art and incredibly powerful; however, its interface was not very user friendly and was not conducive to the established work-flow—hence the need for the development of a new "front end" for the system.

I called the meeting to review the first draft of the spec I had written based on Gail's (the stakeholder) requirements. The project was still in its early phases; and to be honest, I was still not up to speed on the new technology involved. Gail was from marketing and completely nontechnical, but she envisioned the application behaving in a certain manner with a certain workflow and accomplishing certain tasks. She was very sure how the interface should behave, yet she had not consulted with anyone from the editorial group, who were the end-users of the application. That struck me as odd, but I had never worked with anyone from marketing before, and I wasn't sure if I should suggest that it might be a good idea to get feedback from the people who would actually be using the tool. It seemed pretty obvious to me, but I didn't want to push any buttons so early in the project.

Jim, the programmer assigned to the project, was soft spoken and painfully shy. He rarely spoke above a whisper. It was difficult to get a clear answer from him, and even then he spoke in vague, technical generalities that were difficult to decipher. I still trusted him, however, and I was relying on him to step up at the meeting and bail me out of any tight spot I might get in regarding whacky functionality requests that were not in the current spec. Even though I was relying on him to fill in any technical gaps in my knowledge, I was worried because I knew he had his own ideas of how the tool should behave that were not entirely in line with Gail's. Earlier in the day I asked him to give me his feedback on the spec, and he only said that I had "captured the gist of it" and left it at that. It certainly wasn't the reassuring answer I was looking for.

The project took on a high profile due to the extremely high cost of the new list management software and the fact that a custom interface had to be developed in order to actually use it. Two other attendees of the meeting that afternoon were

Dick, the vice president of Technology, who was responsible for purchasing the new list management software, and Stan, the vice president of Application Development, who was the developer's functional manager. Because Dick had purchased the system, he had a vested interest in seeing to it that the interface was developed quickly and the system was put into use as soon as possible. He did not want to be blamed for acquiring a white elephant. Stan was attending the meeting to be sure the project scope was reasonable and not bloated with unnecessary features that would keep his developer on the project past the time budgeted for him.

Competing Solutions

To prepare everyone for the meeting, I e-mailed the spec to all the attendees two days in advance. I wanted to be sure that everyone had a chance to review the document beforehand and alert me to any errors in functionality or workflow I may have created. I did not hear back from anyone, so I assumed everything was in order.

The meeting was scheduled for late in the day, which may have been a mistake on my part but unavoidable due to everyone's schedule. We assembled in the conference room at 4 P.M. I had copies of the spec ready for everyone arranged around the table. As people were getting seated, I made the introductions. Gail, John, and Stan sat on one side of the table, while Jim and I sat on the opposite side facing them. There was a detectable amount of tension in the air; as the group sat at the table, there was zero small talk. I felt all eyes in the room boring in on me as I stated the agenda for the meeting. We were gathered to review the first draft of the spec for the newsletter tool to be sure all the business requirements were addressed and all the features were technically feasible. No one spoke, and I could not tell if they were all bored already or just anxious to get the meeting over with so they could go home.

Because I was not entirely comfortable explaining the functionality of the tool, even though I had written the spec, I asked Jim to explain to the group the scope of the project and how extensive the work would be. He rose from his chair and went to the white board, which is standard procedure whenever a developer wants to explain anything technical. Lines, words, symbols rendered haphazardly across the expanse of a white board are crucial to a developer making himself understood. Jim faced the board as he quietly spoke and drew diagrams of what he was planning to build. No one in the room could hear him, and I noticed Gail craning her neck toward the front of the room as she tried to decipher the mumble emanating from Jim while simultaneously giving me a sidelong glance as if to say, "Is this guy for real?" From the bits we could understand it began to become clear that the tool being described had very little in common with the tool described in the spec. Gail became more agitated and asked why all the features described in the spec did not appear to be included in the interface Jim was describing. This question was directed more at me than at Jim, and as I stammered and struggled to respond, Stan jumped up and went to the white board, saying "I think what Jim is trying to say is . . ." and launched into a description of a newsletter tool that bore no resemblance to the interface described in the spec or to the tool Jim was attempting to describe.

Stan began earnestly drawing on the board and listing all the necessary steps required to build the interface he had in mind. Jim returned to his seat and was silent for the rest of the meeting. Gail began to fire off questions: "What happened to features X, Y, and Z?" she demanded. "We never asked for what you are describing." "Where is the functionality described in the spec?" Try as I might, I could not keep up with what Stan was diagramming; the technology he was describing was beyond my grasp. I could not answer Gail's questions, so I turned in my chair to fully face the person speaking at the board and not have to meet Gail's confused and increasingly angry looks. I leaned forward quietly and asked Jim what Stan was talking about and if what he was describing had anything to do with the spec. He shrugged and said over his shoulder, "Sort of."

Suddenly, Dick, who had been quiet for most of the meeting, took exception to something Stan said and in a sarcastic tone blurted out, "That idea is implausible and makes no sense whatsoever." With that he launched into his own description of how the interface application should be designed and built. A loud, long, technical argument ensued between Stan and Dick, with neither one making much sense to the nontechnical people in the room and neither apparently willing to back down. They argued the point for at least ten minutes while the rest of us sat silently. Finally, Gail asked what this discussion had to do with the spec we were assembled to discuss.

Challenged

Dick turned to Gail and asked, "What spec? You mean *this* spec?" He pointed to the document in front of him and made a face of disgust. He claimed to have read the spec several times but could not understand a word of it. I began to feel my cheeks burn as he went on to say he found the grammar poor and the prose incomprehensible. Was he a closet grammar professor? What did this have to do with the interface application? Why was he indirectly attacking me by criticizing the specification document? In a condescending tone he read aloud a passage from the spec and then sneered, "What the hell was that supposed to mean?" I thought I was going to fall off my chair. I was too embarrassed to look at anyone else in the room, and I was too afraid to speak because of what I might say. I was being personally attacked in a project meeting I had called in an attempt to get everyone involved on the same page. I was angry and more than a little confused, but I knew I had to stay calm as I figured out what to do next.

The conference room suddenly felt unbearably hot and stuffy. No one spoke. I stared dumbly at Dick, who had yet to look at me once since entering the room, not even during his bizarre critique of my writing ability. We had been in the conference room for over 90 minutes and had not accomplished any of the objectives on the agenda. The meeting had exploded in my face in an incredibly unexpected fashion. Stan came to my rescue at last by stating it was obvious there were still a lot of technical issues to discuss and we should meet again after all the technical considerations had been ironed out. Dick said that was fine with him and asked sarcastically who would write the final spec once the details were worked out. No one answered, and they all rose silently from the table and started to leave the room. I looked at Gail, who had downcast eyes as she headed for the door. She did not return my glance. Jim and Stan slipped out quietly behind Gail, and I was left alone in the room with Dick. I began to gather the copies of the spec that were strewn about the table. I was seething, but I said nothing. As I was going out the door, I heard Dick say over my shoulder in what I thought sounded like a sincere tone, "Great meeting."

Lessons Learned

What did I learn that day? For one thing I learned that Dick was not going to get a Christmas card from me that year. Dick saw the holes in the spec I had written and took me to task for it, but he could certainly have expressed his disapproval more appropriately. There is something to be said for manners and decorum in public.

I also realized that I had set myself up for failure from the beginning. The technology was beyond my grasp, and I did not perform the due diligence necessary to be up to speed on the technical aspects of the project. I called a meeting to have the experts, in front of the project sponsor, verify a spec I had written without really knowing if the functionality described in it was feasible. What did I expect? The techies knew better than I what was possible and what wasn't. I was so wrapped up with pleasing Gail that I tuned out the warnings from the developer, however subtle the warnings may have been, about the functionality described in the spec. And in my haste to get the spec approved, I didn't take the time to have Jim explain what he had in mind so I could better negotiate with Gail.

I felt I was responsible for managing Gail's expectations and fearing letting her down and blowing my first high-profile marketing project, I wrote up the spec to include all her requirements and hoped tech would back me up. Unfortunately, the tech group had their own ideas about how the interface application should be built and never took Gail's requirements, or me, seriously.

Summary

Get used to the fact that you will be spending a large percentage of your work-week in meetings. You will also be leading the majority of the meetings you attend. Learning how to facilitate a meeting is a skill that will very quickly become second nature to you. Running effective meetings requires a certain degree of confidence, skill, and sensitivity to group dynamics. Keeping a group of people focused on a topic is a difficult task, but there are some methods you can use that make the task a little easier.

The single most important tool you will use to control your meetings is the agenda. Always create an agenda before any meeting where there are more than four people in attendance. Creating an agenda allows you to discern if the meeting you are calling is really necessary, and it provides you with a road map for the meeting discussion. Never call unnecessary meetings. You know how much you hate attending them, so don't inflict this drudgery on your team or client. It's one of the fastest ways to lose credibility.

Keep in mind that the people you invite to meetings are there for a reason: to share their views, to offer their expertise, and to critique—in short, to participate. The odd thing is, there will always be people who will be reluctant to participate, and you must learn to draw them out and make them a part of the discussion. There are many reasons why some people have a hard time participating in meetings, such as not having bought into the project or meeting topic or reluctance to speak in groups. Before the meeting discussion begins, be sure to state the agenda, and ask the group if everyone agrees that is what the discussion will focus on. Look around the table to be sure everyone is involved. You will know immediately who needs a little coaxing to offer their input when the discussion begins.

Friendly debate is a common occurrence in nearly every meeting you will attend, but tempers can flare when the pressure is on. Stay aware of the tone and focus of the discussion as debates play out. As soon as the discussion turns personal in any way, be it aggressive body language, a sarcastic tone, or a personal attack, you should intervene. Tell the people attending your meetings that personal attacks will not be tolerated. Ask the people engaged in the debate to keep the conversation focused on the topic, not each other. If necessary you can always halt the meeting if tempers and emotions cannot be soothed. Know when the point of no return has been reached in the discussion and pursuing the topic further will only serve to damage the relationships of the people arguing. Above all, when emotions start to show in a meeting, stay neutral. By taking one side over another in a public debate, you run the risk of alienating people with opposing views.

Besides the occasional argument breaking out in your meetings, there are other unproductive behaviors that occasionally crop up.

- The side conversation
- The meeting hijacker
- The personal agenda

These are the most common problematic meeting behaviors you will encounter. Dealing with these situations takes a bit of tact and some assertiveness. Once again, having an agenda is a big help in these situations.

Meetings have a bad reputation because people have been mismanaging them for so long. In the extremely fast-paced world of Web development there simply isn't time for bad or unnecessary meetings. If word gets out that you do not know how to run a meeting or if you call too many meetings, your credibility will be diminished and you'll have a hard time getting people to reply to your meeting invites. Learn how to manage meetings effectively and you will enhance everyone's work experience by sparing them hours of wasted time sitting around the conference table.

CHAPTER 8

Workflow

Workflow is often defined as the relationship between the activities in a project as it moves from start to finish. Workflow encompasses the standards and protocols that your production team will follow as the *outputs* from one step in the process become the *inputs* for the next step. With all of the heavy machinery in place, workflow standards act as the conveyor belt that moves the parts down the assembly line.

Workflow for the Web

Workflow is simply the path that a deliverable follows through your organization as it is transformed from an input (let's say a PhotoShop page mockup) through to output (a finished HTML page). Along this path, the "raw materials" pass across the desks of many people across multiple departments. At each stop on the way, processes are applied that transform the graphics, page mockups, e-mail messages, meeting notes, and handwritten reminders into something of value. The industrial overtones take on a new complexity within Web teams. Rather than describing a digital assembly line, Web team workflow defines the "relationship" between the business units and the key events that affect your work-in-progress. It's a very good idea to define this workflow at two crucial junctures: before your team dives into production and when your team shifts into postlaunch maintenance.

Workflow management is not micromanagement. As you define the workflow you are not telling people how to do their job but instead communicating how their job relates to the big picture. You also assist the project team in setting ground rules for sharing inputs across departments. These are a few ways to lubricate the interlocking parts of your Web team.

- Introduce collaborators long before it's time to pass the baton. (The client's graphic designer and your HTML code jockey should be pals well before the design handoff, when things might get confusing and nerves will be tested.)

- Establish naming conventions for shared assets like content files and graphics.

- Agree on the location and format of assets that are ready to be handed off. (Will the final, approved copy be posted to a special folder on the intranet or to the project Web site?)

Benefits of Workflow Planning

In addition to making the daily workload a little bit easier for your team, a solid workflow will lessen headaches for you as well. A well-designed workflow does the following.

- Decreases the amount of effort required to track milestones and resolves issues related to handoffs.

- Reinforces a culture of teamwork. Familiarity with what's going on both before and after they touch the product increases empathy among team members.

- Bolsters the importance of the project plan. Because workflow focuses attention on dependencies, team members will have a greater appreciation for the impact of missing their own deadlines.

- Eliminates risky assumptions. If the workflow is clearly communicated, costly misunderstandings can be avoided. When asked, most functional experts will say that they do not have any questions about what is expected of them during the process because they "know" their job. This is because they are making tacit assumptions that will become visible when it's too late to make adjustments.

Creating Workflow Standards

Developing and documenting workflow standards is paramount for maintaining an efficient, successful production environment. Still, not every member of the production team, or management for that matter, realizes it. This is because processes are often taken for granted. Subsequently, when you set out to define, or revise, the workflow process(es) at your organization, make a point of informing and including the people whose buy-in you'll need to implement your recommendations. If revising your current workflow process is too controversial, start by simply documenting the workflow process you use now. Chances are, inconsistencies and weak links will come up during the documentation process and revisions will naturally follow.

Work habits can be a highly charged issue, so approach the topic diplomatically and involve as many people as you reasonably can in the process. Explain the following benefits of documenting your organization's production workflow to everyone involved.

- Improving handoffs between different team members
- Creating a better understanding of, and appreciation for, each individual team member's responsibilities
- Providing greater predictability and repeatability on projects
- Exposing any incorrect assumptions about how the process works and providing a forum to correct them
- Presenting your process as a selling point in sales meetings with clients

Code Review: Standards for Developers

As developers write code, they need to follow standards as well. In the same way that copy editors follow a style guide, programmers need their own style guide to ensure that their code will be readable, understandable, and reusable when it is shared with their colleagues. Technical requirements around scalability and performance also play a big part in software style guides, ensuring that programs will deliver results without breaking under stress. These standards are typically enforced through a series of peer reviews that are conducted at critical junctures during the software development process. Code reviews are covered in detail in Chapter 10.

What Processes Do You Need?

Depending on the breadth of your organization's services, you may have more than one type of workflow process. You may produce marketing Web sites that contain static creative content, for example, or e-commerce sites that are database-driven. If this is the case, you may need to define several workflow processes. Avoid getting too specific, though; the goal is to create general guidelines that provide predictability for your team and your clients. Attempting to define every step taken during production can stymie innovation and damage morale.

Documenting Your Current Workflow

Begin documenting the production process your organization currently uses by identifying and describing the following components.

- *Phases.* The overarching phases stages of your production process
- *Deliverables.* Any and all items that are created and shared during production
- *Dependencies.* Which deliverables cannot be started or finished without the completion of some other deliverable
- *Resources.* Employees, freelancers, vendors, and equipment
- *Roles.* Repeatable roles performed on project teams, even if individuals assume multiple roles or change those they perform from project to project. For your standard to be truly useful it needs to define tasks and deliverables by roles, not individuals
- *Roles on deliverables.* Which roles are responsible for which deliverables and which ones contribution to them

You may be surprised to learn that different people on the same project will give you different answers to the following questions. To uncover these inconsistent world views, you'll need to interview at least one key person from each type of specialization within your organization (sales, design, QA)

- What are their deliverables?
- Which specific team member(s) create them?
- Who should review them? Who should approve them?
- What do they need from others in order to create their deliverables? (dependencies)
- At what phase in the project do they start and complete each of their deliverables?
- What is working well for them in the current workflow situation?
- What is not working well for them?

Workflow Analysis

Now that you have an idea of what your production team is doing, think they are doing, and wish they were doing, you are ready to present your findings. A workflow analysis document is a good format for presenting the findings, since it invites the question "How do we address these needs?" and opens a path for recommendations.

The workflow analysis can include some or all of the following items.

- An introduction explaining what you are addressing—defining your organization's workflow process, why you are addressing it (clarification, documentation, revision, project difficulties, etc.), and how you gathered the information presented in the document (interviews, case studies, etc.).
- A summary of the current workflow process. This can include notes of inconsistencies where they exist.
- A more detailed discussion of the inconsistencies you found.
- A chart showing your production phases and where deliverables fall within them. Include dependencies of deliverables where they occur.
- A description of your deliverables—what they are and who authors them (see Table 8.1 for an example).
- A description of your team roles—what they are called and what they do (see Table 8.2 for an example).
- A summary of your findings—for example, there may be several opinions about what the current workflow is and whether it is satisfying your needs or not.

An effective use of the workflow analysis is to present it in a meeting where the participants of the workflow process interviews are gathered to hear your findings and to discuss remedies to the problem areas you identified.

The workflow analysis can provide a structure for brainstorming on a subject that otherwise can appear overwhelmingly complex or contentious. A "Workflow Brainstorming Session" like this can give you the materials you need to put together a recommendation that reflects many points of view.

Workflow Recommendations

You are now ready to develop recommendations on improving your workflow standard. The best practice is to combine the workflow analysis and the recommendations into one document. You should edit down the original workflow analysis to focus on the primary weak spots that the

TABLE 8.1 Sample Deliverables for Information Architecture

Deliverable	Roles
Hypermap: A conceptual representation of the user flow through the site	*Responsible:* Information Architect *Contributors:* Lead Designer, Strategist
Site Map: A graphical representation of the site structure and navigation, showing how many screens there will be and how they link to one another	*Responsible:* Information Architect *Contributors:* Lead Designer
System Architecture Components Model: Provides a summary of the major technical components of the system and how they will interact at a high level	*Responsible:* Object Model Architect *Contributors:* Client, Strategist, Lead Developer
Creative Concepts: Two (or more) interface designs articulating different approaches to the look-and-feel of the site	*Responsible:* Lead Designer *Contributors:* Junior Designer, Creative Director
Creative Direction: The refined, final look-and-feel for the site, arrived at through the review and revision of the creative concepts. This direction informs the design of all site screens	*Responsible:* Lead Designer *Contributors:* Junior Designer, Creative Director
Editorial Guidelines: A description of the recommended tone for editorial content (copy) to serve as a guideline for the writers and merchandisers. Art direction for photography and/or illustration to serve as a guideline for photographers and merchandisers	*Responsible:* Producer *Contributors:* Creative Director, Strategist, Lead Designer
Component-Based Requirements Descriptions: A functional view of the system requirements that maps directly to the object model and the hypermap, thus integrating technical, business, and user experience requirements	*Responsible:* Object Model Architect *Contributors:* Lead Developer, Information Architect

TABLE 8.2 Sample Role Definitions

Role	Description
Strategist	Works with client to formulate project/business strategy. Draft the business strategy documents. Draft ROI documents and cost-benefit analysis. Present project to resource prioritization committees.
Senior Account Manager	Manage communications with the client/customer. Ensure that the project deliverables meet the client's expectations and the terms of the sales contract. Continuous contact with customer throughout the project.
Associate Editorial Producer	Write site copy and ensure that copy is moved through the copy editing process. Perform data entry of content into the content database.

◆ Deconstructing Workflow

One brainstorming technique is to grab a stack of Post-it® notes and sit down with your team to write down all the tasks they can think of. Organize the notes into groups by sticking them on a large white board. Assign each group a name and draw lines connecting the handoffs between groups. After about an hour, you should be left with a pretty clear vision of your current workflow. Once you have documented the current process, you can reorganize the notes to reflect the desired situation.

recommendations will address. Update your introduction and summary, and add recommendations along with the following information.

- ◆ Which problem(s) from the analysis section does each recommendation address?
- ◆ How critical is the implementation of that recommendation to the health of your organization?
- ◆ How difficult will it be to implement?
- ◆ What is needed to implement it (money, new hires, promotions, management support, and so on)?

Using this criteria you can then rank your recommendations based on the ease of implementation and the importance to the organization. You can also include recommendations on the future use of the new workflow standards (that is, its distribution to new employees, partial or full distribution to clients, periodic review and refinement, other areas of your business that would benefit from a similar process review and documentation).

Workflow for the Real World   Not all project managers have a burning ambition to create new corporate reengineering jargon for a major consultancy. Open the Chapter 8 folder on the CD-ROM, and you'll find two whitepapers that address nuts-and-bolts workflow issues.

"Small Project Team Workflow": This proposal defines roles, workflow, and process for a small Web production team that has been brought together to launch a new Web site. This document provides an excellent example of the industry standard "in a nutshell."

"Maintenance Team Workflow": This study addresses the challenges of an overworked and understaffed maintenance team for a large Web site.

Up-to-date versions of these documents are maintained on this book's Web site at *http://www.realwebprojects.com.*

Table 8.1 displays the results of a workflow analysis for the Information Architecture phase of a complex project. This table shows the specific deliverables as well as a detailed description of the roles and responsibilities that are associated with each deliverable.

Content Production Workflow

The most significant workflow issues on a Web development project often relate to the creation and publishing of content. There are several workflow "events" that should be accounted for in any content workflow plan.

- *Harvesting.* Few Web sites contain completely homegrown content. This activity entails researching content syndicators and obtaining appropriate content sources.
- *Authoring.* Create and develop your own indigenous content by writing copy, obtaining royalty-free images, and preparing multimedia.
- *Submission.* Submit content online to editors and managers for review.
- *Review and edit.* As editors and managers will review submitted content, version control is crucial.
- *Approval.* Approved contents should reside in a special location.
- *Categorization.* Content objects are designated according to "type" (feature, news article) and assigned to topics within a subject tree (such as parenting, health).
- *Scheduling.* The managing editor determines when the content will be published and when it will expire.
- *META tagging.* Content descriptors are created for the use of search engines and other indexing tools.
- *Content entry.* This is the data entry into the content management system (CMS), which may take the form of associate producers typing content into form fields to be saved in a database.
- *Publishing.* This step exports content into Web page templates, where it can be previewed in the development environment or made available to the public on a live URL.
- *Archival and deletion.* Content expiry is triggered by an automated process based on live/down dates, moving content into an archive area, or recategorizing content in the database.

Naming conventions are crucial to enabling a smooth transition of digital assets from one group to another. This is particularly crucial for interactive tools, which generally deliver customized, dynamic content. These projects demand an unlikely marriage between editorial workflow and application development.

During the creation of an online "personality profiling tool" based on a user's color preferences, project managers faced a difficult problem. At a crucial juncture in the project, they had to obtain editorial copy from a client and hand it off to production in a format that could be directly understood by the business logic. This was no small task because the assessment tool relied on a "quiz engine" that generated hundreds of possible results combinations, depending on what colors the user had selected. If a user chose blue as her first-ranked color and red as her eighth favorite, she received a customized message about aspects of her personality.

Consequently, the results-processing algorithm was a complex mix of favorite and least-favorite color rankings. The content itself was written by a nontechnical editorial team that was managed by the client. Since the programmers who were writing the results algorithm were unfamiliar with the content, there would be no way for them to determine whether the quiz engine was delivering the "correct" results until it was too late. In addition to making the hundreds of content blurbs understandable to the code, there also had to be a way to automate the process by which the user's color selections were "mapped" to results. This would cut down on crucial development time.

The project plan obscured the complexity of this problem behind a single task that was labeled "Deliver Content to Production." The plan recognized that this step was necessary and allocated time and resources to it. However, an accurate plan was not enough. At its essence, the problem was a workflow issue rather than a planning issue because it raised the following question: "How can we make sure that the input from process A is understood and usable by process B?"

Formatting rules and naming conventions provided the answer. Instead of delivering the quiz results content in one giant document with explanatory text ("This blurb is for people who choose blue as their third-favorite color"), the copy was broken up into hundreds of pieces. Every possible result had a corresponding text file assigned to it. The next task was to somehow enable each result to "find' its mate.

A convention was devised for naming each results blurb according to the color combination assigned to it. For example, the copy for the "Emotional" section of the report for people who selected blue as their favorite and black as their least-favorite color was labeled "emotional_blue_black.txt." The naming convention became more complex as analysis categories were added. Colors were assigned numeric values in order to speed integration with the results algorithm. Positioning and special characters determined whether the color was a favorite, least-favorite, or other type of ranking.

These formatting rules and naming conventions were agreed upon and enshrined in a workflow document that was published to the project Web site. By following these workflow instructions, nontechnical editors were able to deliver text copy that could be imported directly into the database. The copy was immediately understandable to the source code, saving the programmers hundreds of man-hours that would have been spent sifting through reams of copy and translating it into a machine-usable format.

Summary

Workflow recommendations are often met with fear and suspicion. If you decide to suggest workflow reforms, the sound of nailbiting will emanate from isolated cubicles as your colleagues ponder questions like "Are you trying to change my job?" or "Is someone going to get fired after we redefine roles?" When addressing workflow issues on your team, begin by speaking to their pain. Describe a well-known problem that is causing hardship or added work for everyone, and let your recommendations follow from your fact-finding mission. Avoid being labeled a busybody reformer with an agenda who's out to change the world and disrupt everyone else's job. Instead, strive to be an objective problem solver, and you'll have plenty of cooperation as you fix the broken plumbing in the pipes of your project team structure.

When it comes to workflow, the single most important favor you can do for yourself and your team is to sit down with everyone, describe the current state, and put it down on paper. The simple act of defining roles as they currently exist will allow you to expose most of the problems, without coming across as a sinister agent of doom. This simple act will undoubtedly spawn some very interesting discussions and revelations. More importantly, it will expose any organizational booby traps that threaten to snag you as your team is called upon to finally "deliver the goods" in the technical build phase.

CHAPTER 9

Managing the Design Phase

Although the seed from which the Web sprouted may be rooted in technology, the hook that captured the imagination of the masses was, and continues to be, graphic design. The "look and feel" of a Web site will ultimately generate more business (and opinions) than the back-end functionality. Some may argue that without sound functionality, the design is useless. While this may be true, it is also true that the Web is a visual communication medium, and good design is sometimes more useful than whiz bang functionality.

Design solutions can be every bit as challenging and elusive as technical solutions. Like developers, designers will collaborate with the client, team, and themselves before donning the headphones and disappearing behind their Macs for a few days. When they emerge, they usually have several versions of a design solution ready to be discussed at length. Designers come armed with an expansive and metaphorically rich design vocabulary that incorporates everything from Wall Street to 1970s Japanese architecture to Britney Spears. The ability to colorfully describe their work is part of the charm and allure of the Web designer.

Is Information Architecture the Designer's Job?

Information architecture (IA) is tightly wound with the graphic design phase of a Web project. In early generations of Web development the graphic designer *was* the information architect. So was the client, the programmer, the editor, and the HTML programmer. In other words, everyone had a say in the site's architecture. However, it was the designer who, almost by default, was charged with establishing the Web site's structural underpinnings from a navigational and usability standpoint. The prominence of IA as a necessary facet of Web development has grown tremendously over the last few years, and IA departments in Web development companies are now common.

The answer to the question "Is IA a function of the designer?" would probably depend on whether or not you have an information architect on your team. Generally speaking, the information architect has a very broad and sweeping role in Web development projects, and the scope of their role tends to overlap the following resources.

♦ *Project manager.* The information architect works with all the production resources on the team and is responsible for creating and requesting certain deliverables. The project manager helps the information architect manage these deliverables and track his tasks as well as the tasks of the resources he is working with. The bulk of the IA work is done early in the project, but the information architect is involved in all phases.

♦ *Quality assurance.* The information architect is involved in all usability testing of the information system they design. The information architect works closely with the QA engineer on designing tests for various components of the information system.

♦ *Developer.* The information architect collaborates with the development team on the appropriate content categorization structure, database schema, and content management systems. The information architect, similar to the project manager, has a general knowledge of Web technologies—at least enough to be conversant with the tech team. If the information architect's background is technical, then her knowledge will allow greater latitude when designing the tech components of the information system. If the information architect's back-

> *IA on the Web*   There are many excellent resources to learn about information architecture on the Web. Here are two outstanding places to start:
> - The Argus Center for Information Architecture—*http://argus-acia.com/*
> - Webmonkey's Tutorial—*http://hotwired.lycos.com/webmonkey/design/site_building/tutorials/tutorial1.html*

ground is more design oriented than technical, then she will rely on the developer to weigh in on the technical decisions.

- *Designer*. The information architect will collaborate with the designer on many of the display aspects of the Web site. While the information architect is responsible for detailing the client or management's vision of the site, he must be able to articulate it accurately to the designer, who will then create the look and feel.

If you have an information architect on your team, the designer will be more focused on creating the graphic elements of the site, including images, color palette, and typography. All of these elements will be influenced by and derived from the information architect's design document, which will provide the design objectives for the Web site.

If your team does not have an information architect, it would be worth your time to learn as much as you can about the disipline. IA is an extremely interesting topic, and as a project manager your generalist's background will allow you to learn the basics quickly. At the outset of the design phase, work with your designer and other members of the team on creating a design document that is as comprehensive as possible. The document should include the following.

- The Web site's goals
- The client's goals and vision
- Definition of the site's audience
- A comprehensive site map that includes the content categorization structure
- Page maps
- Tone and voice of the content and graphic design
- Navigation system
- Back-end technologies

This may sound like the Web site functional specification, and to some degree both documents will borrow from each other. The design document, however, is more "top-line" than the functional specification and is not technical even though it discusses some technical aspects of the Web site.

Design Production

The length of your design phase depends on the scope of the Web site under development, your established in-house process, the relationship you have with your client, and the design philosophy to which your company subscribes. These factors also come into play in determining how many design revisions the client receives before signing off on a design element.

Revisions and Sign-off: Making the Client Happy

Most Web design companies allow the client at least two rounds of revisions before completing design work on an element of the Web site. Then again, there are some design companies that allow the client to dictate how long the design process will last. It's generally easier for the design team and the client to break up the design tasks into large pieces. This approach may require more sign-off meetings, but at least the client is integrally involved in the process the entire time. Generally the following design deliverables require sign-off.

♦ *The color palette.* This color scheme of the site has a profound impact on everything from usability to emotions.

♦ *The home page.* One of the most debated pages from a design perspective during the build. Everything has to be in sync on the home page: identity, images, color, typography, tone, and voice. Everyone wants to make a good first impression. Oddly enough, often the home page is one of the least-visited pages on large Web sites.

♦ *Landing pages.* If the Web site is using a categorization structure that requires landing pages to allow users to drill deeper into the content, then these pages should be carefully designed and rendered.

♦ *The header and footer design.* Each page template (except the home page) of a Web site generally displays the same header and footer designs. Since these two elements of the Web site are so basic, they often do not receive the scrutiny they deserve. Be sure to get sign-off for these foundational elements.

♦ *Content page templates such as articles, Q & As, quiz and poll interfaces, and search results pages.* These templates make up the bulk of the content display pages and will communicate through their design the desired look and feel of the Web site.

All of the preceding pages actually should be signed off twice. The first time these pages are signed off is during the page-mapping phase. Wire frames of every page of the Web site should be approved and signed off by the client before any graphical representation of the page is created. The pages receive their second sign-off after the design revisions are complete.

Sign-off means many things to many people. To the project manager it means the end of the design phase and time to move on to the technical production. To the designers it means their work was appreciated and approved and hopefully can be refined further before launch. For the client sign-off means the design will pass until they see something they like better on another Web site. Since the client is paying for the time it takes to build the site, they usually feel free to change their mind at any time during the build, and they often will. It's your job as project manager to make the client aware that there are a variety of penalities for not honoring sign-offs. Changes that come after sign-off require the designer to come up with a new design solution that could require code to be rewritten and add to the scope of the project.

None of these issues really deter a client from making changes after sign-off, but all of these issues add time to the schedule and increase the cost of the project—sometimes by a significant amount.

The sign-off procedure need not be complicated. Design review meetings are scheduled for the designer, creative director, client, and project manager to review the current design deliverables. The client is asked if they approve, and if they agree, it is notated by the project manager. Some companies have dated sign-off documents their clients sign, which leaves a paper trail and can be a good idea if you are dealing with a difficult client. However, use your best judgment with regard to how elaborate you want to make the sign-off procedure. Your relationship with the client will also influence this procedure. At the very least be sure to notate the date of the meeting in your project notes so you can reference them should the client request a change or claim a revision did not occur.

Design Production Phases

The design process often begins before the proposal is accepted and the contract signed. During the sales pitch, the client is asked to describe Web sites they like and why. Invariably, the descriptions of sites clients like include "It looks cool . . ." or "It looks professional . . ." or "I like the colors. . . ." Surfers and clients alike demand good graphic design and will make many assumptions about a Web site based on the execution of the design.

These are the basic phases that comprise the design production cycle.

♦ Brainstorming

♦ Multiple idea renderings

♦ Final concept accepted

♦ Production

During the design kickoff meeting, the design team will spend some time brainstorming the myriad directions the design tone of the Web site can take. The information architect or project manager will attend the meeting to contribute technical or usability comments and keep the discussion within the realm of possiblity. The brainstorming process continues beyond the kickoff meeting until the design team feels like a direction has been reached.

Once the team has a basic design direction they are comfortable with, they will begin to create the necessary design assets. The first set of deliverables will be multiple versions of the design that are shown to the client. The client will either select a favorite or work with the designer on creating an ideal solution using elements from each version. Now that the designer has a definitive direction to pursue, the revision process begins.

The number of revisions the design process goes through is decided in advance and indicated in the contract or statement of work. Typically the design process goes through at least two revisions, but this number changes from company to company and project to project. The project manager sets up the revision schedule with the designer and communicates the schedule to the client.

Your goal as project manager is to be sure the revision process runs as smoothly as possible. Be sure to take accurate notes during the design review meeting with the client. After the meetings, verify your notes with the designer to be sure nothing was missed and everyone is on the same page.

The project manager does not have a great deal of input in the design process beyond being sure the milestones are hit and the communication is efficient. However, this does not mean you should not speak up at design meetings and offer your opinion. Often, your generalist background will allow you the perfect perspective to resolve a particular design issue.

When at last the design revision stage is finished and the final design has been signed off by the client, the designer will prepare the necessary design assets. The common practice among Web designers today is to lay out the Web pages in Adobe PhotoShop or Illustrator. These pages are either saved as JPEG files and displayed on a production server for the client or they are printed out and presented on paper at design review meetings. Once the final design has been approved, the designer will cut the actual design shapes (navigation

> ***Design Management Resources***   An excellent resource for articles and information about managing designers and the design process is the Design Management Institute; visit them online at *www.dmi.org*. There are many free articles for download.

bars, headers, buttons, and so on) out of the master file and optimize the pieces for the Web. This work is also often performed by production artists. Once the files have been cut and optimized, the design assets are handed off to the project manager, who in turn hands them off to the HTML programmer.

⇒ KEY POINT

Be aware of last-minute design tweaks the designer may attempt after the final sign-off has been achieved. While the designer's intentions are good, if these tweaks are not scheduled or involve any retooling by the developers once the project is in technical production, they should not be allowed.

Internal and External Design Groups

The differences between working with an internal design group and an agency design team are explained in this section.

The Internal Design Experience

As you progress through your project management career, chances are good that you will work in internal development groups as well as in the agency environment. In either case the design production process is relatively the same. The biggest differences will be the actual design work and the clients. As you would assume, an internal design group may spend 80 percent of their time updating and working within an existing templated environment. The look and feel of the Web site has been established, and the designers spend the bulk of their time on new headers, images, and illustrations, all designed to work within the established framework. The creative director in this type of group is challenged with keeping the design fresh and the designers inspired while working within the existing look and feel.

Projects that flow through this type of environment tend to be easy to manage for the project manager. The process is usually well documented, and after a few projects, things fall into place relatively easily. The clients are all internal, and after a while the project manager knows and understands their idiosyncrasies and expectations.

The External Design Experience

The graphic design department in an agency environment is tightly woven into the reputation of the agency. Clients tend to choose one agency over another not so much because of technical prowess but because of design capabilities and a dazzling client portfolio. Pressure on designers in agency groups can be higher than in internal groups due to the client-facing role they play. In an agency the revenue of the company depends on the designers making the client happy, whereas in an internal group revenues may not be tied so directly to the designer.

The designer's individual temperment will dictate to which environment they are better suited. Some designers respond to the pressure of an agency, and this pressure acts as a catalyst for good work. Others prefer the more familiar setting of an internal group, where there tends to be a bit more flexibility in the timelines and milestones.

While an agency may have a set and well-documented methodology and approach to design, the process will change from client to client. The project manager will be spending much more time managing the client as opposed to the design deliverables in an agency situation. A good project manager learns the designers' strengths and weaknesses. When projects come in, the project manager can consult with the creative director on the resource allocation for the project and help choose the designer who will be the best match for the project.

How Technical Do Designers Need to Be?

As front-end and back-end system designs become more and more intertwined, the need for the Web designer to become technically savvy is apparent. *How savvy* is the question for many designers. Is it enough to just know HTML? Should the designer need to know programming basics in order to successfully design for the Web? Therein lies the debate. How technical do designers have to be today? Some would argue that designers should design and developers should code. This is historically how the two camps worked together: one camp imposing limitations on the other as they both try to push the boundaries as much as possible. But which camp has the greater influence over the other? Which camp *should* have the greater influence?

JavaScript was probably the first exposure to programming logic that designers experienced. In order to use those groovy image rollovers, designers had to edit an existing JavaScript that performed the rollover function. It's doubtful many designers actually became JavaScript experts because there are so many free and easily editable scripts available online, and writing code is not a designer's primary focus. But regardless of the availability of code, designers were now getting their hands dirty with it.

With the addition of Action Scripting in Flash™ the designer was now faced with the need to understand (at least rudimentary) programming logic. Sure, Flash™ actually writes the code, although the designer can choose to do so, but now programming logic and the need to understand a programming language stand between the designer and the finished piece.

As the technical side of the Web becomes more and more complex, should designers have to improve their technical knowledge and at least learn programming basics in order to converse better with the tech team? Or will the facilitation of communication between the tech and design groups continue to be conducted by the project manager? It would seem a little of both. It makes sense for designers to embrace technology further as design and technical development move closer in scope and definition. It may not be enough for the project manager to act as translator in the future of Web development as projects grow more and more complex. The front-end design of Web sites and Web applications will engender more and more integration of the tech and design groups, with the project manager concentrating more on managing responsibilities, tasks, and deliverables and less on technical translation.

This debate will continue to evolve during the next generation of the Web. There have already been essays written on the subject by people who represent both camps: those who believe designers should design and developers should program and those who believe designers should learn how to program to better perform their tasks.

Summary

Like other roles on the Web development team, the designer brings to the project a generalist's knowledge of the overall process. However, in the future this may not be enough. More and more, Web front-end design and technical back-end functionality will be intertwined. Designers will, almost by default and by using tools such as Flash™, become more technically proficient throughout their careers.

The design process consists of the following phases that result in deliverables that are approved by the client.

- Brainstorming the original design direction
- The revision process for all facets of the design
- The final sign-off of the finished piece

The project manager's most important contribution to the design process is ensuring a smooth sign-off process for each deliverable and making sure the client honors the sign-off procedure.

Designers, like developers, have their own quirks that project managers need to learn and exploit in order to get the best work out of this group. Project managers should never be afraid to speak up and suggest a design solution to the designer, but the bulk of the design collaboration occurs within the design group. How a project manager manages the design process will depend on whether he is managing an internal or client-facing design group.

Design is one of the most enjoyable phases of a project. The design process is when people get to be visually creative, and the first inklings of what the Web site will eventually become begin to emerge. Web designers are expressive people who need the freedom to work out design solutions without being too encumbered by timelines and milestones. Be sure your designers have all the freedom they need to create and that their headphones are as big as possible and always turned on.

THE INFORMATION ARCHITECT ROLE IN PRACTICE

Fabrice Hebert is the former managing director of Oven Digital, one of New York's best boutique interactive design shops. Fabrice joined Oven as a project manager and in short order optimized Oven's production process. Oven is well known for its front-end design capabilities. The jewel, so to speak, in its client roster is Tiffany.com. In this interview Fabrice discusses how Oven uses information architects and the Oven design process.

Can you tell us about the role information architects play at Oven?

The information architect department overlaps with all the other departments. Actually, in our methodology we call everything information architecture. This department is the one writing the whole process along with QA. The IA guys are the most crucial component of everything. You can replace site builders and you can replace designers, but you have to have the information architects from the beginning.

The information architecture department at Oven is a three-person department. One of them has a computer designer degree and has a very technical background and a lot of system architecture—stuff like that—so he's the tech guy of the information architects. The other one knows nothing about tech. His approach to information architecture is purely from the front end. And the other guy, the head of the department, is actually experienced in both.

The information architect who is technical is used a lot at the beginning of the project for functional specifications and technical specifications. He also contributes some help in understanding business requirements from the client. Information architecture can overlap heavily with design, and we try to avoid that situation. It needs to be done concurrently. One of the problems we had in the past was when the designers were doing information architecture. So we tried having the information architecture happen before design, and that didn't work well either.

In the end we realized that you have to work concurrently. You have to sit down next to each other and explain specifications. We found when the information technology was too separated from the design process or was too far integrated in the design that we ended up with bad design. There can be a lot of politics, and designers sometimes feel they have constraints put on them if the information architects are somehow assumed to be managing the designers. The only solution to that was to put them on the same level.

Describe the Oven design process for us.

Oven started as a design group; there was no technical ability. For every design project that we do, the process involves using a lot more designers than I think our competitors are using. For every single project that we are doing— Tiffany, for example—you would have eight designers, which kind of, when you look at from a management point of view, you would say that's a waste of money. Well, that's kind of the compromise that we make.

The way it works is that the design department is always very collaborative, always works together, they all sit next to each other, and they all use Internet tools. We actually have a tool that allows designers to plug in comments about other people's designs and then post messages like a message board, and that's great because no design goes out without everybody thinking, "Oh, yeah, this is the best one."

Of course, we use a professional methodology that allows for several revisions. Sometimes we don't hesitate to go through three, four, or five revisions. That's fine with us. The designers spend a lot of time initially writing the creative brief, and even the creative brief is a very collaborative effort. It's done with the information architect and it's done with the project manager. And the creative brief gets sent out to the entire design team so everybody understands. I think it's exceptional because the product you get in the end is something unique.

There is a huge internal decision first, so at the end of the day when we put a design out, we say, "Okay, we managed to get the best design," and the quality is better. That's great because the internal selection makes you think about the reason why the design you presented to the client is the best. In design I think the most crucial thing, when you think about client approval, it's not the design itself, it's how you present it to the client. That's the most important thing. And the fact that our designers spend so much time together—eight people—that's a lot of people in a room trying to argue about the design. In the end they come up with the right solution, and they can articulate that in front of the client very well. And I think that that produces great results. The client is very happy when he can argue about points in the design and have another revision—they like that. That's one of our best selling points as well when we do presentations for clients.

How We Manage Design

David Young is one of the founders of Triplecode, an interactive design studio in Los Angeles, California, that specializes in Shockwave applications and design. David approaches design from a code perspective, which gives him a wider breadth of opportunities for discovering the perfect behavioral and design solution. In this interview he discusses hands-on client management, the de-evolution of interactive design, and why designers could benefit from being more technically savvy.

Could you describe your company's project management style?

What is our project management style? That's a tricky question. Some of it varies a lot according to the client. First we'll meet with the client to get a sense of the brief. What we'll do is take that and begin doing some exploration or sketching to try to address the brief. So we'll take the brief and start playing with what that means. Usually that's a combination of visually what might it look like and especially getting down in code trying to figure out what might the content be that they are trying to communicate.

How do you extract direction from the client during that process?

It's funny because usually the client thinks they have clear ideas of what they want the project to be from the beginning. And it's only after we start working with them for a while and they start seeing some sketches and some ideas and we start talking to them that they and we both realize that the original project that they had in mind may not really be the right solution.

Are you trying to lead them toward a particular destination during this educational process?

No, it's usually more like a mutual education process. We are never experts when we first walk in to what the clients domain is, so we're learning a lot about what they're up to, but they also start seeing, as we start presenting ideas to them, that there are very different ways of designing or making interactive experiences than they might have originally imagined.

It sounds like your approach is more like "What does the information look like?" rather than "What does the page look like?"

Exactly. It's almost like we start at the information level because the visuals are a by-product of what the information is. You can say, "Here is a look or here is a style," and we're just going to use some predefined layout, but then your design doesn't become specifically relevant to whatever the project is.

Most designers start off by "Let's get the color palette nailed down first."

(Laughing) In some cases that is important because you are working with a company with a fixed brand or identity, so those are starting points that you can't really change. But my thinking is, even if you are doing print design, you have to understand what your content is before you can start designing for it.

How would you say your approach differs from how an information architect might approach the project?

I think they are pretty close. It's almost incorporated into our process. Since we're not a big company, we don't have different people doing these different things. We don't have a dedicated information architect. Since we're so small, we do everything simultaneously.

Our approach is a little more sculptural, I think. If you're working in code, you can almost start defining what your information is in a sort of code way by defining data structures or objects. And as you simultaneously reshape what those data structures are, you can start adding interactive or motion behaviors to them.

How does the PM facilitate the communication that goes on between you and the client as you try to discover these information objects?

Well, usually the project manager is also the designer and the programmer. So there's not really an interface there. And usually when we deal with clients, we're dealing with the CEO of the company or the curator of the exhibit, so there are not a lot of layers happening on their side either. That has something to do with the fact that clients choose companies whose structures fit within their structure, too.

There are different scales of groups. When you have 50 people working on the Web site, you have a lot of very different specialized skills. And you also have smaller teams where you have two or three people all sort of doing everything together. So you don't necessarily need these large teams to get something done.

Because we're a small company and a small group, we don't have a single, fixed approach or a project management method. The way that we work tends to get influenced by what the client's needs are in terms of the project itself or the client's management and organizational structure.

How many iterations do you give a client, or do you just collaborate until it's done?

I think it's more along the lines of the latter where we just collaborate until it's done. Usually with the client we know when there's a deadline, and we know we need to get the initial direction approved so we can begin a more formal implementation. But there's a real change from a sketch to something that's really running. Oftentimes once it begins working, and you start to have people interacting with it and using it, you start seeing things you want to change. So there's a lot of revision that tends to take place even in the later stages of the project. I think that because our designs are so code based it's pretty easy to make major revisions later on in a project phase than if there were a more strict design or traditional design approach. In our code we can just change a couple of functions and make fairly substantial changes to the way the design looks or works.

Because you are more concerned with behavior . . .

Right. When you want to change all the graphics, in our experience it hasn't been too hard to do. I'm not sure why it is so easy for us as opposed to other design approaches.

Do you worry about giving your clients too many options and confusing them early on in the approval process?

Usually in the initial phase of the project we're learning just as much about what they're doing as they are about us. So our initial presentations tend to be fairly informal because we don't have a choice that we think is the right one because we don't know what the right one is yet. So we show them a bunch of different designs and the number varies according to the scale of the project, but it's only by showing them and discussing them with the client that we can begin to understand what they do or don't like about different versions.

We then see if they like the look of this one but they like the behavior of that one. Or this one sort of is getting them to think really differently about the way the content might be structured, so you start taking all these different pieces from them and gradually start melding them together.

What generation is Web design currently in?

My background in Web interactive design is pre-Web. I started doing interactive stuff before the Web was around, almost before CD-ROMs were around, where it was just computer-based interactive design, and the bigger question was how do you use the screen for any sort of interactivity? This was in the late 1980s and early 1990s. It seemed at the time you weren't concerned at all with any of this delivery issue and you were writing programs in C or some other more deep machine-level thing. You were really unlimited in what you could create; there were almost no constraints. And also, we tended to work on pretty high-ended machines in those days, beyond what would be considered a consumer desktop machine.

So there was amazing stuff that was being done, and people often forget that before the Web the interactive medium was pretty rich. Then the Web came along, and it was almost like this giant step backwards. Suddenly you were limited with these text-based HTML pages with very few graphics and download speeds, and the computers were a lot less powerful because you'd be on more home computers. And it's almost like now we're finally catching up to where we had been. So in a way it's this evolution, and in a way it's been this sort of de-evolution. There was this weird hiccup of really horrible design that happened for a while or very tightly constrained design, and now we are coming back to allowing the technology to be a little less of the straitjacket that it had been for a while.

What would you attribute that to?

Part of it is that personal computers got a lot more powerful, and obviously things like Flash and Shockwave and to some degree Java have gotten more standardized on people's machines. So you are able to do these things more.

What's on the required reading list for the new Web designer?

The first book I'd shove in their hand is some sort of programming book. I really think they need to learn some amount of appreciation for that. When I taught for a while at an art school, it seemed there was a lot of reluctance from the students to learn programming, and a lot of that was just a weird stereotype: "We're designers, and we don't need to learn math. . . ." And not the acknowledgment that programming in its own way is equally as creative as visual design. There's some sort of scariness that comes from the computer.

My experience with design students has been that the more diverse their background is, the better their design is. The more they know about different things, the more they bring to the way they solve design problems. Whether that's psychology or programming or architecture, its going to allow them to think about more stuff. It's an art thing.

The biggest frustration I have with the usability issue is that a lot of people feel that the primary way you evaluate how successful an online project is is by its usability. And it seems that this has created Web sites that are all equally bland and generic and with very similar navigation and systems to them. My feeling instead is that this is such a brand new field, so we shouldn't lock down yet any strict rules about what works or what doesn't work and that people should be experimenting a lot more.

My hope is that there is still, with the changing of technology, a lot more room for exploring what the Web can be. Maybe it also depends on your audience, too. It depends on who you're designing for. If you design for a big conservative company that tends to do work for more conservative clients, then they're going to want more basic stuff. There is a corporate conservativeness that says we need to be safe in what we do. And yet you can see plenty of examples of companies that aren't safe, that are really successful. Often you hear these stories about a company that broke the rules and did some real different kind of advertising or design and that it changed the whole landscape.

CHAPTER 10

The Technical Build

Anxiety over the Technical Build

At the commencement of the technical build, your project team is armed with detailed specifications, feasibility reviews conducted by experienced tech leads, and formal status meetings for checking progress against milestones. In spite of this technique, the technical build remains a source of great anxiety for several reasons.

♦ Most project managers have a general knowledge of Web programming languages and are uncomfortable discussing the complex details.

♦ No one wants to look dumb when programmers start dropping technical terminology. The urge to nod your head with a phony look of grave recognition is irresistible.

- If anything goes seriously wrong during this stage, you might not find out about it until late in the testing phase, when it may be too late.

- The development phase of a project is fraught with risk, including technical feasibility issues, cost overruns, and missed deadlines.

Mitigating the Fear Factor

There are a variety of tactics that you can use to address any insecurities that you have about the technical build. In addition to familiarizing yourself with technical buzzwords and concepts, you can grope toward a sense of security by building additional milestones into the schedule. You might pound away for hours at MS Project, breaking out a multitude of subtasks in the hopes of capturing and monitoring every potential point of failure.

However well-intentioned these tactics may be, you will need more than a detailed laundry list of milestones to survive this critical stage, and you can't do it alone. Given the array of risks and limitations that plague the technical build, your best insurance policy is to put MS Project away and focus your efforts on supporting code review procedures within your development team. A system of peer-based code review procedures, developed by the tech lead and reinforced though your workflow supervision, will increase the odds of a smooth transition through testing and launch.

Internal code reviews conducted "early and often" provide a self-policing quality control mechanism within the production team. The "Recipe Finder" case study at the end of this chapter describes a project that began effortlessly, only to hit a brick wall during the technical build due to a lack of code review procedures. This necessitated a costly recovery effort that served as a wake-up call to the organization and gave rise to an effective, self-regulating code review system.

Model–View–Controller

Although application architecture is the job of senior engineers, as project manager you should ensure that provisions have been made to separate display, business logic, and data. There are many approaches for doing this, but one of the most successful (especially for object-oriented programming) is the "model–view–controller" (MVC) paradigm.

What Is Model–View–Controller?

The MVC paradigm is a way of separating design, business logic, and data by breaking an application into three parts.

◆ The model serves as an abstraction of some real-world process. It manages data, responds to queries about its state, and reacts to instructions to change state (for example, a relational database or JavaBean).

◆ The view is responsible for displaying graphics and text to the user (for example, the JavaServer Page that dynamically generates HTML).

◆ The controller manages the interaction between the parts of the system. It accepts input from the user and instructs the model and view to perform actions based on that input (for example, a Java servlet or CGI script).

A Generic Technical Build

Most database-driven, dynamic Web applications follow a similar process. The activities that go on during this phase of the project warrant distinct

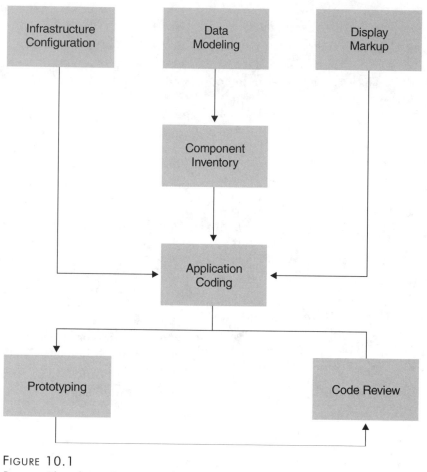

FIGURE 10.1
Process Flow for a Generic Technical Build

milestones in the schedule. If you are not directly managing this workflow process, you should at least be closely monitoring it. The activities for a representative tech build phase are illustrated in Figure 10.1.

A Process for Everyone   Gantthead.com's Process section presents a full menu of processes for guiding your team through the technical build, with recipes for many different types of IT projects that can be adapted for the Web. You'll need to sign up for free membership, but it's worth the two minutes; go to *http://www.gantthead.com/ Gantthead/process/processMain/*.

The Tech Kickoff Meeting

The technical build begins with the "tech kickoff meeting." During this meeting, the technical implementation team meets with the project manager, producer, or product manager and sometimes the project stakeholders to review the functionality requirements and the development tasks that have been set out in the plan. The tech lead and developer(s) review design mockups of the various page templates, read the technical specifications, and review site maps and application flow diagrams. The directory structure of the site is also discussed along with secondary issues like ad serving and Web site traffic analysis requirements. The team should spend a significant amount of time identifying code that can be repurposed, as well as how code from the current project can be genericized for future reuse. The outcome of this meeting is a revised version of the technical specification (drafted by the tech lead) and refined time estimates for each task in the development phase. The project manager updates the project plan if necessary.

Infrastructure Configuration

This activity usually involves the setup of the overall system architecture and development environment. Operations staff prepare the "live" hosting environment by anticipating bandwidth requirements and installing the necessary hardware and software. If necessary, a separate "sandbox" or development environment is prepared for the programmers to test their code. Database administrators are also involved as they prepare to implement the database design.

Component Inventory

The purpose of this activity is to identify software objects within the organization's "code base" so they can be reused to accomplish the task at hand. For example, when building a calendaring application, developers take advantage of software "libraries" containing date-processing functions that allow them to perform routine jobs like converting between different date formats. These "library procedures" are designed to be generic, but if necessary they can be easily modified to handle the current job.

While it is the job of developers to hunt down relevant source code and reuse software modules, you can contribute to this process as well. As a project manager, you should have access to documentation from previous projects that may have used similar technologies or functionality. By researching these applications and bringing them to the attention of the tech lead, you can assist the developers in finding some examples they can draw upon to speed up the development process. This role is especially crucial when working with freelancers or new hires who are unfamiliar with the current code base.

Data Modeling

This activity involves setting up and accessing the data source, which may reside in a relational database, flat text files, or be obtained from a third party via an import of data in XML format. Database administration activities may include the design of a database schema, the writing of database queries, the creation of *stored procedures,* and database tuning.

G *Stored Procedure*   A stored procedure is a group of query statements that reside within the database and perform a certain task. The main advantage of creating stored procedures is that they prevent scripts from using tables directly. This keeps your database tables safe from poorly written queries.

Stored procedures are used to speed up the execution of commonly used queries and to keep the query syntax safely hidden from the business logic of an application. For example, the most commonly used operations on a product database (add a customer, delete a product, retrieve an invoice) could be coded as stored procedures.

Display Markup

This activity may involve the coding of display languages used by the client device (for example, HTML and JavaScript for the browser or WML for wireless display). This raw display code is typically handed off to application developers for insertion into dynamic templates. In more advanced development projects, this step may be extended to include related tasks, like coding JavaServer Pages or writing XSLT code to transform raw XML into HTML that the browser can display.

At this stage a separate quality assurance "checkpoint" is recommended. The purpose of this separate testing step is to review the display markup as it appears across different environments. Typically this involves a thorough test of the HTML in various Web browsers at multiple connection speeds. Testing is conducted by usability experts in the QA department as well as by graphic designers who independently review the work. The design team conducts its own review to ensure that the final version "on screen" matches their original vision in terms of font, color, layout, and other qualities that are subject to browser interpretation.

◆ **Scheduling Tip: Running Activities in Parallel**

In many cases, data modeling tasks can begin during the graphic design phase, depending on the quality of your specifications. Running these two activities in parallel is a slick way to beat a tight deadline.

If the specifications for your application are complete and detailed, give the green light to begin this work ahead of schedule. The schema and the database tables can be created during the final rounds of design approvals because, at this point, the open issues should be merely cosmetic.

After the initial review, designers and HTML coders will get together to discuss the various tradeoffs and limitations the display code imposes on the final look. When both sides are happy with the tradeoffs among download speed, aesthetics, and platform compatibility, the creative director and QA testing director will sign off on the display code.

Application Coding

Here the rubber meets the road, as developers write the business logic of the application, create dynamic templates, and insert SQL statements that will query the database. All the deliverables from the previous tasks are linked together during this stage. Software development should proceed in an iterative fashion, using a "building-blocks" approach. This means that prototypes or working components should be developed early and then tested before the programmer attempts to tackle the next level of complexity.

Ideally, the application should be built as a series of self-contained modules. Each bit of functionality is tested before adding on the next layer of complexity. Good programmers begin with the simplest feature and move on to more complex features. This allows programmers to isolate errors in their code.

Webmonkey Tutorials   Inundated by Web programming acronyms? As a project manager, you don't need a 400-page Java book, you just need a primer that will give you a general understanding of what's going on under the hood. The various Webmonkey.com tutorials (*http://www.webmonkey.com*) provide just enough detail for you to hold your own at the next tech meeting.

◆ Sharing Content with XML

XML (Extensible Markup Language) specifies the logical structure of a document, allowing it to be shared with third parties. XML is "extensible" in that it allows its users to create custom tags to describe how the content is organized. The rules that govern the document are declared in a DTD, or Document Type Definition. For example, if your document is a poem, the DTD might translate it into plain English as "a poem is composed of one title and one or more stanzas, each of which contains one or more lines of text." The XML markup for this hypothetical poem might look something like this.

```
<xml>
    <poem>
        <title>Roses are Red</title>
        <stanza>
            <line>Roses are Red,
            Violets are blue.</line>
            <line>I love project
            management, and so do
            you.</line>
        </stanza>
    </poem>
</xml>
```

Once the content is received in XML, customized style formatting can be applied using XSLT (Extensible Stylesheet Language Transformations). XSLT allows you to define style rules that convert the raw XML into a final display language like HTML.

For example, the set of XSLT instructions for our poem might read (in plain English) as "render the poem's content into HTML, such that the title is displayed in the arial bold font. The text in each line should be colored blue. There should be one line break between each stanza."

The advantage of XSLT is that any third party can apply their own "look and feel" to the raw content. By using a DTD and applying the rules of XSLT, content can be marked up in XML and syndicated to many partners regardless of their technical environments. In other words, XML is the *lingua franca* for content on the Web.

Prototyping

Working prototypes that demonstrate key functionality may also be utilized at this stage, especially if there was no adequate proof-of-concept during earlier tech feasibility discussions. Under "Iterative" models like Rapid Application Development, fully functional prototypes are developed as soon as possible, and new features are added incrementally.

Code Review

Reviews should be conducted periodically as each major feature is added. Performance testing (on both the database and Web server) is also conducted as part of the code review, especially during the final review before the project

◆ **Point–Counterpoint: "Should the project manager play an active role during the application coding phase?"**

"If the project manager has done her job drafting good requirements and specifications, then she shouldn't have to be actively involved. Designing the application is best left to the experts. It's difficult enough without having to deal with the suggestions of someone who just read a *Learn Java in 48 Hours* book and thinks she's an expert. Project managers should limit their activities to communicating and tracking milestones. As they say, having too many cooks in the kitchen causes a lot of problems."

—A senior developer

"While the details of implementation should be left to the experts, project managers can definitely contribute. They need to clear up ambiguities in the requirements. They can make sure that the technology solution fits the company's business strategy and accommodates whatever plans there might be for future enhancements. They sometimes advise on resource tradeoffs and organizational priorities. They should also be managing the overall process and keeping developers on their toes in terms of deadlines. Project managers who ask a lot of questions about implementation details can be annoying, but at least they force everyone to justify their decisions."

—A senior tech lead

is handed off to the quality assurance testing phase. Code review is an absolutely crucial insurance policy that allows developers to identify problems early, before it's too late to save the deadline.

Code Review Guidelines

Code review is especially important for all new scripts and nontrivial enhancements before the code is launched. The goals of the code review are to ensure that the overall system is designed in a scalable, sensible way and also to ensure that the code itself is well structured and well written. Each of the technical review items should show up in the project plan or checklist.

A programming style guide should be used. This can often be obtained from the company or organization that supports the programming language (for example, Sun Microsystems provides a style guide for the Java programming language). A style guide explains conventions for writing code in a clear, readable manner.

The code review should be initiated at regular intervals during the implementation phase. A suggested review interval is every seven to ten workdays, which provides the opportunity to fix systematic problems before the implementation has advanced too far.

For simple projects, the review may consist of an informal walkthrough of the code. However, for more complex projects and final reviews, the reviewer's comments should be written. The reviewer should indicate the severity of the problems uncovered during the review, differentiating between "necessary" and "recommended" changes. Necessary changes include serious bugs that must be fixed before launch. Recommended changes include minor style improvements or simplifications of the code that can be finished after launch.

A separate review of any code that is used to query the database should also be conducted before launch. The purpose of this review is to allow database administrators to "tune" the database for optimal performance under high traffic conditions. The DBA needs to understand how the database tables are being used in order to put performance improvements in place. Also, there are often multiple ways to build a query, and the DBA may be able to suggest improvements to queries. Finally, the DBA may identify some performance issues that are best addressed by implementing stored procedures (and were overlooked during technical design).

After completing a project, developers should enter important details about the project in a searchable knowledge base. This project documentation, typically stored in an intranet archive, provides valuable information to future developers who will be maintaining and enhancing the code.

Creating a code review system is the production manager's responsibility, but as a project manager you can play a crucial role in advocating, establishing, documenting, and enforcing code review policies on each and every project. This effort may entail an internal political battle, but it is a battle that is worth fighting given the time and effort that this practice will save over the lifespan of several projects. If you are outsourcing a major portion of the development work to a third party, ask the contractor to describe its code review procedures, and be sure to track those deliverables by asking for some documentation of the results of each review.

Production Challenges

Although your Web team may include several developers and a tech lead, in practice the day-to-day tasks devolve to individuals working in isolation. The resulting code is often a "black box," whose inner workings are a mystery to everyone on the team except for one or two people. Good tech leads are in high demand, and their efforts may be diluted over multiple simultaneous projects. Consequently, the activities during this highly technical phase are usually a complete mystery to all but a small handful of people in the organization.

♦ **Principles of Good Technical Design**

- ♦ Reuse existing code and database tables where possible.
- ♦ Create reusable, modular code and database tables by identifying features that may be useful in future projects.
- ♦ Database, application logic, and presentation (HTML) code should all be separated out. This will make the code easier to maintain, reuse, and redesign.
- ♦ Identify high-level application flow. Determine which functions and procedures should be stored in a library. Decide

what logic should be built as a component and what elements should be cached or dynamic.
- ♦ Identify potential performance problems. Think about scalability by considering how performance and system requirements will change as more data is added to the system. Consider how dynamic code will hold up under increased traffic.
- ♦ Anticipate enhancements or features that business owners may want to see in the future.

To make matters worse, at this juncture developers are highly sensitive to oversight and criticism. The code a developer writes during this critical time is considered by her peers to be a direct reflection of her competence and intellectual acumen, in much the same way that a world-class chess player is judged by his opening moves. Given this psychological climate and the limited technical knowledge of most project managers, it is very difficult to manage milestones during this stage. Less experienced developers may conceal or downplay the inevitable difficulties that arise. Interruptions by nontechnical people during this phase are usually unwelcome.

Problem #1: The Designer's Blind Date

Symptoms
- ♦ Midway through development, the project sponsor or creative director looks at the work in progress and notices that what they see on the screen looks different from the design.
- ♦ Frantic phone calls and e-mails ensue, asking the question, "How did our 'Mona Lisa' turn into a 'Moaning Loser'?"
- ♦ The designer is overheard saying how she has been painfully reminded of her last blind date: "He definitely looked a lot better on match.com than he did in real life!"

Solutions

◆ Submit the HTML to a quality assurance testing and design review before handing it off to the application developers.

◆ Be sure to obtain the creative director's sign-off before handing the finished HTML over to the developers. Obtaining sign-offs on printed page mockups is not enough. This is because the shortcomings of HTML, browser incompatibilities, and monitor display limitations can all affect how the design is translated onto the screen. Once "application coding" begins, it's very costly to make tweaks to the design markup.

Problem #2: No News Is Not Good News

Symptoms

◆ Nobody on the tech team has any questions about the specifications or requirements.

◆ You sent the specifications as an e-mail attachment asking everybody to "please read this," but you've never been able to hold a tech planning meeting.

◆ The application developer skims over the specifications and says, "It looks pretty straightforward." He is strangely silent or absent during planning meetings.

◆ The lead developer cancels or avoids status meetings. He begins working and delivers terse, vague status reports. You are reluctant to cause a confrontation or be a pain in the neck.

Solution

◆ If the developer is unable or unwilling to discuss her plan of attack, it's probably because she doesn't have one. Round up her manager or a tech lead and schedule a special planning meeting. During the tech meeting, review the specifications line by line. Ask developers to illustrate the system architecture on a white board. Ask questions about how the team intends to implement the requirements to ensure that the technical specifications have been read and understood—for example, "Do we already have some code we can use to build the search engine that is mentioned in the specs?" If you can ensure that everyone understands the requirements and has a solution in mind, you can minimize unpleasant surprises on the eve of a deadline.

Problem #3: "You need Java? Cool! I used to work at Starbucks!"

Symptoms

- The developer doesn't have the technical skills to do the job.

- Your organization was desperate for technical talent and hired consultants, freelancers, or people who were "willing to learn."

- The project team includes only one junior developer or a programmer who is new to the programming language.

- The consultant you're hiring for the job knows all the buzzwords and technical terminology but can't seem to produce any code samples or references.

- The programmer supplies dozens of reasons why certain features "can't be done" but offers few solutions.

- The programmer is working alone. When asked for status reports, the work samples are buggy or behind schedule.

Solutions

- Conduct code reviews early and often.

- Be sure that developers work in teams.

- If you are understaffed, pull someone off another project for a few hours to act as a code reviewer.

- If the current developer is untested, have a contingency plan for bringing in additional help.

- Foster a supportive work environment in which it is okay to ask for help without being looked down on.

- Schedule status meetings with an agenda that explicitly focuses on problems and obstacles rather than reporting successes.

Case Study: A Recipe for Disaster

In the fall of 1999, a leading culinary arts portal undertook an ambitious plan to enhance the centerpiece of its food channel, the Recipe Finder. This project commenced at the height of New York's "Silicon Alley" hiring frenzy, when technical talent was extremely difficult to find. Consulting firms capitalized on the demand for "programmers-for-hire" by hyping the skill sets of their contractors and rushing new hires through abbreviated training programs.

In the race to stay ahead of its competition, the project team was augmented with inexperienced contractors who presented impressive, "buzzword-compliant" resumes. These newbies were thrown into the applications development kitchen, where the *menu de jour* was a customized search engine designed to serve results into a personalized shopping cart.

To make matters worse, the project manager was also new to the job. In his reluctance to make waves among his new colleagues, he stood by while an under-skilled contractor ran amuck with the code until it was too late. A more experienced developer stepped in to save the day; but most of the code had to be rewritten, causing massive delays in the launch date.

Finder Features

The Recipe Finder is an interactive tool that allows users to search a database of food recipes based on their preferences. The tool provides additional features, including a list of "Top Ten Most Requested Recipes" and a shopping-cart-style "Recipe Box" that allows registered members to store and retrieve recipes at a later date.

The Recipe Finder helps users select from their search results list by displaying icons that tell which category each recipe fits into. When users select a recipe, they are presented with nutritional information and the option to add the recipe to a Recipe Box. Users may also e-mail their recipe to a friend, view tips and ratings submitted by other members, and submit tips and ratings of their own. The main features include the following.

- Search a database of recipes by keyword, meal, main ingredients, preparation style, special categories, season, or special occasion
- Display search results with special category icons (vegetarian, no salt, and so on)
- E-mail recipes to a friend
- Store recipes in a Recipe Box
- Rate recipes and share cooking tips
- Accept member recipe suggestions

In addition, the tool interface was placed in an attractive "wrapper" that contains related content. Editorial staff use a publishing interface to assign content to categories, allowing the relevant articles, features, and topics to be dynamically delivered to the page. The attractive left-hand navigation uses sophisticated DHTML to create expandible menus. Relevant advertising from the sponsors of the tool also appears in numerous places.

A content publishing tool on the back end allows editorial staff to add, edit, and remove recipes from the recipe database. The Recipe Finder was developed in Vignette StoryServer, with an Oracle database. StoryServer allowed the development of dynamic page templates as well as page caching. The business logic was written in Tcl, with embedded HTML and SQL statements, as well as proprietary StoryServer commands. The site was hosted in-house.

The business rationale for the project was set by Jane, the editorial director of the site. An accomplished cookbook author and experienced editor, Jane was familiar with the features of competing Web sites. With her print publishing background, she had a clear vision for the tool but was very uncomfortable with the technical details of the software development process. Jane had several business objectives for the tool.

♦ To provide a centerpiece tool for the portal that will increase Web site traffic by providing useful personalized features, tools, and links to related content.

♦ To differentiate the site from competitors with various search and personalization features.

♦ To provide a database of recipes that can be provided by paid sponsors, generating direct revenue.

After a series of informal brainstorming sessions, the project began with Jane's submission of an editorial creative brief. The new features were inspired by a competitive review of leading food Web sites. Jane pitched her project to a committee of department heads at a weekly "priorities" meeting. Her brief consisted of rough page maps, specifying a laundry list of features and editorial copy on a page-by-page basis.

Introducing Tim

At this point Jane enlisted the support of Tim, the project manager. A brand new project manager with two months on the job, Tim had previously worked as the technical production manager for a large Web site. Tim was skilled at drafting technical specifications and communicating technical ideas to nontechnical audiences. However, as a new project manager he was inexperienced at evaluating project risk and had a vague, conceptual understanding of project management principles. With Tim's assistance an effort estimate was calculated, and the project was added to the production calendar.

As the production workload piled up with an onslaught of fall projects, the production team decided to bring in contractors from a reputable consulting agency that specialized in StoryServer development. Given the reputation of the agency and its technical focus, a lengthy screening process was avoided. However, in the absence of industrywide certification standards, it was difficult to judge competency until the contractors were actually on the job.

From this group a contractor named Chris was assigned to develop the page templates that would support the search engine, "Recipe Box" shopping cart, and other features. Chris was a junior developer with six months of hands-on experience, and he had recently completed a training course on Vignette StoryServer technology.

As Chris and the other contractors familiarized themselves with the local development environment, Tim polished off the technical specifications in a series of needs assessment interviews with Jane as well as user interface designers in other departments. Jane presented the specifications to senior management for approval, and Tim's functional page mockups were sent to design. The project was off to an amazingly smooth start.

As the graphic designer worked on creating final page designs, Tim fielded minor feature changes and updated the specifications. As editorial changes began to pile up, the project was split into two phases, with high-priority core features in initial rollout and the "nice-to-haves" relegated to Phase 2. The pros and cons of each feature tweak were discussed in long e-mail discussion threads, and effort estimates were applied against the new features that were included in Phase 2. For example, some debate raged around the issue of where to place a member authentication "wall," since it would reduce page views by discouraging visitors who might be reluctant to sign up for their free membership. As the requirements stabilized, the Phase 2 items were compiled for submission to the priorities meeting as a separate project.

Tim finalized the plan in MS Project, based on the effort estimates of tech leads and his own production experience. As congratulatory feedback about the smooth planning phase rolled in, Tim wondered what all the "scope control" fuss was about, thinking, "This project management gig is a breeze."

The Build Begins

At this point the technical build was ready to begin. Chris assumed a prominent role, drafting a database schema and submitting it for approval to Moe, the database administrator. An experienced database administrator, Moe was responsible for maximizing database performance on interactive tools. Moe's job was to oversee the creation of new tables on the database and ensure that queries would not adversely affect database performance.

As Chris began interacting with the rest of the team, it became clear that he was a very quiet, serious fellow. Since Chris was a technical consultant and an unfamiliar staffer, Tim was reluctant to ask any questions about the schema for fear of insulting Chris. Additionally, the database administrators were swamped with other work. Given Moe's slow response to Joe's schema request, it seemed unlikely that anyone would have time for a superfluous status meeting. Primarily interested in winning friends among his new colleagues, Tim was reluctant to take an assertive role in actively managing these members of the project team.

An e-mail exchange between Chris and Moe went on for a few days as they made changes to the schema. Given the amount of technical jargon exchanged between the two parties, Tim assumed that progress was being made. He certainly didn't want to show his ignorance of "foreign keys" and "inner joins" by having to justify a request for a formal status meeting on the data model.

In the fourth week of development, status reports began trickling in from Chris as he tested the "Rate & Review" and "Top Ten Recipes" features. As Chris moved on to tackle the search engine, radio silence ensued. Tim shrugged it off, assuming that "no news is good news." Other developers in the group assumed Chris was a one-man superstar, since he never seemed to have any questions or problems. He continued quietly tapping at the keyboard and thoughtfully rubbing his brow for another two weeks, while Tim juggled other projects.

As the deadline approached, Tim grew anxious and asked Chris for a status report. Chris indicated that there were "a few issues, but we're really close" and asked for a deadline extension. Tim knew it was important to have the lead developer "on his side," so he lobbied to increase Chris's contract and extend the deadline. Tim pointed out the extensive delays that had been caused by the slow response of Moe's overworked staff. This had significantly hampered Chris's efforts as he tried to build the search engine queries.

Trouble in the Kitchen

Another week passed, with the deadline looming closer. At this point, Chris's contract was about to run out. Al was asked to lend a hand. Al was a senior developer who had been busy working on a related project. As a secondary role, Al had been responsible for answering Joe's questions and providing assistance by request. Al stepped in to assess how much work remained on the project. At this late stage in the project, the remaining work included minor fixes to some of the code, all of the "Recipe Box" shopping cart functionality, and the search results pages. In order to get a clearer idea of the scope of the remaining work, Al opened up the code and took a look inside.

The code itself was clean and well commented, but it lacked basic error checking of user inputs. The programming logic was crammed with convoluted "if-then" statements. Chris also ran into problems on the search results page with handling the output from two queries at the same time. In each case, stock solutions were readily available that could have saved several days of wasted effort. At this point, Moe assumed a more active role, stepping in to review the code from a database efficiency standpoint. Moe offered several suggestions to rework the SQL queries and introduce caching of some dynamic elements. Chris was asked to hand off the project to Al. After reengineering much of the code, Al finally carried the project through to launch, several weeks behind schedule.

Lessons Learned

Chris had run up against roadblocks that were entirely preventable and that he had spent many hours toiling away at in solitude. The combination of Chris's reluctance to ask questions, Tim's chronic reticence, and the lack of a formal code review had wasted weeks of development time.

The solution was clear to everyone: If someone had reviewed the code periodically during the early phases of the project, the project could have been completed ahead of schedule. Additionally, Chris's learning curve would have been accelerated, and he would have avoided the uncomfortable scrutiny to which he was subjected at the end of the project.

Based on this experience, the production team instituted a formal code review process. Guidelines and other documentation were drafted and placed on the intranet, where it could be reviewed by staff and new hires.

Summary

Software development for the Web follows a standard process. However, the "paint by numbers" approach is not enough to ensure a quality end product. Help your tech leads to institute a formalized code review process in order to introduce quality checkpoints that will identify problems before it is too late. Given the complexity of software development work, your best hope as a project manager is to create the conditions for effective self-policing. Code review allows you to harness the collective knowledge and experience of your technical team. Additionally, code review can safeguard against "hidden" bugs that might not reveal themselves during quality assurance testing (QA), like performance or scalability limitations. Since most project schedules do not account for the possibility of major bugs during QA, it is crucial to pass a sound product into testing.

CHAPTER 11

Surviving Quality Assurance

KEY TOPICS

- Why Web QA Is Different
- What QA Tests Are For
- The QA Process
- The Politics of QA

A Common Scenario

The project you have been working on is now just a few weeks away from the launch date, and your head is swimming with details. You have been working 14-hour days for the past month, but you still feel like you do not have a firm grasp of the details or exactly what everyone is working on. You do not want to ask the developers for a progress report because you can tell they are weary of your questions and no longer speak to you in any sort of civilized manner. They communicate only in irritated nods and grunts that could not in any way be characterized as cordial—and that's if they bother to acknowledge you at all. When the business owner is not whining about a feature that had to be cut from the build, he is whining about another feature that must be added now at the eleventh hour. The creative director is complaining to anyone who will listen about how you deliberately kept the designers from seeing the completed templates so they could make their "last-minute adjustments."

You haven't looked at the project plan in weeks because it's too depressing and it no longer has any relevance to the schedule as it has unfolded before you. But one day, out of sheer frustration, fear, and panic, you open the project plan just to see how far afield this project has really drifted, and you see that the milestone you must hit if this project has any hope of launching on time is only a day away. It's the final big effort and the part of the project that always threatens to push everyone over the edge: quality assurance.

You break out in a cold sweat. You can picture the quality assurance (QA) engineers as they eagerly tear into your project and reveal just what a shambles you are attempting to unleash on the world. You picture their sneers and casual yet menacing demeanor as they write up the most insignificant flaws like visited link colors not changing, font sizes too big or too small, seemingly confusing copy, and, worse, missing pages, server errors, crashing browsers, frozen computers—total and utter chaos! You think of the deals, the pleading, the excuses, the promises, and the cajoling you will be forced to do to persuade these people to release the project. You wince as you start to calculate the hundreds of e-mails you are going to have to write to the team, reminding them to check the bug database and fix their bugs. You grow dizzy at the thought of the hours of follow-up with the team and the testing and retesting of all the bugs QA has exposed—all done at a frantic pace as the clock continues to tick.

You think back to the early weeks of the project when, in your infinite wisdom, experience, confidence in the team, and reliance on the spec that existed at the start of the project, you scheduled only five days for the QA and bug-fixing phases of the project. Idiot! Everyone said that would be plenty of time, and according to the production department's project calendar, QA would be able to devote all of their resources to the project when it came in. But that was months ago. Since then the scope of the project has grown to include everything from a third-party metrics reporting tool that requires an as yet to be developed code imbedded in the templates to a new membership database created to accommodate a last-minute marketing request.

Epiphanies are not always blissful, and you are experiencing a painful one now. You are three weeks away from an immoveable launch date, the programmers say they will not be ready to hand off to QA for at least another month, and when you give QA the most recent version of the spec, they will laugh openly in your face and tell you even if they had the available staff to work on the project—which they don't—they'd still need two weeks just to complete the first round of testing.

While the preceding scenario is a tad melodramatic, it is taken from real life. The information in this chapter should help you avoid a messy QA phase in your project and survive the testing and bug-fixing tasks with your sanity and nerves intact.

Quality Assurance for the Web

The quality assurance methodology for Web development projects evolved from traditional software QA. However, the Web development environment imposes different limitations on the QA process that are not present in traditional software development, such as the following.

- *Short development times.* Web development projects tend to run from three to six months.
- *Changing requirements.* Scope creep and ever-changing requirements mean the QA department often does not know what to expect from a project until it is officially handed off to them.
- *Simultaneous development projects.* In most Web development companies and internal Web departments, there are several ongoing projects. Often the QA department is testing several projects simultaneously with a limited staff.
- *Lack of standardized QA practices for the Web.* There are as many different QA processes as there are Web development companies and departments. A standard QA process for the Web has not been established, and the discipline straddles a line between front-end usability testing and server-side functionality testing. At both ends of the spectrum, and everywhere in between, the standards for Web QA vary greatly.

Quality assurance testing employed throughout each phase of a project is typically how software is developed. The developers perform *unit testing* themselves to be sure each discrete piece of the application is functional before it is integrated into the whole. However, the Web development environment is not conducive to this type of testing, mostly due to the rapid pace at which Web sites and Web applications are developed. Therefore, QA on Web development projects can begin to resemble quality control testing, which ensures that the final product is bug free and ready to be released to the public or client.

G   *Unit Testing*   Unit testing means running one component of a system for testing purposes.

Another significant difference between QA for the Web and traditional software development is the level of technical experience the QA engineers possess. Generally, software QA engineers are also developers who have a very high degree of technical knowledge. In the Web development industry,

QA engineers come from a variety of backgrounds. Many end up in the QA department because it suddenly became apparent that somebody had better be testing the site to be sure it is really ready for release.

What Does QA Test For?

If your QA department is like most in the Web development industry, they will join the process toward the end of the project build, and they will be testing for bugs or defects in some or all of the following areas.

- Usability
- Browser and OS compatibility
- Functionality
- Internal standards
- Performance/load handling
- Content
- Security

Usability

Usability bugs are the types of defects that tend to impact the user experience from a navigation perspective. Usability issues include hard-to-use or -find links and navigation menus, unclear site flow, and confusing or difficult tool, page, or form interfaces. Usability is a fast-growing discipline in the Web development industry and should be taken seriously by any professional Web development team. Jakob Nielsen is the industry's annointed usability guru and his book on the subject, *Designing Web Usability: The Practice of Simplicity,* is considered the usability bible. Nielsen recommends spending 10 percent of the project budget on usability and claims this cost will be recouped many times over during the life of the Web site. How your QA department approaches usability issues is a question of your company's standards. Most QA engineers will flag obvious usability problems such as confusing navigation or unclear instructions on a tool. However, there are many more subtle usability bugs, such as architecture or design issues, that may hamper a visually impaired user. These bugs may not be uncovered by QA unless these types of issues are part of the company's standards for usability.

Jakob Nielsen Online Visit Jakob Nielsen's Web site—*http://www.useit.com*—for articles, whitepapers, and books on the subject of Web usability.
   Another Web site that features Jakob Nielsen's writing is the Nielsen Norman Group—*http://www.nngroup.com*.

Browser and OS Compatibility

Compatibility testing across Web browsers and operating systems is one of QA's most important tasks. Because Web sites display differently from computer to computer and browser to browser, they must be checked for compatibility on all the popular Web browsers, browser versions, operating systems, and screen resolutions. A site may display perfectly on Netscape Navigator version 6.2.1 running on the Windows 98 OS with a screen resolution of 800×600 pixels per inch but horrendously on Netscape Navigator 4.08 running on the Macintosh 7.01 OS and a screen resolution of 1040×768 pixels per inch. A mature QA department will know what to look for when doing compatibility testing and will have documented the analomies across browsers and operating systems. They will also know how style sheets are handled in the various browsers, which is a difficult design component to optimize for. A good QA department will also have up-to-date metrics on which browsers, operating systems, and screen resolutions are most favored by their audience and on the Web in general.

QA should always test for the lowest common denominator in terms of user configuration. Company standards come into play again with regard to what exactly the lowest common denominator is for a user. Does the company support people who use a 9,600 baud modem connected to a Macintosh Quadra running Mac OS 6.5 and Netscape 1.2? Probably not. QA will help the company determine where to draw the line with regard to what user scenarios are supported. Most large Web sites no longer support versions of MS Internet Explorer and Netscape Navigator lower than 3. The percentage of Macintosh users on the Web is dwarfed by Windows users, and most Web sites and design companies do not optimize for the Macintosh audience. Microsoft Internet Explorer is the Web's most popular browser, probably due to the ease with which it handles style sheets and its tight integration with the Windows OS, which is the dominant OS in the PC market.

Functionality

Functionality testing used to involve simply putting data into a Web form and getting the correct result set or page back. As Web sites become more and more complex and database-driven, functionality becomes the norm, QA testing tasks expand and change. Even with the increased complexity of Web sites, most QA departments still only perform functionality testing from a user's perspective. Does the page load in a reasonable amount of time? Is it the page that was requested? Are the quiz results accurate? Generally, QA does not look beneath the hood of the application or Web site to be sure the code is optimized and the database schema is as efficient as possible. These optimization tasks are left to the developers to perform, and QA will work to expose any deficiencies in the code simply by using the Web site.

Internal Standards

Most professional Web development companies or departments will have standards for design, functionality, and performance to which they must adhere. Part of QA's responsibility is to make sure these standards are met. These details run the gamut from internal tracking tags being implemented on every page to correct logo usage. The company standards are normally documented and available on the company or department intranet. The QA department is often responsible for creating and maintaining these documents.

Performance and Load Handling

Another crucial area of testing concerns Web site performance. The QA department will have established benchmarks for performance that include download times and the allowed wait time for a Web application's results page to be delivered. The QA engineers will time all pages and applications to be sure standards are met. Slow load times and applications *"timing out"* usually are a sign of a bug or the need for the code to be optimized.

G   *Timing Out*   When a Web page does not load into the browser after a prescribed amount of time and a 500 error (server error) is displayed, the page is said to have "timed out." Similarly, if a Web application does not return results after a reasonable amount of time and instead displays a blank page or a 500 error, the application has timed out.

Load testing or stress testing is an area where the QA department may or may not be involved. Some companies require developers to conduct performance or stress tests during development that involve running scripts that simulate varying degrees of traffic and load on the application and the Web servers. Often these tests are done in collaboration with the system administrators who are responsible for the server's performance. If your company does not require developers to perform stress testing, then this chore should fall to QA. There are many commercially available scripts that can aid the QA engineer in performing these crucial tests. Again, help from the system administrator will be required to install the scripts and load test the servers.

Content

Even though most content displayed on a professional Web site has been proofed by a copy editor, QA still combs through the site and makes sure *i*s are dotted and *t*s are crossed. During the mad rush at the end of a project, the content is often the last thing to be put into the templates. Mistakes happen. Be sure your QA department checks for errors in grammar, spelling, and punctuation, and for illogical or clumsy prose.

Security

Security holes are most often the responsibility of the system administrators. They maintain the company firewall and servers and make recommendations to the developers on how to best code for security. E-commerce sites present the most security concerns, and QA will be checking that all sensitive data entered into shopping systems are protected and secure.

How Does QA Test Web Sites?

Most QA departments have an established testing regimen through which they run new Web sites and Web applications. The regimen will consist of testing for all or most of the elements just described, documenting bugs, following up with the project manager when a round of testing is completed, and rechecking the bugs once they have been squashed.

The QA Process

When you were developing your project plan, you consulted with the tech lead and QA staff on their estimate of the length of the testing phase for your project. They based their estimates on the functional scope of the project (the spec at that time) and on the availability of resources at the time the project was handed off to QA. You plugged this time estimate into your project plan and continued on with the build.

If you are extraordinarily lucky, your project has progressed smoothly, the scope has not increased dramatically, you have hit all your crucial milestones, and you are now only a few days away from the QA handoff. You check your project plan and see that today's task is to alert QA to be ready for the coming handoff. You e-mail QA and tell them what time and on what day you expect to hand off the project. You set up a meeting with QA, during which you give them the most recent version of the spec and describe any outstanding issues, such as missing content or unfinished coding.

The QA department will appreciate the update on the project details and will be doubly glad you are not trying to hand off something that is incomplete. This is QA's first task in managing their phase of the project: to be sure nothing comes into QA that is not completely developed. The goal is to hand off the Web site to QA after the technical build is finished. From the moment the project is in QA until the end of the first round of bug testing, there will be no coding or design tweaks. Rarely does this happen; but because of the inevitable scope creep and resulting time slippage that happens during the build phase, it is important that the technical build is complete and that the only coding during the early rounds of QA testing are minor tweaks and bug fixing.

Early Quality Assurance Milestones

Even if your development process does not include unit testing or code reviews by developers, two QA milestones should be scheduled during the course of the build: design and HTML. Be sure QA tests and approves these components before they move along the development path.

- *Design QA.* The Web site design—specifically page layout and navigation elements—should be approved by the QA department before the project progresses to the technical development phase. Testing the design elements of the Web site before the back-end functionality is built will ensure that the final design is consistent with the specs and scope of the project. This is also a chance to make sure the Web site is conforming to the company standards for design and usability. Exposing problems at this early stage in the build will save time and keep the project within budget.

  If you think all the design deliverables will not be completed by the date scheduled, then work with the creative director or designer and the QA lead on a rolling handoff schedule of design elements. This will allow the project to progress to the technical build and avoid a potential bottleneck.

♦ *HTML QA.* When the page designs have been rendered in HTML, be sure these templates are tested and approved by QA. The HTML templates of the site provide the structural framework required to support the dynamic code and functionality. If your QA department does not perform code reviews for advanced programming languages, they at least should be able to test and check the HTML code. The HTML should be checked to be sure it conforms to current World Wide Web (W3C) standards. If your company does not require the HTML to comply with these standards, at the very least be sure all the links are working, images are in place, and style sheets are functioning. Cross-browser and OS testing should occur in this QA phase as well.

The Bug Database

Similar to the issue log, a bug-reporting tool or bug database is an indispensible communication tool used during the QA phase to log bugs in a centralized location under the project name. These tools come in many shapes and sizes and provide varying degrees of functionality. There are incredibly expensive products available that do exactly the same thing as a bug database or tool you could build yourself with MS Access.

Regardless of how you acquire your bug-reporting tool, off the shelf or home grown, there are some basic features that must be included if the tool is to be used successsfully.

♦ *Severity ranking.* The QA department will have a ranking system for the severity of the bugs they find. The severity is a measure of how much the bug hinders the user from interacting with the site. For instance, a ranking of High describes a bug that totally disrupts the user experience, such as a page not found or a server error. A less severe bug, such as a broken image, would receive a ranking of Low.

♦ *Type of bug.* Similar to bug severity, the reporting tool should display the bug type. Web site bug classification is fairly standard across the industry, but there are still variations particular to individual companies and departments. Bug types include Display, Navigation, Functionality, Copy, and Usability.

♦ *Description.* It's important that the bug behavior be described briefly yet as concisely as possible. This will help the bug owner to determine if what is being described is a problem with the site or a user error.

♦ *Status.* Once a bug is reported, it needs to be monitored by the development team and the QA department. The goal of the development team during the QA phase is to change the status of bugs from "Open" to "Fixed." The status of a bug can also be "Waived" if it is discovered that the bug is not really a bug after all.

♦ *Author.* The QA engineer who discovered the bug should identify herself and provide her e-mail address in this field so the bug owner can contact her for any necessary clarification.

♦ *Owner.* It's important to assign the bug an owner, whether an individual or a group. For instance, a broken image may be assigned to design or HTML. A server error obviously would be assigned to the programmer or programming group.

♦ *Date.* Bugs should be assigned a date when they are logged. This allows the project manager the ability to monitor the progress of the QA process.

There are some other nice-to-have features that help move the process along, such as the ability to e-mail bugs to team members. A link to the bug location is helpful as well. The tool should also allow for varying levels of permissions. "Guests" can view bugs but not change the status of them, whereas a team member with more privileges can change the status of a bug when it is fixed.

It's also important to be sure the reporting tool is easily accessible. The most successful bug-reporting tools are served from the Web or the company intranet. Tools that are not dynamic, such as those built using a desktop application, must be stored on a company server, which often means the tool will not allow simultaneous access. Building your bug-reporting tool as an online application will save you time and headaches during busy QA phases.

Finally, the bug-reporting tool should be easy to use and understand. The goal of any communication tool is to keep everyone on the same page and in tune with each other and the effort at hand. You don't need to buy a reporting tool with so many whizbang features that it becomes a hassle to use. If you build the tool in-house, keep it simple, and provide only the essentials to get the job done.

The Testing Process

Where the rubber hits the road is in QA. The standard testing procedure is described in this section.

Handoff

Generally the project is handed off to QA by the project manager once the technical development is complete. A handoff meeting is scheduled, where QA is fully briefed on the project before they start testing. Possible attendees to this meeting are the QA lead or testing engineer, the developer, the tech lead, the producer, and the stakeholder or client. During the handoff meeting, the project manager will present any outstanding issues of which QA should be aware, discuss how the scope of the project has grown or diminished, indicate expected outcomes or results of certain dynamic features, and most importantly, review the time alloted in the schedule to allow QA to complete their testing. An up-to-date draft of the spec should be handed off to QA along with the project.

If your project is on schedule and a testing engineer has been scheduled, then testing should begin immediately. If you miss your QA handoff date, then the project will enter the QA queue, and testing will begin as soon as an engineer is available. In busy Web development companies or departments, hitting your QA milestone is imperative to making your scheduled launch date.

Rounds One, Two, and Three

QA testing occurs in rounds. The QA department should have an established testing procedure they follow for all projects. They may begin by testing usability and then progress to functionality testing or begin with security testing or load testing. The QA engineer will run the project through all the required tests and log all flaws and bugs. Once the first round of testing is complete, the engineer will inform the project manager, and testing will stop until all the bugs have been fixed. The project manager should have his team fixing bugs as they are reported. Everyone on the team should have access to the bug database and should be checking it frequently. The project manager should be monitoring the bug database closely and following up with his team to be sure they are checking the bug report. When the first round of testing is complete, the team will attempt to fix all the remaining bugs as quickly as possible. When the fixes are complete, the project manager will alert QA, and the second round of testing will begin.

During the second round of testing, the QA engineer revisits all the reported bugs to verify they were fixed. Occasionally, fixing bugs will create new bugs, which are revealed and reported. During this round the team and the QA engineer work closely together to clear up any questions the QA engineer may have about the design, copy, or functionality.

When the second round of QA is complete, the QA engineer, developer, and project manager meet to review any outstanding bugs or issues. If the Web site is in good shape, then the site is ready for the final round of QA. Until now all testing was conducted on the production servers where the Web site was developed. In order to get a true sense of how the Web site will perform, the final round of testing occurs in the live environment. The Web site is soft launched to the live servers, where the QA engineers can get a truer sense of the Web site's behavior. If required, the Web site will be password protected until it is ready to be launched to the public.

Soft launching a Web site is an important step in the QA process. Often a Web site that has been stable in the development environment will break once it is live. This is usually due to paths to databases, applications, and design elements changing once the site is on the new servers. It can take a full day for the developer to stabilize the site once it has been migrated to the live servers. More serious bugs are often exposed in the live environment as well. Do not attempt to launch your site in the live environment without first going through a thorough soft launch period of testing.

The Blessing

When the final round of testing is complete and the Web site is stable in the live environment, QA will meet with the team to present their final report. At this meeting the QA engineers will give the project their blessing and allow the site to be launched, or they will recommend that the site not launch because of a still outstanding bug or flaw. This meeting provides the opportunity to negotiate with QA on what the term "launch ready" means for this project. Even up to the last minute before launch there will be small imperfections that are still being chased down, such as misspellings, broken images, and broken links. If these issues are known, are being addressed, and are not on the home page, *and* you can promise QA they will be fixed before launch or immediately after, then you have a good chance of convincing QA to allow you to launch. However, if there are major problems, such as the search functionality not working, then you should get an estimate from your developers on how long the fix will take and alert your client or the stakeholder. You can also expect QA to be extra thorough when they retest the broken functionality. Receiving the blessing from QA is the first step in the launch procedure.

◆ **Black Friday**

A good rule of thumb is never launch on a Friday. Even if you have all the confidence in the world that your Web site is completely sound, do not risk launching over the weekend because should something go wrong (and you can almost be sure something will), it can be difficult to track down your team. First impressions count, so be sure your site is launched at a time when you have full coverage by your team.

The Politics of QA

Sometimes standards and process clash.

That's Not a Bug, That's a Feature!

A common problem for both the QA department and the project manager is that no one wants to admit he or she made a mistake. This can be especially true for developers whose pride can often get in the way of a delivering a bug-free product. It is a rare project where there are no disputes between the QA engineer and the developer, the copywriter, the designer, or especially the project sponsor as they try to rush the QA effort.

As project manager you are caught dead center in these disputes. Within minutes your feelings for the QA department will turn from love to hate and back again as you struggle to settle bug disputes and calm frayed nerves. Because the QA phase occurs at the end of the build when your team is tired and anxious to get the project out the door, small bugs can take on gigantic proportions. Use all your leadership skills (and this may be difficult because you will be tired as well) to motivate the team to stick together and cooperate with QA through the bug fix phase. Help the team through this phase by monitoring the bug list carefully and double checking QA's work as well. If there are a large amount of reported bugs, offer to assist in fixing any bugs that are within your technical or editorial capabilities.

Who Needs Code Reviews?

One of the most frightening and illogical assumptions in the Web development field is that developers, due to their commitment to quality and their incredible skill, do not need their code checked for bugs. The argument almost works. The commitment-to-quality part is quite noble, and of course, who could doubt a developer's skill as images of 1950s lab-coated geeks with crew cuts humming "The Star-Spangled Banner" come to mind. But the reality is this: Web projects are intense, pressure cooker affairs where the specifications constantly change and the hours are incredibly long. Everyone on the team will pass through periods where quality is far down on the work survival priority list—certainly well below Diet Coke and finding a favorite CD, two items that get people through the toughest parts of the build with their sanity intact. No matter how committed to quality a person may be, his energy and concentration will fluctuate during the course of the build, leading to mistakes and oversights and, hence, a need for QA and code reviews.

Another argument developers will use to avoid QA and code reviews is that these testing procedures make them feel they are not trusted enough or competent enough to do good work. This argument verges on the personal, and it must be handled correctly. The argument has nothing to do with QA or competency, but it is actually about an unwillingness to be supervised and the inability to work in a team environment. Some developers would prefer to be left completely alone and to code in solitude. This approach may work in some software development environments, but building Web sites is *the* most collaborative form of software development. If this argument should crop up on a project, don't engage the individual; it's not your battle. Kick the issue to the tech lead or even the CTO if necessary. This argument is a signal that there may be some deeper issues brewing in the tech department, and a closer look at the overall process may be required. It could also simply be the sentiment of one individual, in which case you shouldn't worry too much because that person will be moving on soon enough, willingly or otherwise.

Case Study: Burning QA

In this case study, we watch as a project manager in a publishing company resorts to a manipulative tactic to get her project released from QA and subverts the established practices of the organization. Where is the dividing line between putting personal relationships ahead of company interests?

Landing the Client

Michelle was a project manager working in the interactive department of Axelrod, a large publishing company. Axelrod published several trade magazines for the financial community, and each magazine had a companion Web site. Axelrod's online advertising department recently acquired Pennywize, a large national bank, as a new client. The pitch centered around the creation of a debt reduction calculator that would be displayed in a standard Web banner. The idea was that a person would enter her debt amount, how quickly she wanted to reduce the debt, and how much she could afford to contribute each month to pay down the debt. The user would enter all of the information directly into the banner ad, which was doubling as a tool front end. When the user clicked Submit, she was sent to a results page that presented different payment scenarios for paying off the debt within the amount of time selected. The user could also choose to enter new figures into the tool from the results page to see other payment scenarios. The results page also displayed marketing messages aimed at driving the user to the Pennywize Web site, where she could open a checking or savings account online.

In addition to the interactive ad, the bank would become the sole sponsor of all the financial tools on Axelrod's Web sites. This sponsorship would provide millions of page impressions over the course of a year for the Pennywize Web site. It was an impressive package and the bank liked the idea of the debt reduction calculator, but past experience had shown no quantifiable success with online advertising or sponsorships. Before they committed to the total package, which was potentially worth more than a million dollars in ad revenue to Axelrod, they wanted to do a three-month test of the debt reduction ad. If the ad drove significant amounts of traffic to Pennywize's site and a significant percentage of people who clicked through became Pennywize customers, then the bank would sign on for the entire program and a three-year commitment.

As with most projects that originated from the ad sales group, there was a hard and fast deadline that could not be missed. The launch date was timed to coincide with a large print ad campaign Pennywize was rolling out in the Sunday edition of several large metropolitan newspapers. The campaign was slated to begin in three weeks. Fortunately, the project was not a difficult one for Michelle's team, who had built far more complicated online financial tools.

The Handoff

The tool was ready for the QA handoff on the designated day according to Michelle's project plan. The design and HTML had already been tested by QA the previous week, and Michelle had provided complete specs to the QA engineer soon after the project kickoff meeting. Juan, the QA engineer who would be testing the tool, estimated that the first round of QA would take three days. Michelle and Juan had been working together at Axelrod for the better part of three years. They had worked on many challenging projects together and had a keen understanding of how the company worked and how to manage the development process.

Michelle did not expect any major flaws in the tool, so she budgeted two days for bug fixes after the first round of QA was over. The second round of QA should only take one day. The second round of QA was nothing more than the QA engineer verifying that all the reported bugs were fixed. This schedule would allow the tool to be launch ready on the Friday before the newspaper ads ran in the Sunday editions.

Michelle was well aware of the fact that launching anything on a Friday was forbidden. There was usually not enough coverage in terms of people being reachable in case something went wrong with what had launched. However, in this case the timing was unavoidable. The ad had to be live on the site when the Sunday editions hit the newsstands, and Michelle did not want to ask people to come in to work on a Saturday night to launch the ad and all the attendant functionality. Launching the ad required the work of the advertising production group, the application development group, and the system administrators. A launch of this type could never be done on a weekend.

Round One

The first round of QA went smoothly enough. There were no fatal functionality bugs and only a few cosmetic bugs, but otherwise the ad tested fine. Unfortunately, on the day the first round of QA ended, Cynthia, the account representative from the ad group, wanted to alter the design of the ad and change some of the copy on the results page. Michelle had not counted on any last-minute changes, but she didn't think this would be a problem or would disturb QA. She asked the programmers to make the changes at the same time they were fixing the bugs. Michelle did not tell Juan about the changes to the ad or the results page because they did not affect functionality, only design.

Two days later Michelle handed off the ad to Juan for the second round of testing. According to her team all the reported bugs had been fixed. She felt sure the second round of QA would take less than a day. Michelle handed off the project to Juan by e-mail, as was the practice. She mentioned in her handoff e-mail that all reported bugs had been fixed and that the design had changed a little bit. An hour after she sent the e-mail she received a reply from Juan informing her that due to the design and copy changes, the project would require another round of testing. Juan explained that even minor changes to the display elements of a project always required a new round of testing. It was the process. To compound the problem, the testing could not even begin until Monday or Tuesday of the following week because of a large project that was scheduled to begin QA immediately.

Michelle was shocked. She had explained to Juan how important this project was to the company, and she could not understand how the design changes that had been added at the last minute could require a whole new round of QA. She became angry at the thought that Juan was delaying her project because of the "process." She was upset, but at the same time she knew that if she had taken the time to let Juan know about the design changes, this situation might have been avoided. She e-mailed Juan and asked him if there was anything he could do to get the ad through the second round of QA today. She told him the new design did not change any of the functionality—it was just display changes. Juan responded that the other projects coming into QA had tight deadlines as well and that even though the design changes were slight, rules were rules. And anyway, Michelle was planning to launch the ad on a Friday, which was against company policy.

Round Two

Michelle knew Juan was correct in wanting to perform a new round of testing on the ad, but she also had the best interests of the company at heart. She knew Juan did as well, and that was what was making her angry. She decided, however, that this battle was one she could not fight. She had always had a good relationship with Juan, and she valued his service. She contacted Cynthia from sales and explained the situation with QA. Cynthia did not seem terribly concerned. She told Michelle to explain to Juan that this was the most important client in the company and that the ad could not miss the launch date. Cynthia asked Michelle why she had sent the ad through QA anyway because the ad group rarely did that. Michelle explained that anything that goes on the live site had to pass through QA. Cynthia replied that this was the first time she had heard of that rule. So much for process, Michelle thought.

Michelle was right back in the middle of the QA mess. She decided to try a ploy that she always hated when it was used on her, but she felt it might be the best tack in this situation. She would e-mail Juan again and explain the importance of the client and ask him to please forgo the new round of QA, complete the second round of testing ASAP, and release the ad so it could launch the next day, which was a Friday. "Surely," she wrote, "you understand how important this project is to Axelrod as a whole but especially to those of us in the interactive group." This last line was gratuitous, and she knew it. It might even be viewed as a veiled threat, but she wanted the e-mail to have an impact—especially since she was going to cc Cynthia, the Axelrod CTO, and the vice president of sales. It was a cheap shot, and she knew it. By including executives on the e-mail she would be presenting Juan in an unflattering light and would invite others to pressure him into subjugating his process in order to get the ad project out the door.

Michelle had to decide where her loyalties were strongest: with the company or with maintaining her relationships with her coworkers. She decided that in this particular instance she should side with the company and do what she thought she had to do to get Juan to finish the testing in time to launch. She sent the e-mail and decided to let the chips fall where they may. If the CTO was a reasonable manager, he would see how both sides had a valid argument and make the right call. The right call in this case, Michelle reasoned, was launching the ad.

Was the Sacrifice Worth It?

Despite her knowing better, Michelle felt a sense of satisfaction in sending the e-mail. She knew there was probably a better, more diplomatic way to handle the situation, but she was undeniably angry at Juan and, to be totally honest, out for a little blood. She felt a pang of regret nearly instantaneously after sending the e-mail, but she had to go all the way with her decision now, which would more than likely mean explaining to the CTO how Juan had become an obstacle in getting the project to launch. She was also a little angry at Cynthia for fobbing off this problem on her, and she regretted not being able to get Cynthia to take responsibility for getting the ad through QA.

Juan had a perfectly reasonable response to Michelle's e-mail. Without losing face or appearing guilty of anything more than not having the capacity to handle the workload, he was able to put the problem back on the business owners. He responded to Michelle's e-mail by explaining that should sales or the CTO make the decision to launch the ad project, then they had to acknowledge that the price would be delaying the other projects that desperately needed to get through QA. Juan positioned it as a "this or that" proposition. You can have the ad, but you lose the other project, which also has revenue attached to it. By presenting the problem this way, Juan was able to show that he valued the company's interests over the process and understood the business ramifications of either decision.

For a couple of hours neither the CTO nor the VP of sales responded to either Michelle's or Juan's e-mail. Cynthia weighed in with an e-mail imploring Juan to finish testing the ad so it could launch. Finally, the CTO sent a simple one-sentence e-mail to the group: "Finish the Pennywize ad, and launch it." And with that, the debate was over.

Michelle felt a mix of emotions. She believed she was vindicated because she had sided with sales and knew her project was more important than process or any other project that was in the QA queue. At the same time she felt enormous pangs of guilt at having used an underhanded tactic to get her way with Juan. The project was launched the next afternoon according to plan. Juan sent Michelle an e-mail stating that the ad was ready for release—and nothing more. Michelle was by now feeling so guilty that she tried to read between the lines. "He didn't sign it. He *always* signs his e-mails. What does that mean?" Finally, she sent Juan an e-mail apologizing for having resorted to cc'ing his superiors in order to get her way. She knew he knew what she had done and that knowledge was feeding her guilt. Juan validated her feelings by not responding to her e-mail. Ever.

Summary

QA is the final gateway the project must pass through before launch. It can be a trying process, especially in light of the fact that by the time the QA phase rolls around, the team is often tired and ready to move on. The project manager will be called upon to help the team chase down and fix bugs and at the same time help the QA engineers monitor the bug list. At least once during the QA phase, a dispute over a bug will crop up between QA and a team member or the stakeholder. When this occurs, the project manager will be called upon to play referee and help settle the dispute amicably.

Most Web QA teams test primarily for usability and adherence to company standards. Functionality testing is usually limited to the user experience—for example, does the search functionality return the correct results?

QA generally will not look beneath the hood of the Web site but will leave code checking and optimization to the developers. However, QA should at least be in the loop with regard to more technical testing, and part of their process should include being sure the technical tests such as load testing and code reviews are completed.

Establish a good relationship with your QA department, and gain their trust. Prove to them you are just as committed to upholding the standards they have worked so hard to institute. Having a good rapport with QA will provide you with some helpful leverage when the time comes to negotiate for the release of your project.

CHAPTER 12

Getting It Out the Door

The Final QA Phase

Launch should be viewed as the transition from the development phase to the maintenance phase. It's important to keep that point in mind as your project heads into the launch phase, and all you can think about is getting away from the office for a week or two to rest and regroup. By the time the project is out the door, you and your team may very well be ready for a break from the project, the client, and each other. However, there is still some work to do and some deliverables to manage before you move on.

Launching a Web site is always a great feeling, especially after a long, arduous build. And the launch phase needs to be managed just as carefully as the rest of the project to be sure you and the team do not stumble at the finish line.

The Soft Launch

The final round of QA occurs in the live environment. Even if your company does not have a QA department and all the testing is performed by the developer, it is still good practice to soft launch the site before the public release or any marketing or press releases go out. A soft launch is when the Web site and its entire directory structure and functionality are moved from the development server to the live server where the site will reside. If there is a development database, then the table structure is migrated to the live database as well.

The soft launch is conducted by the developers in coordination with the system administrators and the DBAs. The goal of the soft launch is to allow the Web site to stabilize and be thoroughly retested in the live environment. QA and the development team will test all the functionality as well as verify that all the display elements of the site have remained intact after the migration. A common migration problem stems from paths to image directories, style sheets, and databases not being updated in the code when the site's location changes, causing the site to break.

Don't rush the soft launch period. Allow at least a few days for the site to be retested and stabilized on the live server. During this time the editorial people may still be entering content into the site, proofreaders may still be combing the content for errors, and the developers will still be fixing bugs.

The following e-mail is a good example of the type of correspondence among the team that occurs during this phase in the project. This e-mail is from the project manager to the tech lead and director of application development at an interactive agency, summarizing the final development phase and the prelaunch QA process.

```
All:

Late this afternoon the client signed off on the final release of the
system. Sure, the usual minor content bugs continue to trickle in as we
go from soft launch into final QA, but we have a very happy client who
keeps dropping quotes like "This thing is sooo cool" and "You guys were
amazing!"

I wanted to thank both of you for working with your team to accommodate
a schedule that was stretched to the limit by a demanding and eccentric
client. Jane and Steve made this happen, and here are a few highlights,
going from front end to back end. I'll start with Jane.

Jane developed a slick prototype of the quiz in record time, soothing the
client very early in the process and avoiding any major soul-searching/
second-guessing headaches down the road. She stepped up to the plate and
volunteered to take on additional responsibility for the entire front-end
and free results experience, removing a great deal of the pressure from
App Dev and allowing Steve to focus on the daunting task of building the
algorithm. Jane delivered a very streamlined system, using JavaScript
and other client-side goodies to create absolutely minimal performance
```

overhead. Jane worked some very late hours, blasting through a massive number of last-minute copy and design edits, the highlight of which came last night when we both worked on the bug list until 11 p.m. after participating in the infamous sushi-eating contest, which Jane won! She can down 20 pieces of yellowtail and redesign ten templates in a single night!

Steve displayed some tenacious attention to detail wading through a very knotty algorithm that generated quiz results for hundreds of possible combinations. He led the effort to develop a naming convention and content workflow that allowed a nontechnical editor from the client to create hundreds of text files that could be seamlessly imported into the quiz system (also enabling yours truly and the producer to get down and dirty by doing some serious content entry). The logic for the quiz engine was essentially bug-free in spite of the mind-numbing details. Steve also identified combinations that the client's algorithm did not account for and pointed them out in time for us to address. Managing the technical coordination with our partner site was also a crucial role.

During the next week we'll have a chance to do the final QA testing and some stress testing as well. It wasn't an easy project, and we still have some Phase 2 enhancements ahead of us, but based on the outcome so far, I'm very optimistic that we'll make our public launch date without any major problems.

Yours,
Project Manager Sam

The Walk-Through

As the soft launch period wraps up, you more than likely still have some small bugs and open issues on the bug list. Meet with the QA department and your team to discuss the remaining open issues and create a plan of attack for either eliminating these bugs before launch or taking care of them very soon after.

Once you have a plan to clean up the bug list, schedule a meeting with your client or the stakeholder of the Web site for a final walk-through. The walk-through is when the project manager and the client or stakeholder of the project click through the site together to be sure everything is in order and the site is launch ready. If the project has been managed well and all the proper sign-offs have occurred, the walk-through should generate only minor comments or tweak requests from the client. Obviously a major functionality change request at this point would hold up the launch and add significantly to the cost.

Because the site has been soft launched for a few days, the client more than likely has been checking out the site on their own and has prepared a list of questions, tweaks, and possibly even some bugs that got past QA. The walk-through meeting can be conducted face to face with the both of you viewing the site, or it can be conducted over the phone. You could even conduct this meeting by instant messenger if that is more convenient. The goal of the walk-through is to be sure the client is completely satisfied that the final deliverable has met the expectations set forth in the specifications. The client's final sign-off is the expected outcome of this meeting, not more work or large-scale changes. If the client begins requesting changes more significant than a minor tweak, then you will either have to scrub the launch or create a Phase 2 for the project.

Launch Deliverables

As the project nears completion, it's time to start thinking about managing the handoff process to the client. Unless the contract calls for the same team that developed the Web site to also perform ongoing maintenance, you will have to prepare the new team for these duties.

Turning over the Keys

A complete handoff package should be assembled prior to the launch date so the team or person who inherits the site is fully briefed and can perform all the necessary maintenance tasks. Schedule a meeting with the maintenance team to review the handoff package and answer any questions they may have.

A very helpful service you can perform for your client is to evaluate the capability of the people who are slated to take over the site. You want to be sure they have the technical ability to manage the day-to-day technical maintenance tasks. If they do not, it would behoove both you and your client to raise this red flag. The solution could be that the development team needs to provide more training on the functionality of the site, or the client may have to hire a new team or Webmaster.

The handoff package should include the following.

♦ Site map

♦ Wireframe mockups

♦ Style guide

♦ Project documentation

♦ Application manuals

♦ Maintenance plan

Site Map

This document is most often created in Visio and displays the hierarchy of the site. The site map should display the flow and navigation of the site from page to page, including search and application results pages.

Wireframe Mockups

Every template used in the site should be represented by a black-and-white illustration. This provides an easy-to-read inventory of functionality and placement of elements on the page without the finished graphic design elements. This allows easier planning for future redesigns of the display templates.

Style Guide

This is an important document that will be used by the maintenance team to create new areas of the site and keep the look and feel consistent with the original design. The style guide consists of the following elements.

- *Color swatches.* Every color used in the design of the site should be displayed with its name and hexadecimal equivalent.
- *Style sheets.* All style sheets used on the site should be printed out and included in the style guide. The style sheets should be listed by name and associated location or template.
- *Type specs.* If style sheets were not used in the development of the site, then the style guide should list all the fonts used in the site, as well as any specific formatting and where the formatting was used.
- *Other HTML formatting.* Any other HTML formatting not covered by the style sheets should be listed and the location where it is used notated.
- *Images.* All image files should be listed in this document. Besides the image name, each listing should also include the names of the templates or piece of functionality where the image is used (such as a navigation bar rollover).
- *Directory structure.* Create a printout of the directory structure that displays the hierarchy of the site on the server. This printout should include all directories and subdirectories that make up the back end of the site.
- *Nomenclature.* The naming convention for files and directories should accompany the directory structure. Normally the programmers create these naming conventions.

♦ *Code samples.* The developers will provide code snippets from various elements of the site. These code snippets will provide examples of the correct syntax use for the maintenance team.

Project Documentation

Assemble all the important documents you created during the life of the project. These include the final specification, the project plan, and all sign-off and change order forms. You could also include the issue log and QA bug list if you like. The more complete the better. These documents will provide the maintenance team with the necessary back story, which will allow them to solve problems or fix bugs that may arise during normal use of the site. These documents will also provide the maintenance team with templates for the ongoing documentation of the Web site.

Application Manuals

Be sure to write thorough and easy-to-understand manuals for any Web applications the project has called for. The most common manual will be for the editorial tool component of the content management system (assuming one was created for the project). Include screen grabs and other helpful illustrations as well as any specialized naming conventions and directory paths the users of the tool will have to know.

Maintenance Plan

Part of your preparation for the final handoff of the site is to create a maintenance plan for the site once it is in the client's possession. During the discovery phase of the project, you worked with your client to establish exactly how much maintenance the Web site will require once it's launched. You asked questions such as How often does the content need to be updated? Will the site require new content categories and subcategories in the future? How often do the images need to be updated? Are there plans for more advanced functionality in the near term? The answers to these questions are what shaped the final specification and scope of the build.

Before launch, work with your client on creating a simple maintenance document that reiterates the preceding questions and provides not only the answers to questions of frequency but describes the areas of the site and the associated files that need to be accessed for the maintenance to occur. The maintenance plan can be part of the handoff package. Be sure the programming team taking over the maintenance of the site also has a copy of any manuals that were created for the use of the editor or producer of the site.

Another important part of the maintenance plan is the identification of the people who will be taking over the maintenance of the site. Everyone on the client team should be identified by name, role, and title if appropriate. Contact information for each team member should be included in this document as well.

All of these documents should be assembled into a binder with a table of contents. It is also a good idea to assemble these documents electronically and burn them to a CD. The binder and the CD will be the physical deliverables that comprise your project.

 Handoff Package Sample The Chapter 12 folder on the accompanying CD-ROM includes examples of the various documents you will have to create or include in your handoff package, including a site map, page maps, and a style guide. An up-to-date version of this document is maintained on this book's Web site at *http://www.realwebprojects.com.*

Going Live

It's the big moment at last; but don't lose sight of all the final details before you go public.

The Launch Moment

It's a scene you've pictured in your mind for weeks. The team is crowded around the developer's desk as he prepares to flip the switch that will cause the site to go live. Everyone is nervous, joking and rechecking the bug list. Champagne is at the ready. You all count down to the launch moment: "3 . . . 2 . . . 1 . . . Launch!" The floodgates are hurled open, and millions of happy surfers are now streaming onto your site as the champagne corks pop. The client beams, the team cheers, and you're carried out of the office on the shoulders of your coworkers, pumping your fist in the air exultingly.

Well, maybe. Keep in mind that if you are following a careful launch regimen, then you have already soft launched the site onto the live servers and have already been testing the site for a few days. Most times the actual launch occurs when a phone call or an e-mail from the client arrives giving you the green light to go live. The official launch can be a rather anticlimactic moment if all you are waiting for is final approval. In many cases the actual launch task consists of little more than swapping out the temporary home page for the real home page.

➡️ KEY POINT

Just before the site goes live, it is important to send out a "Launch Notify" e-mail to the client, the system administrators, the project team, QA, and the customer service department. In the e-mail state the exact time and date the site will be live and what the expected traffic loads may be like for the first few days. Also, be sure to include contact information for all the members of the team who will be on call to handle any problems that may crop up in the first week postlaunch.

Regardless of how low key the actual launch moment is, it is still a time to celebrate. Even on the most contentious projects the moment of launch will bring smiles of joy and accomplishment to the faces of your team.

The Customer Service Plan

When the Web site goes live, the frontline of the organization is the customer service representative. Any professional, commercial Web venture should have a trained customer service staff—even if it's a staff of only one individual. Before the site launches, it is your responsibility to meet with the customer service team to be sure they are completely up to date on all the site's functionality and any potential areas for user questions or difficulties. As soon as the final specification is signed off, you should send the customer service team a copy. Be sure customer service participates in all regular status meetings during the build phase of the project.

The only way customer service can do their job efficiently is if they are completely familiar with the entire Web site. Take the time to establish a good rapport with your customer service team, since they will provide you with a wealth of information, especially once the site is live and they begin fielding questions from users. Customer service works hand in hand with QA postlaunch to stay abreast of all bugs or parts of the site that are not user friendly. QA and customer service should have a formal process in place for monitoring the site once it's live. This process should also include an escalation procedure when things break. Be sure you are on the e-mail list from customer service that reports user feedback so you can stay informed of what parts of the project are successful and what parts are not from the user's perspective.

The Escalation Procedure

This procedure should be created well before launch and signed off by all members of the team who are involved. The escalation procedure details exactly what happens in the event of problems that may occur on the site once it's live and who should be contacted and in what order. That 3 A.M. phone call to the tech lead to report something minor like a broken image is not good escalation management. However, should the site be generating a server error instead of the home page, it's imperative to know whom to contact first and by what method: e-mail, beeper, cell phone, home phone, or signal flare.

Work with the team leads on who should be on call and on what schedule—for example, is the weekend on-call person different from the weekday on-call person? You also need to establish what types of bugs should be escalated up the chain. As mentioned before, broken images can wait until the next business day, but what constitutes broken functionality? Do erroneous search results require a 911 call, or can this wait? The degree of complexity and functionality of the site will determine how you set up your escalation procedure. At the very least, the entire team's contact information—e-mail, office phone, and cell phone—should be posted on a public project Web site and included in the launch notify e-mail.

The Warranty Period

Once the site is live and has been handed off to the maintenance team, you will still be responsible for monitoring the site and fixing bugs for a predetermined amount of time. This amount of time can be from one week to one month and is considered a warranty period. This is a great time to have your development team create any documention that is still necessary. You can also use this time to begin transitioning from the project that just launched to new projects. It's important to keep your team assembled and focused on the project that just launched and not immediately become immersed in a new project. Unfortunately, this is much easier said than done. Build the warranty period into your project plan, and be sure all the resource managers are aware of the duration of the warranty period for your project to avoid a scheduling conflict.

The Postmortem

This meeting is covered in more depth in Chapter 7, but it bears mentioning here, since this will generally be the final team meeting once the Web site has launched. The postmortem is an opportunity for every team member to contribute his or her impressions and interpretations of the project from a process perspective as well as suggestions for improving the process. One thing you have to consider carefully is when to schedule this meeting. Two weeks after launch is usually the best time. Try to conduct this meeting before the warranty period has ended and people have moved on to other projects. You want to be sure the details of the project are still fresh in everyone's mind.

Remember that the postmortem is not a gripe session. Keep any personal feelings out of the meeting, and be sure everyone approaches the meeting with a positive state of mind and an eye on improving the process.

Case Study: The Most Expensive Launch that Never Happened

This case study chronicles the experience of a project manager attempting to manage the integration and launch of an e-commerce system. Several factors are working against the project manager, including an incredibly tight and highly publicized deadline, a nonresponsive vendor, and a clueless executive management team. The project manager is caught in the middle of a variety of forces that ultimately lead to his undoing.

The Setup

ConSports was a content publishing Web site specializing in sports-related news and information for athletes and participants of nearly every sport imaginable. The site was advertising supported and growing quickly, but the founders wanted to expand the site's revenue capability by selling sports equipment online.

Despite the fact that ConSports had an in-house technology staff that included Web developers, system administrators, and DBAs, the founders of ConSports believed they would be better off outsourcing the development of the e-commerce system. The founders did not want to distract the ConSports developers from their current daily maintenance tasks with a long, complicated development project. By pure chance AdRev, the company that provided ConSports' ad serving technology, wanted to begin developing e-commerce systems for their clients. One thing led to another, and before long ConSports was AdRev's first client for e-commerce development. Based on ConSports requirements, AdRev presented an $8 million proposal for the development of the system. ConSports agreed immediately.

A minor detail left out of the negotiations between ConSports and AdRev was the fact that AdRev had no experience in developing e-commerce functionality despite what they told ConSports. ConSports did not believe any due diligence was necessary because AdRev was its closest and most trusted vendor. AdRev took advantage of this situation, and with the initial payment of $3 million they now had the funding necessary to gain the required technical knowledge to build the e-commerce system they promised—or something close to it.

Lou started working as a project manager at ConSports on April 1 and immediately began planning for the delivery of the e-commerce system from AdRev. He worked backwards from the previously established launch date of July 1 and tried to identify all the necessary tasks and internal milestones necessary, all the while keeping in mind that the biggest task would be the installation and rollout of the e-commerce system that was scheduled to be handed over on June 1. AdRev was developing not only the e-commerce back-end functionality but also the front-end templates that would display the shopping cart pages.

Lou was worried about the lack of a QA department at ConSports. He took a little comfort in the fact that AdRev had promised every aspect of the system would be thoroughly tested before release. He also understood that ConSports would simply have to install the system on its servers, connect to the database, and be ready to go live. From AdRev's perspective it was the simplest of integration projects, but from Lou's perspective, if he was not able to test the system to his satisfaction, he would be the person with the most exposure should problems arise.

He attempted on many occasions to meet with the AdRev project manager to develop a more detailed plan for the handoff and installation of the e-commerce system. Unfortunately, the AdRev project manager was too busy with other projects. As he turned down meeting requests, he promised a thorough walk-through before the system was handed off.

Smells Like Teen Spirit

Two weeks before the scheduled delivery of the system Lou received a call from a project manager at AdRev. He was told the handoff would have to be delayed by one week due to a previously scheduled upgrade of the AdRev development servers. Unfortunately, the upgrade could not be rescheduled. Lou quickly calculated how this delay would impact his launch plan. He told AdRev the system could not be delayed any further or the highly publicized launch date would be jeopardized. Lou also insisted that they meet in order to hammer out the details of the handoff, and he wanted a demonstration of the system. The AdRev project manager agreed, and they scheduled a meeting for the following morning.

The next day Lou and two senior ConSports developers arrived at the AdRev offices. They were looking forward to trying out the system and meeting the AdRev development team. Lou had never seen any documentation describing the system AdRev was building, and for that matter, neither had the developers. As far as Lou knew, no one at ConSports had ever seen any specifications provided by AdRev.

The three of them stepped off the elevator on AdRev's floor exactly at nine o'clock. The office space beyond the little reception area was filled with rows of tables and desks jammed together, most of which held flickering computer monitors. Colorful vinelike ropes of data cables and phone wires hung from the ceiling to the floor in several different places throughout the open office space. A thin layer of cigarette smoke hung in the air above the desks and tables. The uniform of choice at AdRev was oversized tee shirts complementing extra-baggy jeans. Lou thought the total effect was something like a high school cafeteria being used as a base of operations for a technology company.

They waited in the reception area for 20 minutes until Tim, the AdRev project manager in charge of the ConSports project, got off the elevator and briskly walked through the reception area. The receptionist called his name and told him he had some visitors. Tim introduced himself to Lou and the developers and apologized distractedly for being late. Tim appeared nervous and jumpy as he gave the group a quick tour of the office before ushering them into a small conference room.

Lou explained that they were anxious to see the e-commerce system and to test its functionality. Tim assured them that they could take the system for a test drive right away. There was a computer in the conference room, and Tim typed a URL into a Web browser and waited for the page to load. After a minute or two, the page request timed out. Tim hit the reload button on the browser, but the page timed out again. He opened a different browser and tried again, only to experience the same results. Finally, he picked up the phone, dialed a number, and began speaking to someone in hushed tones. When he hung up the phone, he explained that the system was down at the moment, but the developers were working on it. They anticipated the system to be up and running in a few hours.

Lou was angry but did his best to keep his cool. He asked Tim to set up another demo for him as soon as possible. The team from ConSports left the AdRev offices disappointed, angry, and with a growing unease about AdRev's capabilities to deliver the system.

Escalation

Lou was not able to reach Tim for the next three days. Finally, on the fourth day of calling, Tim answered his phone. Lou wanted to know what was going on at AdRev and demanded a demonstration of the system that very afternoon. Tim apologized sincerely and said they were still unable to provide a demo because they were right in the middle of QA testing and the system was not available. Also, the server maintenance was scheduled to begin the next day, so the system would not be available for another week. Lou was sure Tim was not being truthful, but he felt helpless to do anything about the situation. He had not been part of the vendor selection process, and his bosses, Zameer and Keith, the founders of ConSports.com, had only good things to say about AdRev. All he could do was make them aware of the delay and hope his team had the stamina to install, test, and launch the project by the target date. Instead of risking an unpleasant confrontation with Zameer and Keith when he informed them of the AdRev situation, Lou sent them an e-mail and outlined the problems the project was facing. He never received a response.

When the delivery date passed without any word from AdRev, Lou began working on a contingency plan that would require work to be conducted around the clock in order to hit the launch date. In preparation Lou pulled two of his developers from other projects and dedicated them to testing the e-commerce system once it arrived. Lou asked the developers to write test scripts to simulate a load on the system so they could measure the performance. He also met with the marketing team, and together they devised as many complicated user scenarios as possible to test the usability of the system. He was as prepared as he could be. All he needed was the system to be delivered within the next few days.

Two days later Lou received a call from Tim at AdRev. The system was ready, and he wanted to meet to discuss the handoff details. They met later that day at the ConSports offices, and Tim described the handoff procedure. AdRev would FTP some of the files to ConSports, while other parts of the system and the database would be backed up and delivered on tape. Lou asked if the system had been thoroughly tested and if there were any outstanding bugs they should be aware of. Tim assured the group that the system had passed a very stringent QA regimen and it was ready to be released to the public. And to ensure a smooth installation process, he and an AdRev developer would personally be on-site every day during the installation and implementation period.

The Devil Is in the Details

True to Tim's word, the following day AdRev delivered the e-commerce system files. The digital backup tape arrived with a user manual and documentation that described the directory structure, the database schema, and wireframe page maps of each of the system's display templates. The only thing missing was Tim and the AdRev developer. By noon ConSports had the complete system in their possession, and the developers began the installation process. Lou was so relieved to have the system finally in-house he didn't care that Tim or the AdRev developer had never shown up. His team was sharp enough to get through the installation without any help from AdRev.

The ConSports developers completed the installation within 24 hours. They now had 15 days remaining until the launch date. Before the developers could test the system, the massive job of entering the sports equipment inventory into the system had to begin. There were 10,000 items to enter into the system, and all of them included an image and a product description. The testing and product entry would have to happen concurrently, which could lead to a variety of problems should bugs develop, but Lou was left with no alternative.

A team of freelance product entry people had been hired to enter the products into the system, and they sat in the developers' area to facilitate communication should problems with the system arise. The manual that provided the basic instructions for using the system read like subtitles for a badly translated foreign film and was nearly indecipherable. It took the product entry team the better part of two days to figure out the order entry process. Frantic calls to AdRev support, Tim, or anyone else at AdRev failed to provide any answers.

By the time the inventory entry procedure began, there were only 12 days left until launch.

The Clock Continues to Tick

As soon as there were a few items entered into the system, the developers began testing. To their joy and amazement the system seemed to work well, and the ordering process from the user's perspective was intuitive and simple to complete. Lou was everywhere at once: He would enter products for a few hours, test for a few hours, proofread the product descriptions that were about to be entered, and keep Zameer and Keith up to date on the progress.

On the third day of product entry the e-commerce system servers crashed. When they were rebooted, the product entry team found they had lost the last several hours' worth of work and would have to reenter close to 100 items. The product entry procedure consisted of finding the correct image in the image directory and linking it to the product page, typing in the product ID number, and then copying and pasting the product description from MS Word into the product entry GUI. Once the product description was entered, it had to be formatted with simple HTML tags. The entire process for a single product could take anywhere from five to ten minutes to complete.

Lou and the developers began trying to figure out why the system crashed. Once the system was rebooted, it worked fine. Meanwhile, the developers covering the QA tasks were logging more and more bugs. The majority of the bugs had to do with typos in the product descriptions or missing, broken, or incorrect images. Lou realized the product entry people, in the interest of saving time, were not previewing their work before saving the pages. Lou assigned one of the product people the task of fixing the content bugs. He also asked the rest of the people entering the products to be sure to preview every page in order to catch their own errors.

So Close, Yet So Far

With seven days to go until launch, there were close to 6,000 products entered into the system. The bug database had close to 300 records in it, and Lou spent the majority of the next few days and nights fixing content bugs. Lou calculated that at the current rate of product entry they would be able to have all the product entered by the launch date; but there would still be hundreds of bugs remaining in the bug list.

Just as Lou completed this calculation and updated the schedule, the e-commerce servers crashed again. The system was rebooted, only to discover the entire last day's worth of product had been wiped out of the system. Lou was furious as he conferred with his developers on what could be causing the crashes. One of the developers thought these were the classic symptoms of a memory leak. The system worked fine once rebooted, and then as more and more memory leaked out or was used up inefficiently, the system crashed.

Lou called Tim and told him he wanted to meet with the AdRev developers immediately. An hour later Lou and the developer who diagnosed the bug were sitting in an AdRev conference room. Tim sat across the table accompanied by someone who appeared to be a high school kid, who was introduced as the senior developer and architect of the e-commerce system.

Lou began to describe the problems they were experiencing. It appeared there was a memory leak somewhere in the system. The kid claimed that he did not know what Lou was talking about. The ConSports developer began to describe how the system would be fine once it was rebooted and then gradually performance would suffer until the system finally crashed. Based on these symptoms, they contended that it had to be a memory leak. The kid smiled as the problem was described to him. He sat silently for a moment as if not sure what to do next and then said, "Yeah, we know. There's a leak in the virtual memory, and we couldn't figure out how to fix it."

Lou was furious and demanded an explanation. The kid just shrugged, and Tim said this was the first time he was hearing about the problem. As Lou left the room, he turned back to Tim and told him AdRev could forget about getting paid the balance of the development fee. Tim only smiled and nodded.

Back at the ConSports office, Lou, Zameer, Keith, and the head of marketing took stock of the situation. There were now six days to go before launch, and they only had half of the inventory loaded into the system. There was a severe memory bug that had to be fixed before the site could go live, and there were still over 200 minor bugs that needed to be addressed.

Zameer asked the developers if they thought they could isolate and fix the problem. The developers believed they could, but it could take a few days, and then the system would have to be tested again and the product entry would have to finish. If by some miracle they did make the launch date, due to the high-profile marketing campaign, the potential traffic load on the servers might bring the system to its knees. Lou had requested a soft launch period of two weeks before the big marketing push, but Zameer, Keith, and the marketing department ignored his warning and went ahead with their plans for a multimillion-dollar campaign promoting the new e-commerce service on ConSports.com. Now they were faced with the fact that if they launched, it would be with only half of their inventory and no guarantee the system would survive the load.

"I Thought I'd Be on the Beach by Now"

On the table in front of Keith was that week's issue of *Sports Illustrated* open to a full-page ad announcing the launch of the "Greatest Sporting Goods Store on the Web, ConSports.com!" Keith looked at the ad and then said out loud to no one in particular, "I thought I'd be on the beach by now!" The final decision was to postpone the launch until the system was deemed sound. The developers promised to work around the clock to repair the memory problem. Once the memory bug was fixed, the remaining product could be entered into the system and one last round of testing would occur. They estimated the launch would only have to be postponed by one week, two at the maximum. The delay would mean $3 million in advertising dollars down the drain and another $2 million spent on ads promoting the new launch date.

At 6 A.M. the next morning Lou's phone rang. Zameer was on the line and hysterical. He told Lou all the ads on the site were missing, and some of ConSports' biggest sponsors had already called demanding an explanation. Lou said he'd be right there. Upon arriving he found Zameer, Keith, and the head of marketing waiting for him. "What did you say to AdRev?" Keith demanded of Lou. Lou thought for a minute and replied that he only described the problem with the memory leak. "Did you say we were not going to pay the balance due for the commerce system?" Keith asked. Lou remembered his parting words and nodded. "I was pissed off," he said by way of explanation. "Who gave you the power to make threats on our behalf?" Zameer asked. "AdRev is refusing to serve our ads until we pay the balance due for the e-commerce system, and guess what? We don't have any money!" As it turned out, the extra marketing dollars that needed to be spent plus the loss of the revenue from sales ConSports was hoping to make in the first weeks of business had wiped out the ConSports cash reserves.

"There's nothing left," Keith explained. To make matters worse, ConSports' biggest new sponsor, an athletic shoe manufacturer, had read about the problems ConSports was experiencing in that morning's *Wall Street Journal* and decided to cancel its sponsorship deal. The writing was on wall: ConSports was going down—but not before Zameer and Keith fired Lou on the spot.

ConSports immediately began legal proceedings against AdRev, claiming they were in breach of contract. AdRev countersued ConSports on identical grounds. As the problem escalated in the press, more sponsors abandoned ConSports. The e-commerce system never launched, and within a year ConSports was out of business completely.

Lou retired from the industry with the intention of writing a novel, but he never finished. Within six months he was back at another dot com, working on a project with a tight deadline and everything riding on a successful launch. Only this time he was determined to see the project through to the end and to avoid threatening any vendors on his employer's behalf.

Summary

The launch phase of a project can be incredibly hectic. There is a lot at stake during the final days of a project build, and people are on edge. No matter how tired you may feel, you need to be as focused now as you were at any other time during the build. You will have to inspire and motivate your team to be focused as well. If you have managed your project carefully, you should enter this phase of the project confidently, and your nerves should be fairly calm.

Soft launching for the final round of QA will go a long way toward ensuring the site is stable and ready for public release. Work closely with your team and client during this phase to be sure all the major bugs are squashed and the client is confident the final deliverable meets all expectations.

Keep in mind that simply making the site live to the public is not the only task during the launch phase. You will be assembling a handoff package that will include all the pertinent documentation for the maintenance team that will be inheriting the site. The transition needs to be managed well to ensure a smooth handoff to the client. Meet with the maintenance team in advance of launch, and answer any questions they may have about the design or functionality of the Web site.

Another important and often overlooked task during launch is meeting with the customer service team that will be fielding user questions and comments. Be sure the customer service team has a copy of the final specification and they are thoroughly familiar with all aspects of the Web site. Make yourself available to answer any questions they may have about the site, and be sure to pay attention to any suggestions they may have with regard to usability. Customer service representatives are closer to the end user than anyone, and their experience can be invaluable.

Launch is what you are working toward on every project. Launching Web sites is what you do better than anyone. Coordinating the entire effort and all the disparate elements and resources for this one moment is one of the primary reasons there are project managers on Web development projects. Every time the moment comes, savor it. The moment may be composed of nothing more than the official nod from the client that the status of the site is now "live," or it could be as dramatic as a last-minute bug fix being conducted minutes before the CEO of the company unveils the site in front of an auditorium full of shareholders. Launch is victory, and you should celebrate accordingly. Enjoy the moment because your next project is probably only a few days away.

CHAPTER 13

Leading Organizational Change

KEY TOPICS

- Common Organizational Structures
- The Project Management Role
- The Project Management Office

A project is a microcosm of the organization, and it can be a most effective proving ground for organizational reform. The role of project management is often vaguely defined, but this situation has a silver lining. Your fuzzy location on the organizational chart provides you with considerable latitude, as well as the danger of stepping on toes. This chapter encourages you to take advantage of your hands-on position to implement change "on the ground." By the end of this chapter, you will learn how to use your project as a success story, a source of inspiration for senior executives who are trying to make the case for a more efficient organization.

The Invisible Team Member

In addition to designers, developers, and QA testers, your project team contains a silent but powerful player who can determine the destiny of every project: the company's organizational structure. Most employees of a corporation are prisoners of the "org chart." As functional specialists, the scope of their activities is limited to well-defined parameters. Designers design. Salespeople sell. Sure, they'll have input into how the designing and selling gets done, all right—when they make director in six years!

Project managers can take advantage of their "fuzzy" role to advance their vision of best practices. As inventors and enforcers of process and protocol, project managers are uniquely positioned to recommend and implement changes. Few advocates of organizational change are as well positioned as the middle-level project manager. Highly paid management consultants write whitepapers in the hope that executives will "sign off" on them (whatever that means!). Senior executives issue mandates based on the latest issue of the *Harvard Business Review* or the opinions of their golf pro. These mandates are left to "trickle down" to the rest of the company through the medium of fearful or politically motivated VPs and directors. Project managers on the other hand can truly lead by example, making change happen "on the ground" by immediately adopting best practices and implementing them in their own projects.

A track record of delivering results creates instant credibility with senior management when it is time to speak up and recommend changes. Projects are the proving ground for new methods, and no one is better positioned to report objectively on the effectiveness of a new workflow than the project manager. The project manager represents the interests of the project, rather than the interests of a functional department. Consequently, astute executives come to rely on this impartial source of "local knowledge," which filters its way up the corporate food chain anecdotally. Organizational changes can often originate with watercooler anecdotes like the following.

> "The project manager has been saying all along that the team had a really hard time with multiple designers and no creative director. The collaborative approach just isn't working with the big egos in our group. He says it has dragged out the design process by two months!"

With their unforgiving analysis of successes and failures, project postmortems yield a rich crop of hard evidence that can be used to justify recommendations to the rest of the company. While being situated at the business end of a "dashed line" on the org chart feels precarious, it also provides the best vantage point for organizational pioneers who want to make an impact.

◆ Life Outside the Organizational Chart

"Annex 149" was a drafty storage closet that had been home to the Microsoft Exchange Server. As the workload blossomed, this corporate version of the backyard toolshed now provided low-budget cubicle housing for a production team that was bursting with consultants, programmers, and a new project manager named Kirstin, who had been on the job for five months.

Allen, an ex-ColdFusion developer, stepped out from behind a shriveled Chia head and four *Star Wars* figures to drop a profound thought on Kirstin, who had just visited his desk for a report on the status of a code review: "I have tremendous, unbelievable respect for project managers."

Allen was a rather dull fellow and not at all the sarcastic type, so Kirstin allowed herself an embarrassed shrug. Alex, however, was just warming up: "I respect you guys because your job sucks. I would never want your job. The way that you have to deal with salespeople, editorial, and marketing people and design people throwing random stuff at you all day—you guys have the worst job. Not to mention *clients*."

Initially embarrassed, Kirstin went back to her desk and took a few minutes to digest these words. As she looked at her thriving Chia kitten, she realized the irony of Alex's observation. Having to work "up close and personal" with clients, designers, editorial, marketing, sales—and everybody in every conceivable department of the company—exactly what she *loved* about being a project manager. The opportunity to get out of her office and lead people from every corner of the organizational chart was exactly why she had chosen to become a project manager instead of an HTML programmer. Even though she was a junior employee, she was at the epicenter of tremendous forces of organizational change, as her company moved ahead with large technology initiatives.

Kirstin's leadership role on cross-disciplinary project teams placed her in a unique position. For all practical purposes, she "floated" outside the neatly stacked organizational chart boxes. Sure, the director of the Interactive Group wrote her reviews, but somehow her connection to the rest of the company was blurry. She was a "dotted line" that cut across every department, not just Creative or Technology. Her place in the grand, rapidly changing scheme of things was confusing and at times infuriatingly vague, but it was exciting nonetheless—more exciting than HTML programming anyway.

Common Organizational Structures

There are many different ways to structure the relationship between a project manager and the rest of the organization.

Functional Organizations

The "silo" model segregates staff according to functional specialty (typically sales, design, editorial, marketing, production, technology, and QA). Functional, or "line," managers absorb project tasks into their normal departmental workflow. The project is divided into segments that are doled out to the departments. Each piece of the project is coordinated by its respective functional owner. The project manager is a member of whatever department is sponsoring the project. The project manager's primary loyalty is to her line manager. For example, a junior editorial producer might be responsible for developing the content area of a Web site. She reports to the editor-in-chief, but she will require the assistance and cooperation of other departments. The project is sponsored by editorial, but she will be asking Design and Marketing to assist her.

This organizational structure also complicates communication. All job requests must be cleared through the respective line managers. In order to get anything done, you may have to play ventriloquist: Place the functional manager on your lap, and ask him to repeat whatever instructions you have for his team. Repeat seven times, once for each department that's involved in the project. Project tasks often take a back seat to whatever departmental tasks are going on. The project manager is reduced to the role of a supplicant, roaming the halls looking for a handout as line managers cut slices from the man-hours "pie" and staff work on the project *pro bono* in their free time. Bribery carries the day until senior executives intercede to force the project along.

The Functional Matrix

This fuzzy scenario includes a project manager with limited authority who is coordinating a project across several departments. The veneer of authority is deceptive: The project manager feels "in control" at the early stages of the project as she happily initiates important e-mails and calls meetings. Once again, the project manager's primary loyalty is to her line manager. For example, a junior project manager in the IT department may be responsible for ensuring Y2K compliance. She reports to the director of Operations, but she calls upon the assistance and cooperation of other departments. The project was sponsored by IT, but she depends on the cooperation of functional managers in Facilities, Production, and Legal. Although it was nice that the electricity stayed on after December 31, 1999, her primary concern was the approval of her boss, the director of Operations.

Once implementation begins, however, this type of organization starts to show its true colors. During the later stages of a Web site design, for example, your client may begin reading *Wallpaper* magazine. This results in a sudden request for a brand new design with "1960s retro futuristic airport chic." You've only contracted to do three versions of the design, but you want to do the extra work in order to generate "good will" with the client on future projects. As you lobby unsuccessfully for last-minute resources, you realize that you are merely a "liason," facilitating communication and keeping track of the project schedule. Your requests for additional work fall on deaf ears—as an outsider, you have no real leverage with the project team.

In a functional matrix, the project runs smoothly as long as the initial requirements are well documented, resource assignments are preapproved by line managers, and scope doesn't change. In other words, you're in big trouble. Communication "liasons" have a hard time rallying systems administrators to pull all-nighters load testing the servers the week before launch. Once resources are stretched thin, line managers will have other pressing work for their staff. Soon you're right back where you started: relying entirely on the good graces of the line manager to secure the necessary resources. After a short-lived whiff of influence, you're back to a "functional organization," and the schedule is held hostage by competing demands on resources.

The Project Matrix

This is the most favorable arrangement from a project management perspective. Under this structure, the project manager has full responsibility for the tasks that appear in the plan. For the duration of the project, the project manager has day-to-day or "operational" authority, while administrative authority is retained by the department head. Functional managers focus on "people issues" (training, promotion, performance evaluations). Staff go to their managers when they require advice or technical assistance, but progress reports are made directly to the project manager.

In essence, staff are "on loan" from their functional groups for the duration of the project. This allows the project manager to focus on the interests of the project and secure the necessary resources to achieve the deliverables. Ideally, the project manager will be a member of a separate project management office (PMO), which is "chartered" by senior management. Since the PMO is an autonomous group that is accountable to a very senior executive, the project manager is empowered. Due to the autonomous nature of the PMO, she is in a peer relationship with the line managers. In this way, she is uniquely positioned to enforce the plan without being bogged down by personnel management. Her loyalty is to the project, and her authority is independent. This structure is illustrated in Figure 13.1.

The Project Unit

In this specialized case, the project manager is in charge of a self-contained "unit" composed of core personnel from several functional areas. A temporary reporting structure is created for the duration of the project. This structure is typically used for long-term, large consulting engagements that may occur

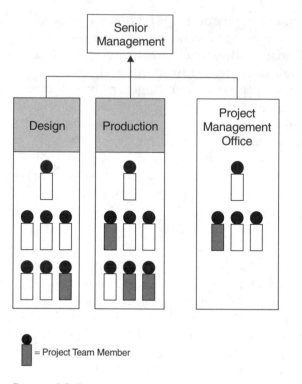

FIGURE 13.1
Project Matrix Organization with a Project Management Office

on-site at the client's location. The project team may be temporarily detached from the parent organization, reporting to a unit of the client's organization. The senior project manager must now deal with personnel and HR issues (vacation, performance evaluations, sick pets, and so on). Given these distractions, the project manager is now "big sister" as well as "big brother."

Early Stages of Project Management

The ability to maintain a clear vision of "where this project management thing is headed" is a crucial success factor in pulling your colleagues toward the adoption of best practices. The "primordial soup" of project management at a New Media organization usually consists of a few motivated account managers, editorial producers, or extroverted programmers who are scattered throughout the organization. These people draft schedules and specifications in an effort to deliver projects that are handed down by their managers.

Project management intiatives within most companies follow a remarkably consistent growth pattern. In interactive agencies, account managers grow into the role as they bring their company's creative resources to bear in support of the client's needs. In companies with a strong technology focus, the project management role usually arises as a means for technology managers to control scope or rein in the requirements of ambitious project sponsors. As the project management effort grows in size and sophistication, there may be a number of project managers scattered throughout various departments in the organization.

As the role becomes better defined, there is increased pressure to represent the interests of the *project* rather than the interests of the functional department. Friction between department heads and project managers is a common "growing pain" at this stage because functional managers are primarily concerned with staff retention and cost reduction. Their decisions are based on several criteria.

- The need for long-term staff development and training
- The desire to minimize resource expenditures from their department's budget
- The desire to increase the department's standing and influence within the company

These objectives will often conflict with the interests of a particular project. For example, the production manager who is concerned about his team's job satisfaction will try to assign employees to challenging projects, stretching them beyond their current skill set. As the project manager, however, you will seek to assign the fastest, most experienced worker.

"Yeah, Samir is the fastest, but he's been stuck in 'HTML Hell' for two years. If he doesn't get a chance to start learning JavaServer Pages, he's going to quit and join his buddy who's taking down six figures with some startup gambling Web site. Unfortunately, I promised him the last time that there would be no more rush client work and he could start learning JSP. Now, we've got a new hire who's been using Adobe GoLive, and this is a great opportunity to wean him off of it and get him to start doing some real hand-coding in JavaScript. So I need to use the new guy, or Samir is going to freak out, and we'll lose our best HTML guy to zanycasinoworldparadise.com, which would be really personally embarrassing."

Naturally, no one wants *his or her* project to be used as JavaServer Pages boot camp! To make matters worse, if the revenues associated with client work are small, the line manager would rather expend resources on internal projects. For example, the redesign of the company intranet will have more impact for the department internally than the "Bad Hair Day" community site

◆ Managing the Managers

You will need the cooperation of functional (or "line") managers in order to effectively staff your project team. You also need their support to implement your vision for the development process. As you assume a leadership role, obtain buy-in on staffing and organizational initiatives with these tactics.

◆ Tap into the department manager's prime motivators when "selling" your vision for change. Cite the positive impact your project will have on staff development, cost reduction, and the prestige of the department.

◆ Establish a "prioritization committee," which is responsible for creating a high-level resource schedule or calendar that cuts across all projects. This will alleviate resource conflicts between project managers and line managers.

◆ Require project stakeholders to advocate/promote their project internally and publicize the rationale. This will lubricate resource prioritization and remove some of the burden from the project managers.

◆ Ensure that the project has the necessary management approvals before seeking resource commitments from line managers.

◆ As a last resort, put the "fear of God" into department heads by introducing the possibility that subcontractors or consultants might be necessary if in-house capabilities are found to be lacking.

that the client wants to set up for $50,000. The fact that "nobody ever uses the intranet" and the redesign will suck up 2,000 man-hours makes little difference when annual performance reviews come around.

The Project Management Office

As project managers throughout the company recognize common goals and the need for a consistent development process, the establishment of a project management office (PMO) is the final step. This evolutionary leap consolidates project management functions into a centralized office that services all of the various departments. The benefit of this centralization is to allow project managers to cross departmental lines and respond to the needs of a growing company regardless of its organizational structure.

The PMO structure brings several important benefits to an organization.

◆ It involves a consistent, companywide project planning methodology that will allow company operations to scale rapidly without suffering from communication and organizational breakdowns.

◆ There are consistent quality standards for all Web-based products and services.

- The objective cost-benefit analysis of projects aids in prioritization and decision making and promotes the more efficient allocation of resources.

- A growing institutional knowledge base, acquired through detailed documentation of processes, templates, and best practices, develops.

- Formal training on project management skills, techniques, and tools. In project-based Web development organizations, these skills are crucial for everyone in the company, regardless of their department.

- Project managers are provided with a career path and active mentoring.

- The PMO serves as a neutral and independent watchdog, ensuring that best practices are followed and that projects are conducted and analyzed in a climate of objectivity.

- Project managers can represent the interests of their projects and the company as a whole rather than their respective departmental interests.

Making Your Case: Project Management Whitepapers In the Chapter 13 folder of the CD-ROM, you will find three documents that can assist you in making the case for the establishment of project management in your organization.

The "Project Management" whitepaper: This document explains what project management means for Web-centric companies. It includes a definition of project management for the Web, business objectives, benefits, and a basic development process. The whitepaper is targeted at middle managers.

"The Project Management Office" proposal: This document presents a blueprint for the establishment of a PMO and also provides the business justifications. The proposal is designed for presentation to senior executives.

"Proposal to Centralize Web Production" whitepaper: This whitepaper advocates the migration from a functional or "silo" organization to a functional matrix by pooling Web development resources.

Up-to-date versions of these documents are maintained on this book's Web site at *http://www.realwebprojects.com.*

Establishing a Project Management Office

If you have joined with senior management in an effort to establish a PMO, you will be called upon to supplement your traditional job description with three additional roles.

- Politician
- Pragmatist
- Publicist

These roles will help you to overcome the aversion to change that you will face from people in your organization who are affected.

Politician

As the politician, you will need to craft a message about the benefits of project management. Make your pitch as attractive and acceptable as possible. This message must be repeated at every opportunity. Like a candidate running for office, you will need to tell project stakeholders what they want to hear in terms of the benefits.

- ◆ Faster time-to-market for projects
- ◆ Decreased costs
- ◆ Overall increase in capacity and output (getting more work done)
- ◆ Improvement in the quality of work
- ◆ Greater stakeholder satisfaction with features and functionality

Pragmatist

The need for project management makes sense to most people. However, even if people in your organization accept the logic of project management, they may struggle with the project prioritization process. There will also be a struggle over the means by which projects are assigned to project managers. Project prioritization and resource allocation are emotional issues becasue they touch directly on the distribution of power and authority. Those who complain the loudest are usually the most wary of losing their power.

Although you may not be directly involved in the prioritization process, you will need to find a way to participate actively. This is because your success will be affected by the projects that receive resources. If doomed projects are chosen for implementation, the result will reflect poorly on the value of project management. Avoid taking on a "lemon" as a pilot project by getting involved in the evaluation process. The best way to do this is to contribute to estimating costs, benefits, and ROI. The trick here is to take the emotion out of the equation. This is done by a comparison of various projects on an "apples to apples" basis, which means that all participants should concentrate on the financial aspects of each opportunity. In addition, you should strive to be seen as an expert in the prioritization process so that you will be viewed as a key advisor when initiatives are launched.

Publicist

Although it might seem uncomfortably self-aggrandizing at times, you simply must communicate successes (even small ones) as widely, frequently, and consistently as possible. To avoid the perception of "blowing your own horn" while at the same time winning over converts, you should highlight the efforts of other participants in the process, emphasizing cooperation as the key to success—for example, "Thanks to our outstanding developer *and* our new process, the project was launched on time." Good propaganda efforts will serve to drive home awareness of this "new way" of doing business, as well as the sense that it is breeding success. This will cause a "bandwagon" effect among project stakeholders, creating the perception that failure to join the trend will be dangerous to their initiatives.

When objections arise, raise the level of these three activities even further. State your case, explain the benefits in a practical way, and keep harping on the benefits and successes.

We Are the Champions

Your champions in senior management can take a similar, but slightly more tactical role in support of the effort. Project management leadership can focus on these specific activities to assist the team.

- Push for cultural change.
- Insist on the creation of, and adherence to, a consistent methodology.
- Take emotion out of the equation.
- Buffer the project managers and allow them to focus on delivering projects successfully.
- Advertise successes.
- Seek recognition for project managers as both functional and technical leaders.

Throughout the process of establishing a PMO, your champion needs to buffer you and aggressively push for the adoption of standards and process.

Case Study: Establishing Web Project Management at a Media Company

This case study relates the experiences of a global media company (which we'll refer to as "BigGlobalMedia, Inc.") as it struggled to build a coordinated network of Web sites from a diverse media empire consisting of magazines, newspapers, cable TV progarams, and other properties.

The Early Days: Everyone Has a Silo

BigGlobalMedia, Inc. embarked on its Internet strategy with a collection of independently branded sites devoted to the numerous print magazines that were owned by the conglomerate. Each media group had its own independent Web team, with its own producers, editors, assistant producers, Web developers, and designers. The IT department had its own group of application developers and systems administrators, responsible for maintaining the corporate site, intranet, and desktop support. All told, there were six isolated pockets of Web developers across the company.

This arrangement provided each department with a great deal of creative control over its Web site. However, this ad hoc system lacked uniform quality standards and a coherent development process. There was a great deal of duplication of effort, poor knowledge sharing in terms of features, and chaotic competition between the different channels for scarce development resources.

From a technical perspective, it was a disaster. Three of the media groups had very little technical expertise or supervision and were poorly positioned to solicit or receive assistance from the other groups. There was little project documentation. Designs and requirements changed late in the implementation phase, "spaghetti" and duplicate code proliferated, maintenance was increasingly time consuming as the Web sites grew, and site performance was a problem. Furthermore, people felt isolated. The entire development staffs of two departments resigned because they did not see any growth opportunities within the limited scope of their departments.

Consolidation: Joining the Pool

The graphic designers who were scattered across the various departments felt isolated as well. When a new creative director was hired, he gradually began to pull the designers together into a centralized Design department. This transition had gone well and helped to ensure high-quality design standards across the company. The creative director's easygoing personal style allowed him to pull designers away from the channels and into a central department without alienating anyone. Design's success helped mobilize a similar movement to create a centralized Production department that would join its counterparts in corporate IT as part of a new Technology group led by a CIO. Figure 13.2 illustrates these changes to the organizational chart.

Each of the six affected departments had concerns about centralization.

Would they get as many resources as they had before? Not necessarily, since resources would be allocated according to companywide priorities. Man-week assignments were made to departments depending on the relative priority of their projects. This ensured that talented developers would be assigned to challenging, high-priority projects and furthermore incentivized project sponsors to come up with creative, revenue-generating ideas and advocate them aggressively at prioritization meetings. Departments could get more or fewer resources, and this would change over time depending on the importance of the projects that they were generating. There would be more flexibility and more coverage.

What about the close working relationships that project sponsors had with their development team? Although there would still be close collaboration between the business owners and developers, the new Technology team needed project spon-

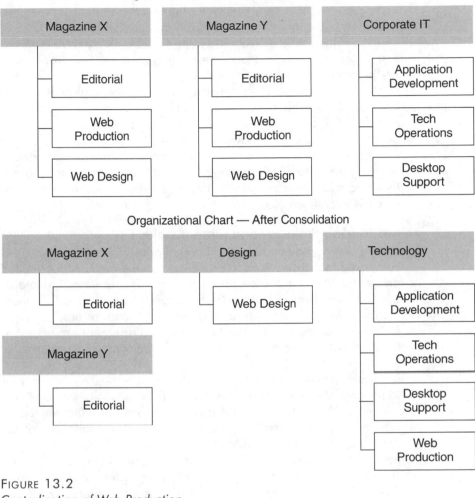

FIGURE 13.2
Centralization of Web Production

sors to be more organized and not waste development time. Also, there was no guarantee that a particular developer would always be dedicated to a particular site, so new relationships would have to be forged.

Would Production be responsive to emergencies and high-priority issues specifically related to projects that were sponsored by Marketing? The Production team worked out processes to handle this and set up contacts and e-mail aliases to facilitate communication. However, work on urgent issues would fall into place along with the rest of the company's priorities. Revenue potential, brand, and other strategic ROI factors went into the calculation of priorities.

How did the Web developers feel about moving? Most of the Web developers welcomed the move to a central Production department. A few developers initially had concerns about being less involved with the business side, where they had enjoyed significant creative input in product development. The advanced developers in the original IT group were concerned as their ranks were flooded by ex-"Webmasters," whose expertise was focused on front-end technologies like HTML and JavaScript. The relationship between the original IT staff and the channel Web developers was poor, due to the history of a separate organizational structure and the general lack of technical supervision outside of corporate IT. The IT developers for their part had grown accustomed to being insulated from interaction with project sponsors and were reluctant to face daily interruptions and scope changes. Bringing the Web developers into the fold was a step in the right direction, but it took years for members of the new Production department to gain the respect of some veteran IT developers.

Introducing Project Management, Take 1

Getting management buy-in for the Production consolidation was a cakewalk compared to the introduction of project management. At the time, there were two project managers in the company. Frances, in corporate IT, wrote specs and managed deliverables and timelines for large enterprisewide initiatives such as Y2K. Carmine, in the Production department, kept track of project assignments, status, submission dates, and due dates. These two divergent project management functions did not provide a very good model to point to when making the case to senior management.

Management's first attempt was to hire a tech-savvy project manager, Deana, to manage the Production department. They reasoned that one person should be able to do both technical and project management. Deana focused on working with the editorial content producers to introduce the idea of written specifications, timelines, and process. Unfortunately, most of the Editorial management team was new to the Web. Coming from a print magazine background, most senior editors were used to "handing off" a concept to Production and were unfamiliar with the day-to-day collaboration and feature specifications required by Web projects. While Deana evangelized project management to senior editors and wrote specifications, one of her reporting managers, Sam, worked with the developers and interviewed job candidates. Contrary to management's expectations, one person could not do it all. After three months of hard work that yielded little progress, Deana resigned.

Introducing Project Management, Take 2

Deana's departure made people take notice. Why hadn't she been able to get any traction? What had been the source of her frustrations? Deana had taken a top-down approach with Editorial and focused on the more bureaucratic aspects of project management rather than the benefits. She had also been an outsider who did not understand the process and the dynamics that she was trying to change and who could not draw on existing relationships to implement this change. The deck had been stacked against her, and it was a significant blow to the company when she left.

Sam took over management of Production. He resolved to achieve the same goals that Deana had, but through different means. He identified a junior developer, Tanya, to make the transition into project management. Tanya had shown an interest in project management when working with Tech on a project earlier in the year. Frances mentored Tanya as she put together specs, timelines, and flowcharts. She had done pretty well and was interested in doing more.

Questions and Concerns: What's Project Management, Anyway?

As Sam prepared to move Tanya into this role, he had to address concerns from the developers.

"Tanya's technical skills are not as advanced as ours. How can she manage our projects if she doesn't understand the technology as well as we do?" Tanya didn't have all of the answers; but she did understand the technology well enough to know when she needed input from the senior developers. In some cases, tech leads were assigned to work with her and the developer to ensure that effort estimates were realistic and that all technical considerations were identified.

"Does this mean that we report to Tanya, the new project manager?" Developers still reported directly to Sam. Tanya's primary responsibility was ensuring her projects' success, not managing staff. This presented some unique challenges to Tanya. As the "manager without authority," she would have to motivate her team and convince them of the importance of her projects.

"How does Tanya's role differ from Sam's?" Sam and Tanya worked closely together and supported each other. Sam provided the force of authority that Tanya needed to ensure the cooperation of her team. Sam focused on managing the Production team and setting standards for technical implementation. Tanya's focus spanned all phases of the project, from concept to launch.

"With Tanya writing specs, does that mean that we will have no input into the concept or storyboards? What about Design's input?" Developers were not required to get involved during the concept phase; but they were invited to contribute ideas and be actively involved if they were interested. Project kickoff meetings included the developer and the designer, providing the perfect forum for developers to present creative input before the specs were finalized.

On the Job

Sam and Tanya started working through the project lifecycle, developing processes and standard milestones. They created a project checklist for developers to follow. Sarah, the creative director, put together a one-sheet outline of project implementation phases and jazzed it up with a little caricature at each phase. It was comprehensive, yet simple and fun enough for the Editorial staff to pin it up on their bulletin boards for reference. Tanya had the toughest job: convincing the Editorial staff to follow the new process.

Her experience at BigGlobalMedia Inc. was a tremendous asset to her as she faced this challenge head-on. She had been a developer long enough to understand the technical issues that the developers faced. Also, she had a lot of experience working with tech-phobic Editorial staff. She knew how to speak their language and how to express complex technical concepts in ways that were non-threatening and accessible. She had a reputation as someone who was easy to work with. She began by working with the Editorial staff, not the senior management. Once they realized that she was helping them define what they wanted and could walk them through technical issues and translate technical jargon, they were sold. In return for her assistance, they had to agree to follow the process, help meet timelines, and provide intelligent sign-off for designs and specifications. It seemed like a pretty good deal all around. Soon Tanya had more work than she could handle.

Two Steps Forward, One Step Back

So much change in such a short period of time caused some stress in the new Production department. Some developers did not like the increased supervision by Sam and Tanya. Suddenly there was a development process, which was great; but there were also milestones, status updates, and code reviews. Sam could see how well the developers coded, and Tanya could tell which ones were on schedule. Developers who were used to the old days of the "Wild West" had a lot of adjusting to do.

There were similar problems with editors from the various media groups. The biggest obstacle was getting, and keeping, sign-off on specifications. Some business owners had grown accustomed to having their own development staff at their beck and call. They seemed to be addicted to those last-minute, time-consuming tweaks that should have been worked out during the design phase. Some tried to avoid project management by sending numerous requests directly to the maintenance team. Other business owners were not sure what level of detail was needed in a specification, and this required some education and hand holding.

A match was struck amid this explosive situation with the entry of project manager number two, Raul. Raul was a recent junior developer hire from a leading equipment manufacturer and a huge fan of process. It seemed to Sam that Raul was a good candidate for project management. He was not working out too well as a developer, and, besides, Tanya needed some help. Raul loved process, but he could not work effectively to put process in place. He was often overheard wildy gesticulating, waving his arms in the air with a raised voice, "This is not a spec!" and "This is impossible!" He was very adept at shooting down misguided efforts but had a hard time facilitating better solutions. He did not have Tanya's patience, teaching abilities, or people skills. Everyone involved found the situation frustrating, and Raul submitted his resignation within a few weeks.

In the meantime, some developers decided that they'd had enough. A handful of resignations trickled in. Editorial turnover was high as well. This was during the height of the Internet bubble, and there were plenty of opportunities elsewhere. While it was hard to lose valued employees, the loss made it easier for the company to adapt to the change in process. Those who were unwilling or unable to adapt left. The newly hired employees did not question the new process that had been established.

Success

Tanya hired two more project managers, and the projects started to roll in. As everyone got into the swing, it became obvious that we were working better and faster. Senior management noticed and decided that the new Project Management group should report directly to the CIO. Production was just one phase of a project, so why should the project managers report to Production? It was official: Project Management was a success!

The consolidated Production team made huge strides. No longer working in isolation, they mentored and brainstormed with each other to implement solid solutions. As the new process made their efforts more efficient, they were able to focus on building things well, not just quickly. Over time, they reworked and reduced the code base, vastly improved the content publishing UIs, addressed the performance and maintenance issues, and created a shared knowledge base.

As projects began moving smoothly through the pipeline, a few business owners were effectively acting as their own project managers. This resulted in an increased level of efficiency, and it became an important objective for everyone to "internalize" the process. Once everyone learned the methodology, there would be no need for project managers   right? Wrong. Even the business owners with the required skills had fatal flaws. Some could not refrain from making changes that they thought of at the last minute and just had to have. Others just did not have the time to track all of the details. Then of course there were others who just didn't have the skill set or interest in project management. After all, that's not what they were hired for.

Lessons Learned

The lessons from this case study are:

- ◆ *Birds of a feather*. People perform better when they have access to others who perform the same functions. This facilitates learning and the adoption of standards and best practices. The centralization of developers into a single pool accelerated learning curves and created a fun, collaborative environment.
- ◆ *Pooling resources made simple*. Everyone is worried about losing dedicated resources. Convincing arguments include access to more resources as needed, reduced risk from employee turnover, and the increased ability to respond to company priorities.
- ◆ *Project management can mean many things*. Ensure that your definition of project management is explicit and meets your company's project needs. Expectations of what project management is all about run the gamut from "schedule managers" and "meeting notetakers" to senior architects and consultants.

- *Focus on the immediate benefits.* When selling the concept of project management, focus on the most immediate, tangible benefits to your audience.

- *This is a cultural change.* This kind of change is stressful and difficult. It will take a while for process change to take root. Be prepared to support people emotionally, and give them a forum to voice their concerns. Turnover can accelerate the acceptance of change.

- *Try a grass-roots approach.* The more buy-in you have from the front line, the better. Introducing project management by fiat is problematic, in part because senior management may not understand the benefits or impact. Make sure the people "in the trenches" receive immediate benefits from having a project manager on their team.

- *Attack from the inside.* Relying primarily on an outsider, unfamiliar with the people and existing process, is not the best way to introduce the sweeping process change that project management can be. A trusted insider will likely have a much easier time of it.

- *Not for everyone.* Not everyone has the temperament and ability to be an effective project manager. Technical and communication skills are required but not sufficient. Take your prospective project manager for a "test run" project if you can. Furthermore, not every project manager can effectively introduce project management into his organization. He may be able to work well within a structured environment but not have the patience to set one up.

Priorities Meeting ROI Worksheet   A streamlined prioritization process is key to a successful consolidation of production and project management resources. At the moment that resources are pulled away from the direct ownership of business units and placed in a "pool," departments begin to squabble over who gets the biggest share of the pie.

A high-level priorities meeting where department heads present resource requests is the obvious answer. However, disorganized priorities meetings can degenerate into a chaotic state of "committee rule," wherein nothing is decided and open-ended feuding ensues.

The Chapter 13 folder on the CD-ROM contains a "Priorities Meeting ROI Worksheet," which forces project sponsors to state their case before the committee, using a consistent return-on-investement calculation. This small document can play a crucial role in the consolidation of production and project management resources at your company.

An up-to-date version of this documentation is maintained on this book's Web site at *http://www.realwebprojects.com.*

Summary

Junior project managers may not be able to issue edicts that can change their organizational structure overnight, but during a project they are the masters of their domain. Once the project is underway, functional specialists will have their heads down as they focus all their energies on creating designs, writing code, and testing their work. This climate presents an opportunity to create customized rules, structures, and procedures that can be adopted by the rest of the company. Don't underestimate the potential of a model project, which can provide enough momentum to overcome the fear, politics, and endless debates that plague organizational reform initiatives. A well-executed project is the most powerful argument for change. The best place to validate your proposed reforms is at the project postmortem, not the corporate boardroom. Lead by example!

APPENDIX A

Project Quick-Start Guide

Brochureware

A graphic designer's dream? A low-tech cakewalk? Not so fast. Brochure sites look easy on paper. Their sole objective is to communicate a "quick hit" of brand identity through the use of a design-heavy splash page or home page. Their only informational function is to display a basic company profile and contact info. They usually contain a few brief pages: "About Us," "Our Products," and "Contact Us." Brochureware sites have anemic back ends, usually composed of a simple mail script for shooting off a fill-in form from the "Contact Us" page.

While Brochureware sites are simple from a functional standpoint, they conceal an Achilles' heel with regard to scope creep: low-budget graphic design. Clients expect brochureware sites to be slapped together quickly on a shoestring budget, yet they have high expectations when it comes to visual impact. Beware runaway design revisions!

Protect yourself before you take this "easy" bait.

- ♦ Tie the graphic design closely to the client's print marketing materials.
- ♦ Obtain an inventory of art assets that can be repurposed so that you do not have to purchase stock art or replicate the client's print marketing materials from scratch.

♦ If the client does not have a corporate identity, execute on this as a separate project. Do not try to wrap logo design and corporate image into a low-budget HTML job unless you are being paid for it.

♦ Structure your design fees in installments. Protect yourself from endless design revisions by including the first three treatments in the initial concepting fee and then bill the client for each additional revision on a pay-as-you-go basis.

♦ Identify the branding/design decision makers and establish a clear approval process up front, or the project deadline may get killed in endless committee deliberations.

♦ Insist on having the bulk of the editorial content up front. Continuous content tweaks can be the death of a low-budget project.

♦ Have a low-cost content management solution ready in your back pocket so that when the client begins making the inevitable manual edits and content tweaks you can up-sell them to the convenience of making their own changes.

Business-to-Business Portals ("Vortals")

Business-to-Business commerce sites (also called vertical portals, or "vortals") provide information and services to a specific industry. B2B portals are gathering places for members of a specific industry that serve as a resource for news and research. In addition to this content function they also support business-to-business services by uniting buyers and sellers and enabling transactions. The features provided by these specialized communities usually focus on supply chain management. They all perform the same function of bringing buyers and sellers together, increasing market liquidity, and reducing the cost of doing business online.

The scope and complexity of B2B portals are daunting. If you are managing a large B2B project (gulp!), get some experienced help now! While you are hiring an industry-specific project team, keep the following tips in mind.

♦ *Set standards*. B2B portals are marketplaces where numerous trading partners can gather and exchange business documents. Adhere to XML-based standards for Web services (SOAP, etc.) and make sure your project contains activities for defining common DTDs (document type definitions) and other shared protocols. Java 2 Enterprise Edition (J2EE) is the framework of choice for platform independence and interoperability, although .NET provides some excellent support for XML-based Web services.

Portal Partners

Ariba—*http://www.ariba.com*

Commerce One—*http://www.commerceone.com*

Epicentric—*http://www.epicentric.com*

IBM—*http://www-3.ibm.com/e-business/i*

Microsoft—*http://www.microsoft.com*

VerticalNet—*http://www.verticalnet.com*

- *Outsource.* Vortals are extremely complicated sites combining content management, e-commerce, and legacy supply-chain management systems. Leading vendors provide XML-based approaches that work well in this heterogenous environment.

- *Use industry experts.* As you select outsourcing partners, realize that specific industry ("domain") expertise is central in determining the right mix of content, services, and transactions that will reflect real business practices.

- *Don't skimp on information architecture.* Since they contain both industry content and supply-chain transactions, vortals require a complex navigation structure.

E-Commerce Web Sites

A discussion of e-commerce and the many important details and tasks that comprise an e-commerce Web site project are beyond the scope of this book. In this section we will highlight some of the important points you need to be cognizant of when beginning an e-commerce initiative. There are many good books that cover e-commerce exclusively, and some of these titles are listed in our Recommended Reading section.

Putting the "E" in E-Commerce

During your career as a Web project manager you will participate in an e-commerce project of one type or another. It could be a full-blown catalog site for a large retailer, it could be the addition of commerce functionality to a brochure site, or it could be a subscription offering or special for-fee promotion on a corporate site. You may even end up working at an agency that specializes in e-commerce initiatives.

One of the original tenets of the Web was that commerce, electronically enabled and easy to implement and manage, was going to make those clever enough to get in on the action filthy rich. While the dreams of many turned out to be the reality of a very few, the Web still offers business an alternative channel for commerce. Many still believe e-commerce should be, and one day will be, the Web's primary function.

What Kind of E-Commerce?

The term *e-commerce* has grown in scope over the last few years to encompass practically every aspect of doing business online. E-commerce here refers to Web sites that allow the users to purchase goods or services online.

The online shopping universe breaks down into two large categories: B2C and B2B. B2C, or business-to-consumer, sites run the gamut from behemoths like buy.com to tiny one- or two-item mom-and-pop shops using a service like Yahoo! stores.

B2B, or business-to-business, sites also run the gamut from great to small. B2B e-commerce sites, like the name implies, sell goods or services to businesses as opposed to individual consumers. The B2B side of e-commerce has proven to date to be a more successful model than B2C sites. B2B sites have allowed businesses to purchase stock and supplies from vendors without the need for a dedicated EDI (electronic data interchange) system in place.

The E-Commerce Project Plan

An e-commerce project plan contains all of the same elements as a non-commerce Web development project plan, such as creative briefs, functional specifications, timelines, and so forth. However, e-commerce project plans also contain specifications and scope documents for additional elements such as the commerce engine functionality that includes the "shopping cart" Web pages and the payment capture and authorization process. Another area of the project plan that requires more attention than that of a noncommerce initiative is the customer service plan and the required functionality both online and off to support it.

The Business Components

E-commerce projects require the financial and business components of the project to be thoroughly researched and completed early in the development. The marketing, sales, and senior executives will all be involved in building the business case for the project. If the client is a startup, then the business case should be well documented in their business plan. However, if this is an internal undertaking and a new venture for your company, be sure the business people take the time to perform the due diligence necessary to validate the project. The following documents are especially important in any e-commerce project and will comprise the majority of the business cases for the project.

- *The feasibility study.* This document is about taking a good, long, and objective look at the project and making a clear, unequivocal decision on whether the project should be undertaken or not. Is this project worth doing? Will people buy our widgets online when they can get them just as easily at every widget store in the country? Can we really sell our widgets online for a lower price than our competitors? Do we know anything about selling widgets online?

- *The creative brief.* The creative brief should provide a high-level detailing of the site and is an important document in the business case. The creative brief should describe the desired shopping, order taking, and checkout processes as well as what products will be featured on the site and how they will be displayed. The creative brief should also describe how the commerce aspects of the site will be supported, such as new items added, prices changed, shipping costs calculated, and so on. Will there be an online tool that allows a person to maintain the site? How many people will this require? How technical should these people be? Describe any editorial content that may run in tandem with the products or on a separate area of the site. Also, describe the type of functionality that may be required to support these areas as well.

- *Return on investment.* One of the outcomes of the feasibility study should be the raw data that will allow the business people involved in the project to determine the ROI on the project. The questions that should be answered by the ROI document are How much will it cost us to sell our widgets online? How many widgets will we have to sell in order to recoup our investment? How long will this take? How much does it cost to acquire a customer? How much does it cost to keep a customer? How much does it cost to fulfill the order?

- *The marketing plan.* Just building the site is not enough. To be successful you must have in place a marketing plan that details the marketing activities for the following: how the site or brand will be established in the public eye, how customers will be acquired or driven to the site, the types of media to be used to market the site, what new products will be developed for the site, and the cost of the total marketing mix.

The marketing plan may actually require additional online functionality to be developed, implemented, or outsourced. E-marketing initiatives such as e-mail campaigns may require separate development projects but should still be included as tasks and milestones in the overall e-commerce project plan.

Be sure that when the business case is complete, it is formally presented to the client or executive who will be funding the project and liable for its success or failure. Be sure to receive sign-off on the business case before moving forward with any aspect of the project build. Don't settle for a middle manager telling you the plan will be approved "eventually" because nine times out of ten, what is finally signed off by the executive committee or client will not be what was originally presented.

E-Commerce Nuts and Bolts

The common components of an e-commerce system and the associated deliverables are described in this section.

The Commerce System

At the heart of any "commerce-enabled" Web site is functionality that allows users to choose items, add them to an electronic shopping cart, and pay for the chosen items. Easily the most common piece of prepackaged Web software available, commerce applications vary widely in levels of sophistication, functionality, and cost. Commerce functionality is also one of the most available outsourced pieces of functionality as well. There are many application service providers who can provide every aspect of the shopping functionality for your Web site. Again, the features, functionality, and cost vary widely.

In the early stages of the project you may be required to select a vendor for the commerce functionality of the site. More than likely it will take you several days, if not weeks, to narrow down the field of potential vendors. The first thing you need to decide is whether the commerce functionality of the site will be developed in-house using a programming language such as Java, JSP, or Microsoft Active Server Pages, or if you will be implementing a prepackaged software solution that requires little more than loading it onto your servers. Or you may be outsourcing all of this functionality to an e-commerce service provider. Before you can make a qualified decision, you need to know the basic moving parts of any commerce engine. Here are some of them.

- ◆ *The "store."* How the store or shopping area of the site is categorized is an important part of the early planning process. A store that features one or two items does not need a complicated categorization scheme, but a site that is going to feature hundreds of items across hundreds of categories, many of these overlapping, needs to carefully consider how the categories and associated items will be laid out. The commerce system must allow for easy categorization for both the person who is entering the product data and the shopper who will eventually be searching the site for the widget they so desire.

◆ *The product pages.* An important element of the store is how the product is displayed within its category. Does the commerce functionality allow for each item to be displayed and ordered from its own individual page, or is the product grouped together on one master page? How lengthy is each product description? Does the commerce system allow for easy maintenance of these pages? The product pages are where the sale is actually made, so these pages must be easy to find, use, and order from.

◆ *The shopping cart.* The shopping cart functionality must be intuitive and easy for shoppers to use. The shopping cart functionality not only allows users to add items to their virtual cart but it must follow the user as he trolls the virtual aisles of the store, always just a click away for the user to modify his order. Shopping carts come with a variety of bells and whistles such as the ability to suggest complementary items or supplies for the products being purchased.

◆ *Payment functionality.* In addition to giving shoppers the ability to store their goods in one place, the commerce system must also allow users an easy, intuitive, and fast payment or checkout process. This is where many commerce systems fail. Often it is more work to go through the payment process than the shopper perceives the item as being worth. The notion "time is money" has never been more apt. The competition is only a click away, and if their checkout system is easier to use, guess who will win the return business?

◆ *Credit card/payment authorization.* Most online retailers require credit cards as the primary method of payment. Behind the scenes there is usually more than one player involved in the online payment process. The commerce system provides the first step: secure capture of the credit card information. This information is then either stored securely on the retailer's server or encrypted and electronically handed off to a partner that provides the credit card validation and authorization. If the retailer has the capability to process credit cards in-house using a preexisting system, it may choose to do this process manually at a later date. If the retailer only conducts business online, then it will more than likely choose to have the credit cards processed in real-time.

Real-time processing normally consists of the encrypted credit card information being handed off to a vendor providing the authorization service. This vendor decrypts the data and validates the credit card using a zip code or address lookup process to be sure the card holder information matches the credit card information. The validation may also include contacting the card-issuing bank to validate that the funds are in place. Once the validation process is completed, the authorization vendor responds to the retailer's server with either an accepted or denied authorization.

The outcome of the validation process is displayed to the user on a Web page.

Fulfillment—the Achilles' Heel of E-Commerce

One of the greater distinguishing components of an e-commerce project, besides the shopping and ordering functionality, is the actual order fulfillment process. Again, complete coverage of the fulfillment process is beyond the scope of this book, but it's important to discuss having a plan for order fulfillment as part of the overall project plan.

Many e-commerce sites, both large and small, were undone by not having a well-thought-out and feasible order-fulfillment plan in place. Success often spelled doom for many early e-commerce sites as orders poured in day and night without any chance of the retailer having the inventory or capability to fill all the orders.

Besides having the necessary inventory on hand to support a new sales channel, the online retailer must decide if it has the capability in-house to "pick, pack, and ship" orders or if this function should be outsourced. Developing the business processes, hardware, physical space, manpower—in short, the infrastructure—necessary to handle a large volume of orders introduces tremendous costs into the ROI equation. Many large retailers that already have a catalog or direct mail sales channel more than likely have the fulfillment capabilities already established. However, a bricks and mortar retailer making the switch to bricks and clicks will have to carefully consider its fulfillment options and plan accordingly.

Never Underestimate Customer Service

A common omission by many e-commerce projects is a customer service plan. What many businesses performing commerce online have learned—some too late—is that the customer service aspect of the business is every bit as important as the quality of the Web site, the commerce system, and quality of the goods for sale. Customer service has evolved into a completely separate and massive industry called customer relationship management (CRM), complete with million-dollar software packages and consultants ready to teach you how to manage your customers and turn them into return visitors.

Customer service for an e-commerce project, at its most basic, consists of helping customers find and purchase goods from your site. Once the goods are purchased, customers must be able to interact with the retailer should a problem develop with the sale transaction or the goods themselves.

Most successful e-commerce sites employ online customer service or help links that take users to how-to or FAQ pages as well as provide toll-free numbers for customers to call and speak to a human customer service representative, usually during business hours. Both of these types of customer service functions need to be thoroughly planned for and documented in the specifications of the project. How robust these processes are will be dictated by the project budget as well as the scope of the overall site.

Managing customers once they have purchased items from your store is as important as helping them to do so. Will the Web site contain a customer service area where customers can fill out a form to request help or describe a problem? Will a toll-free number be provided to customers wishing to contact the retailer? Who will answer the customer inquiries? These are important parts of the project plan that need to be figured out long before the site is launched.

Security

Because e-commerce sites are dealing directly with sensitive credit card or other types of payment data, the security aspects of the site are of extreme importance. Will the credit card information be stored on the retailer's servers or simply encrypted and handed off to the authorization vendor? How robust is the encryption scheme? What level of browser security should the shopping cart allow for? These are only a few of the security issues that must be worked out with the technical developers of the site, the authorization vendor, and the ISP hosting the Web site.

This is a very detailed aspect of e-commerce Web sites that should not be taken lightly, and again, due to its extreme breadth and scope of detail and functionality, is beyond the scope of this book. That being said, the security aspects of the Web site should be major milestones on your project plan, with the tech lead on the project helping you establish the required details.

E-Marketing Projects

While there are many types of e-marketing initiatives available to the marketer, this section focuses on e-mail marketing projects.

The Message IS the Medium

E-mail marketing is an exploding industry, with everyone from Joe's Garage to General Electric having at least one mailing list it markets to on a regular basis. The odds are pretty good that at some point in your career as a Web project manager you will manage an e-mail marketing campaign.

Running an e-mail list management campaign or project can be relatively straightforward once you know the steps involved. These are the basic components of an e-mail campaign.

- ◆ The list
- ◆ The database
- ◆ The list management software
- ◆ The message
- ◆ The metrics

The List

The list is the most important deliverable you will have to manage. The list can be rented from a list provider, supplied by the client, or captured on your Web site via an opt-in form. The list is the heart of your campaign or project and needs constant maintenance to keep it up to date and free of dead e-mail addresses. All the marketing components will be executed against the list. These include mailing, segmenting, testing message components, testing offers, and measuring response.

■➡ KEY POINT

One of the most important aspects of the mailing list is that all the list members have *opted in* to receive contact from your client or company. There is no point in executing an e-marketing campaign if you are simply spamming a list of people who have not given you permission to contact them. As everyone knows firsthand, our e-mail inboxes are cluttered daily with unwanted, unsolicited spam. Don't join the fray just because it's easy.

The Database

Every professional list management system has a powerful database back end that stores the mailing list as well as all the necessary demographic data about the list members. The tables in the database allow the list management software to "slice and dice" the data to arrive at the necessary measuring metrics. In addition to the list and demographic data, the database will store information generated by the e-mailing campaign such as amount of messages sent, number of messages that "bounced" or were undeliverable, and even how many clicked on links embedded within the message.

The List Management Software

The software that is used to create and manage e-mail marketing campaigns is known as list management software. The software's primary function is to manage the information in the database that impacts or is derived from the list. List management systems come in a variety of sizes and with different feature sets. There is a list management system for every budget and size of list. There are also many application service provider list management systems on the market that can save a company money by avoiding the cost of purchasing and hosting the list management system, not to mention the bandwidth costs for sending millions of pieces of e-mail.

The following is the basic feature set on a good list management system.

- A robust database
- A simple GUI for creating campaigns and messages
- The ability to send multiple message formats, such as MIME, ASCII, AOL
- The ability to segment the list into subsets for testing purposes
- The ability to run complex queries against the database for marketing purposes
- A simple GUI for generating metrics analysis reports on the list as well as on mailing campaigns
- A robust engine capable of pumping out large quantities of e-mail within a short timeframe

Generally, a professional class list management system will require either a DBA or a system administrator to maintain the back-end functionality. The person responsible for managing the back end of the system will add or delete entire lists; create and delete database fields, rows, and tables as required; and monitor the system's performance.

If the list management system provides a simple, intuitive GUI for creating and managing campaigns, then the project stakeholder or client is usually the person who will be managing the campaign creation and reporting. However, if these aspects of the campaign are provided by your company or department, then you may be the resource who mans the GUI.

The Message

What good is all this hardware and software without a compelling message to send? The message is at the heart of any e-marketing campaign and is another important deliverable to manage. A good list management system will be able to send messages in the following formats.

- *MIME.* Stands for Multipurpose Internet Mail Extensions. This standard allows messages to be formatted for a variety of e-mail systems. Not all e-mail systems and e-mail clients can handle HTML-formatted e-mail and can only display text. Typically, a MIME-formatted e-mail file contains both message formats, HTML, and ASCII text. The message is typically encoded in base64 encoding, which wraps the entire message in text. If the e-mail system or client can handle encoded MIME messages, then the system will display either the HTML portion of the message or the ASCII text portion of the message. However, this is far from foolproof. There are some e-mail systems that will only display part of the message in HTML, and the rest of the message will be displayed as "garbage characters." This can be very frustrating for the e-mail marketer, but unfortunately it's something that is beyond control unless you relegate yourself to only sending out ASCII text messages or use a separate encoding and decoding program to ensure proper functionality.

- *HTML.* E-mail formatted in HTML is becoming almost standard for e-marketing campaigns and e-mail newsletters. The response rate on messages formatted in HTML is much higher than simple ASCII text messages. Besides allowing for fancy formatting and attractive design using images and even style sheets, HTML e-mail allows the marketer to embed links into the message that can be tracked by the list management system and provide performance metrics.

- *ASCII text.* The original standard. All e-mail systems and clients are capable of handling messages formatted in ASCII text. The advantage of using ASCII for your messages is that you will experience very few, if any, broken, corrupt, or unreadable messages. The drawbacks are that the response rate for ASCII messages is appreciably lower than HTML and it is difficult to track URLs placed in the message body. The placed URLs must be copied and pasted into a Web browser by the user instead of simply being clicked on as they would in an HTML-formatted message.

- *AOL.* Version 7 of the AOL software is supposed to be able to handle HTML e-mail better than past versions. The AOL e-mail software has

traditionally only been able to handle the most basic HTML formatting, such as bold or italic tags. HTML tables did not work with the
AOL e-mail client nor did link tags. Many marketers simply created
a subset or segment of their list for AOL users and sent them a text
message. Even with the new version of AOL, the rule of thumb
should be to test your HTML message before sending it out to your
list. You may want to create a text message that contains very basic
HTML formatting for your AOL recipients regardless of what version
of the software they are using. Or send your AOL list as ASCII text,
just to be safe.

The message may be created by the marketing department, a producer, a
copywriter, or the client. If the message is being sent in multiple formats, then
there will be some workflow involved, and more than one resource group
may be involved in the production. If the marketing campaign is managed by
a marketing person using the list management GUI, then it may be only a
single person who is involved in the message creation and workflow.

The Metrics

The goal of every e-marketing campaign, besides accomplishing a sale, is to
measure the response to the message or the offer. Normally the same person
who is responsible for the mailing campaign creation is also reponsible for this
deliverable. The metrics reports allow the marketer to fine-tune the message
or offer, which will increase response rates, click-throughs, or sales on ensuing
campaigns. Most list management systems come with metrics-reporting functionality. The most common metrics reports are the number of messages sent
and the number of messages bounced. The system will be able to track these
metrics for each subset of the list or lists. More advanced metrics reporting
includes number of messages opened and number of clicks on links embedded in the HTML messages.

The Campaign Process

The basic process involved in most mailing campaigns, from weekly newsletters to one-time-only e-mail marketing blasts, consists of the following
tasks.

- The business case and campaign goals
- Generating or acquiring the opt-in list
- Setting up the database fields

- Message production
- Campaign mailing production
- Generating reports

The Business Case and Campaign Goals

Before your company or your client begins an e-marketing campaign initiative, be sure the business case—the "Why are we doing this?"—has been documented. Part of the business case is establishing at the outset what the goals of the campaign will be and how success will be measured. Some goals of campaigns are customer acquisition, branding, product sales, product launches, CRM, and research. Success metrics could include increased sales, increased membership, brand awareness measured by open rates, and response rates to offers or survey questions. The client or project stakeholder should be the person responsible for creating the business case. This should be the first deliverable on your project plan.

Generating or Acquiring the Opt-in List

It's imperative that you only mail to people who have opted in to be contacted by your client or your company. If the project you are working on does not already have a list, there are several reputable companies that provide list rental for just about every demographic group and segment imaginable. If you are working with a list that was generated in-house using an opt-in form on a Web site or via another marketing initiative, the mailing may be more successful because the message is expected and relevent to the recipient.

The list is an important deliverable in the process. If it is coming from a third party, it will be delivered to you either on disk or as a compressed file via e-mail. You will have to be sure the list is handed off to the DBA or system administrator so it can be loaded into the list management database. If the list has been generated in-house, then the data should already be in the list management system, and if not, a task for importing the data into the list management system needs to be added to your project plan.

Setting up the Database Fields

Before the list is imported into the database, the DBA must set up the proper profile and demographic fields. These fields are used by the list management system for segmenting the list, measuring response, and personalizing the messages. The following are the most common user fields.

- First name
- Last name
- E-mail address
- Home address
- Zip code
- Phone number
- Opt-in status (yes, no)

Business demographic fields could include the following.

- Current customer (yes, no)
- Current member (yes, no)
- Favorite product

Depending on the size and complexity of your list management system, the profile field creation could take anywhere from an hour to a full day. Be sure to check with your DBA to establish how much time this task will take.

Message Production

The message production can happen concurrently with the database setup and list import. If your campaign calls for messages to be created in HTML, AOL, and ASCII formats, then you will have to add a design effort to your project plan. The design effort is managed exactly as a Web design effort, and the deliverables will be the same: page maps, color palettes, type specifications, graphic images optimized, and design mockups and specifications. The client or stakeholder should be allowed at least one round of revisions as well.

Once the design elements of the message have been created, they are handed off to the HTML developer. Again, the process is exactly the same as it is for designing a Web page. The HTML developer will build the files, and they will then be handed off to the person or resource group responsible for importing the messages into the list management system.

Campaign Mailing Production

The campaign mailing production tasks will vary, depending on how automated your list management system is. These are the basic tasks in building the mailing campaign.

- *Segmenting the list.* The most basic type of list segmentation is for the type of message format the user can receive—for example, AOL,

ASCII, or MIME. A separate subset of your list will be created for each of these, and the list management software will allow you to be sure the people in each segment receive the correct message type. Other common types of list segmenting are different subject lines, different offers, and geographic segmenting.

♦ *Importing the message.* The message files (AOL, ASCII, MIME) are imported into the list management system through the GUI. This is a relatively straightforward task. Once the message is imported into the list management system, the campaign may call for link tracking in the HTML-formatted messages. The list management system should allow you to create the special URLS or redirects necessary to tally clicks on embedded links.

♦ *Reply-to and bounce e-mail addresses.* The list management system will require you to provide it with two e-mail addresses. The reply-to address is the address e-mail is sent to should a recipient of the message hit the reply button in her e-mail client. The bounce e-mail address is the destination folder where bounced or undeliverable messages are collected. These addresses are later removed from the master list as part of the list maintenance process.

♦ *Opt-in and opt-out Web pages.* An important part of any e-mail campaign is the provision of Web pages where users can choose to join (opt in), be removed (opt out), or update their profile information. These page are often served by the list management system and run off of the same database that keeps the data loop closed and efficient. If your opt-in and opt-out pages are served outside of the list management system, then a data transfer or import functionality or task must be added to your process.

♦ *Scheduling the mailing.* Once all the preceding pieces of the campaign are in place, you will schedule the date and time the mailing will occur. This is a common automated feature of list management systems. Once the date and time are set, the system will send out the messages to the appropriate list and list segments at the scheduled time.

Generating Reports

Measuring the response of the mailing campaign is one of the most important tasks in the campaign. Most marketers pull reports at different intervals once the campaign has been mailed. These intervals are usually 48 hours, one week, and then from two to three weeks out. The biggest response occurs within the

> ▶ *E-Marketing Resources* There are several excellent online resources to learn more about e-marketing. Two of our favorites are *http://www.clickz.com*, which provides information, how-tos, and many articles on this subject; and *http://www.internet.com/sections/marketing.html,* which provides many links to various e-marketing sites.

first 24 to 48 hours of the mailing. Every list management system generates reports differently. Some make exporting the data easy, and others only generate the reports within their own GUI. The better systems will allow you to run custom queries against the database to measure more granular metrics, such as how many people in a certain geographical area responded.

Conclusion

Successful management of e-mail marketing campaigns is not difficult once you understand the steps involved. The most crucial element of this type of marketing at the professional level is the type of list management system you use. These systems run the gamut from low-priced packages that run from a desktop machine to full-blown systems requiring their own set of servers for the software and database. It may be easiest to get into e-mail marketing by using one of the many ASP list management vendors on the market today.

Like any Web initiative, an e-marketing campaign is time and labor intensive. Be sure you have all the basics covered, such as a business case, the necessary staff resources, and the opt-in list before you launch the campaign. Create a project plan for your e-marketing initiative just like you would for any Web development project, and manage the milestones just as stringently.

International Web Sites

Going global with your Web site requires familiarity with two concepts: internationalization (commonly shortened to "I18N" because of the 18 letters between the I and the N) and localization (similarly, L10N).

Internationalization

Internationalization is the process of reengineering your back end so that it can recognize and process any language. It also involves making source code changes so the software can understand different currency, measurement, and date formats. Once the back end has been internationalized, it's not too difficult to translate content into the target language.

Localization

Localization refers to the process of translating and culturally adapting any front-end content, including user interfaces, help files, and other documentation. The concept of a "locale" is important because it captures the notion of regional culture. Culturally specific content includes image iconography, color, and fonts, as well as plain text.

Back-end Inventory

As you embark on a globalization project, take an inventory of all the back-end systems used by your Web site. The purpose is to identify any points of failure between systems that are communicating with each other by relying on a common character set. Make sure that all of your systems can handle multiple language character sets, currencies, and so on. These systems should be able to support 16-bit Unicode, which is capable of representing over 65,000 characters (think Japanese!).

Code Cleansing

Internationalizing code means stripping out any hard-coded references that are locale-specific. Hard-coded text strings (such as "click here") should be stripped out and placed in an external file or database where they can be translated. The code should then reference the database to pull in any locale-specific items. Typically developers on an I18N project will create custom search/replace tools and utilities that comb through the code and pull out text strings.

Content Management

The key to localization is to strip out hard-coded items from your Web site templates and export them into a content management system. Publishing tools should be built for local editors so that they can tweak the translated copy for cultural relevance. Content may be categorized into three tiers: global (to be shared across all sites—such as company logos), regional (within one language grouping), and local (subject to cultural nuances in presentation).

Graphics

In addition to a graphic redesign that takes into account the cultural meanings of colors and icons, a review of your functional images is necessary. This art review is crucial to rooting out graphical "submit" buttons and other text that appears as a graphic.

Editorial Muscle

Many project managers make the mistake of treating I18N as a technical problem when it is really all about taking a thorough inventory of your content assets and applying editorial manpower. The planning phase during which you will take this inventory is particularly laborious. During localization you will need to use a combination of machine and human translation. Automated scripts can do the heavy lifting and seek out hidden strings, but human editors will need to review the final product. This labor-intensive activity requires in-country content teams to perform legal reviews, marketing impact studies, and so on. This effort is usually underestimated, and many I18N projects suffer a manpower crisis as the true scope of the content effort emerges. Make an exhaustive inventory effort before committing to a launch date, and you may find yourself on an exotic trip with an expense account when it's time to "oversee" the launch.

Intranets

Building an intranet is analogous to building a Web site. The tasks and the process are the same as many of those already covered in this book. Whether you are managing the project internally or you are building the intranet for a client, you will soon find that the biggest challenge of an intranet project is not managing the actual build but managing the various interpersonal and inter-departmental relationships. The technical aspects of a large corporate intranet can be every bit as complex, if not more so, than a large corporate Web site. In this section we will outline some of the key differences of intranet development and Web site development as well as some of the tasks you will need to concentrate on through the lifecycle of this type of project. We'll also cover the important features a corporate intranet should include.

It Doesn't Get Much More Political than This

The biggest challenge you will face on an intranet project is smoothly and delicately managing the political battles that will inevitably be raging around you. Intranet projects suffer from multiple internal owners with competing agendas. A Web site build may have multiple owners, but all of them tend to be focused on the business goals of the site, not their own agendas. Whether you are working on an internal intranet project or you are working for a client, you will have to establish from the very beginning of the project who the primary stakeholders are and who makes the final call on important, critical decisions.

Traditional intranet project stakeholders are the IT group, the corporate communications group, or human resources. Due to increased functionality in Web and intranet technology, corporate intranets can now be effectively utilized by many groups within the organization. This is a blessing and a curse because now the stakeholder pool has grown and with it the number of competing agendas.

What many companies and agencies have learned is that the best way to manage decisions on a large-scale internal communications project, such as an intranet build, is to create a governing body or steering committee. Representatives from each stakeholder group sit on the committee and represent their group's interests. Because large-scale corporate intranets represent many large internal groups such as finance, legal, and HR, each of these groups may end up with their own individually branded site or channel within the intranet. Therefore, a stakeholder from each group must sit on the committee to enable fair representation across the company. This model has proven very successful for many companies and reduces the level of political infighting.

Whose Site Is It Really?

The answer, of course, is the employees who work at the organization. Keep this thought in the front of your mind during the intranet build, especially in the early planning stages. The goal of an intranet is not to entertain but to provide information quickly and easily. Finding out in the early planning stages what time-saving features the rank and file employees of the organization want in the intranet will save the company a great deal of money by improving and increasing productivity.

A successful method for gathering requirements for corporate intranets is to conduct user surveys. The survey can be sent out via e-mail or an intracorporate office memo. Whatever the method, collect as much data as possible before your company blows a million dollars on an intranet that is never fully embraced by the intended users and is bloated with useless features.

Who's Going to Take Care of It?

It's rare when a company will hire staff just to maintain the intranet from a content and technical perspective. Because intranets are typically developed and hosted by the IT group, this group is often also responsible for updating the site and adding new features and content areas. This situation leads to an intranet site that only gets updated or properly maintained when the people in the IT department have the time to do so, which is not very often.

Be sure to include in your project plan a comprehensive content and maintenance plan, and identify the necessary roles. Decide whether the intranet will require a content management system or editorial tool and, if so, who will be responsible for updating the content. If the intranet is going to be maintained with an editorial tool, will this tool be used by a single group such as the communications department or will it be distributed across all departments who require regular content updates?

If your company or your client's company does require a dedicated team to maintain the intranet, the roles are the same as those of a Web development team.

- *Developer.* If the intranet is an integral and important part of the company culture, the IT department should dedicate a full-time person to the intranet team.

- *Designer.* If the company has an internal design team, then it may be possible to dedicate a person to the intranet. If there are no designers on staff, a person can be hired to provide design support for the intranet, or this work can be farmed out to an agency.

- *Project manager.* If you are an internal project manager, you should be ready to devote some time each month, or maybe even each week, to managing new intranet initiatives. If you work for an agency and you are managing the intranet build for a client, identify who in the client organization will be managing the intranet and provide some basic project management training.

- *Content team.* Because the bulk of the content displayed on a corporate intranet is developed across many departments, it may be hard to bring in an outside team to take over these tasks. However, an intranet producer can be the primary contact for all content created within the organization.

Features

The discovery work you do early in the project, such as interviewing the stakeholders and conducting user surveys, will shape many or most of the features that will be incorporated in the intranet. These are some of the more common features found on corporate intranets.

- *Access to documentation.* This is the most common feature of most corporate intranets, especially from an HR perspective. The intranet provides the ability for employees to download HR and financial forms easily.

- *Calendaring functionality.* This feature could increase the number of repeat visitors to the intranet. Allow users to maintain their own schedules on the intranet, as well as post meeting invitations and other events on specific days and times. This feature may be already available on the company e-mail system, but if not, make it a useful part of the intranet.

- *Search.* Like any text- or content-heavy site, an intelligent search engine is a crucial piece of functionality. Some people prefer to search for information, whereas other people like to drill. Be sure to have a good search scheme in place for the people who like to locate information by searching.

- *Time management.* Many intranet or corporate portal packages contain functionality that allows employees to maintain their timesheets for the week, month, and year. This is a convenient feature for both the user and the HR and payroll departments.

- *Security.* Generally, intranets provide gateways or links out to the internet, but there is rarely access into an intranet from outside without user ID and password authentication. Because there is normally a great deal of sensitive information contained on the corporate intranet, security is one of the most important features on an intranet project.

- *Message boards.* Message boards give employees a place to interact and voice their opinions about various work- and nonwork-related issues. While being a great feature for fostering communication and release among the staff, in order to be successful the message boards need to be moderated on as regular a basis as possible, just like any other electronic community. Rules of play should be established and posted on the intranet.

You'll Need a Marketing Plan Too

Work with the marketing department to create an internal promotional campaign for the intranet that will not only announce the launch of the intranet but will motivate employees to use the features available there. If necessary, create an incentive campaign to get the staff to begin using the site. Remember: The most important goals of management for the corporate intranet are to increase productivity and reduce costs, but the employees may need some help getting into the habit of using the intranet, and incentives are a great way to jump-start enthusiasm.

Intranet Resources

There are some great resources for learning more about intranet and corporate portal development online. One outstanding site is IntranetJournal.com, which is packed with useful articles and reviews of the latest intranet technology.

An oft-cited book about intranet development and features is *The Elements of Intranet Style* by Eric Brown and James W. Candler. The content of this book is not tech-heavy nor full of corporate business jargon. It's a good primer on the basics for any intranet project.

APPENDIX B

Technology for the Web Project Manager

What You Really Need to Know—Frameworks

Web software development is more than just programming languages. Web sites are supported by complex systems made up of disparate software components and hardware tied together with numerous protocols. The environment that allows all of these moving parts to communicate with each other and the outside world is referred to as a Framework. *Frameworks* determine the hardware, programming languages, and protocols that form the life-support system of a Web site. The organization of the hardware, software, and protocol environment into Frameworks provides several benefits.

- A complete environment for Web site development, hosting, interoperability, security, and maintenance so that developers do not have to build customized systems from the ground up every time they launch a new site

- Standards, consistency, and predictability across enterprises

- Software components or building-blocks so that developers can share and reuse code without having to reinvent the wheel for every bit of functionality

- A model or standard architecture that allows us to easily visualize how the entire system works

Without standardized frameworks, the Web would dissolve into a useless Tower of Babel, as a myriad of one-off systems attempted to communicate,

Where to Get Framed
- JavaBeans Component Architecture—*http://java.sun.com/products/ejb*
- What Is Java?—*http://java.sun.com/java2/whatis/*
- *New Architect Magazine*, May 2001. "Choosing Between .NET and J2EE Frameworks" by Al Williams—*http://www.newarchitectmag.com/documents/s=4419/new1013636374/*
- Open Source–LINUX—*http://www.linux.com*
- Open Source–PHP—*http://www.php.net*
- The Open Source Initiative—*http://www.opensource.org/*
- O'Reilly Publishing's Web site: "Microsoft .NET vs. J2EE: How Do They Stack Up?" by Jim Farley—*http://java.oreilly.com/news/farley_0800.html*

both internally and externally, through customized interfaces. The need for standardization of systems, languages, and protocols is a major force behind industry consolidation. This consolidation has yielded several major Web development frameworks: Microsoft's .NET, Sun's Java 2 Enterprise Edition, Open Source, and CORBA. While making software development efficient and easy, Frameworks also limit the parameters of what is possible. Each Framework has benefits and drawbacks that organizations must carefully weigh before they embrace the system of their choice.

Microsoft .NET

Microsoft's .NET Framework accommodates many programming languages and provides powerful tools for integrating XML-based Web services. The main limitation of .NET is that it will only operate on Windows platforms. The .NET Framework is composed of four major features.

- The Common Language Runtime (CLR), a compiler that translates many different program languages into a kind of "mother tongue" that is universally understood by any .NET application.

- A prepackaged library of classes and services that developers can use. For example, .NET has excellent support for XML-based Web services.

- A new version of Active Server Pages called ASP+.

- A new object-oriented programming language called C# ("C-Sharp").

At the center of .NET is the CLR "virtual machine," which compiles many different programming languages into a universal interpreted language (IL). The IL will only run on Windows. With the IL, .NET goes a step beyond traditional Active Server Pages. Traditional Active Server Pages had to be interpreted by the server individually for every request. This placed a heavy performance burden and disguised some programming errors.

With .NET, every page is compiled into an IL file. The IL serves as a kind of universal intermediary language. Since all .NET components and services understand IL, it is possible to code dynamic Web pages using many different programming languages. .NET also introduced C# as a master programming language for this new environment. C# closely resembles Java. Like Java, C# requires that every program be defined as a class.

Sun Microsystems' Java 2 Enterprise Edition

Sun's Framework relies on the Java programming language. With its Java Virtual Machine (JVM), a universal language compiler that can be run on top of practically any operating system, Sun makes the claim that Java is a "write once, run anywhere" programming language. The J2EE Framework is known for its two unique features.

- *JavaServer Pages (JSP).* On the presentation side, JSP allows Java code to be embedded in HTML pages. When compiled, the JSP draws dynamically generated HTML pages and sends them to the browser. JSPs let you create Web pages that contain server-side Java but generate ordinary HTML and display it directly to the client.
- *JavaBeans.* The logic of J2EE applications is encapsulated into reusable components called Enterprise JavaBeans (EJBs). These components maintain state (by storing data) and carry out logical functions (called methods). Enterprise JavaBeans also reduce the complexity of developing middleware by providing automatic support for services like database connectivity.

The Open Source Initiative

Open Source frameworks use software that is freely distributed, freely modified, and may not be tied to a particular product. Special software licenses (most famously, the General Public License, or GPL) are used to ensure that the development and distribution of the source code is in keeping with these principles.

◆ The Great Debate in a Nutshell

Passionate techies can easily come to blows over the ".NET versus J2EE" debate. Keep these concepts in mind during your attempt to make sense of the flying jargon.

◆ .NET is language-neutral and Windows-dependent.

◆ J2EE is Java-dependent and platform-neutral.

Is it really that simple? Of course not, but these pithy lines will sound good at a job interview, and they may help keep your head from spinning as the debate rages on.

Open Source epitomizes the idea of collaborative development within a community of volunteers. The basic idea is that with a global community of programmers constantly making improvements, the software should evolve at a very high speed. Members of the open source community believe that this rapid evolutionary process produces better software than the traditional closed model, in which only a very few programmers can work on the source. For example, the open source database system PostgreSQL adds major features every few months, whereas major upgrades to commercial software products can take years to introduce. This unprecedented rate of revision stems from a worldwide army of loyal and enthusiastic developers who brainstorm fixes and test the latest tweaks, quickly reporting results from all kinds of applications, configurations, and platforms.

Open Source does not mean that the software cannot be used in commercial applications. For example, several companies like RedHat sell Linux-based products by creating "brands" of Linux, called distributions. They can charge money for these packages as long as the product is distributed along with its source code and as long as anyone who buys the product is allowed to make changes and share their modifications. This means that it is okay for you to make copies of Linux and give them to your friends, and you can even tweak a few lines of the source code while you're at it—as long as you make your improvements publicly available to anyone who might ask. Here are some examples of successful Open Source products that are in widespread commercial use.

◆ Apache HTTP Server, which runs more than 50 percent of the world's Web servers

◆ Perl, which is still the most common programming language used by server-side applications

◆ Linux, a successful Open Source operating system

> *Dropping Knowledge on Yourself*
>
> W3Schools—*http://www.w3schools.com*. Inside W3Schools you will find a large number of free Web building tutorials, from basic HTML and XHTML tutorials, to advanced XML, XSL, and WAP tutorials. The tutorials are presented in a clear, no-nonsense, "just what you really need to know" format.
>
> Webmonkey—*http://www.webmonkey.com*. This site offers a how-to library and a quick-reference guide that have been teaching people how to build Web sites on their own since 1996. The tutorials are presented as articles written in a breezy, conversational style.
>
> Web Developer's Virtual Library—*http://www.wdvl.com*. For those with some hands-on experience, this site takes a slightly more technical approach. The WDVL offers in-depth tutorials on available software technology and suggests pointers to additional resources.

- PHP, a general-purpose scripting language that is especially suited for Web development and can be embedded into HTML
- PostgreSQL, an object-relational database system that is Open Source

Object-Oriented Design

Object-oriented (OO) design is a way of thinking about software that organizes everything into objects. An object is a software model of some real-world entity, like a customer or an invoice. Objects are organized into classes, collections of objects that share common attributes and behaviors. Objects can inherit characteristics from their parent classes. In order to design an OO system, your team must take an inventory of the objects that the system will contain and identify the behaviors and responsibilities of those objects, as well as how the objects will interact with each other.

To understand objects, classes, and inheritance, we can use the simple example of a dog named Roark. If we were to think about Roark in object-oriented terms, he is a particular "instance" of the class "Dog." As a member of the Dog class, Roark inherits certain attributes and behaviors. For example, he has fur and four legs. He also has behaviors, or methods, such as eat, sleep, and fetch.

There are many advantages to thinking about Web applications as collections of objects rather than lines of coded instructions. Most of these advantages have to do with inheritence, reusability, and modularity. For example, by simply saying that Roark is a member of the Dog class, you know quite a bit

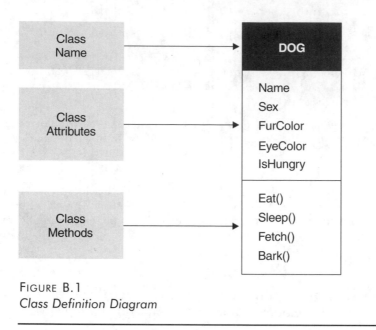

FIGURE B.1
Class Definition Diagram

about him already, like the fact that Roark doesn't talk, but he can bark. You also know that if you send him certain instructions that are understood by all members of his class (like the command "Roark, sit!"), he will probably understand you.

When working with your team to model an object-oriented application, the class diagram is an extremely useful tool. This modeling technique describes each object along with its methods (behaviors) and attributes. These models can also define the relationships that exist between the objects in the system. A typical relationship between objects is the "parent–child" relationship. An example of a parent–child hierarchy can be seen in the class progression: Animal > Vertebrates > Mammals > Dog. If we were to write a simple class definition diagram for our new Dog class, it might look something like Figure B.1.

CRC Cards

CRC stands for "class–responsibility–collaborator." As you work with your team to design an object-oriented system, CRC cards provide a convenient format for expressing complex information about classes. The goal of this technique is to come up with a set of 3 × 5 index cards that describe all of the classes that make up the application. Each card lists the name of the class, the responsibilities of the class, and a list of collaborator classes that provide information or services. The idea is to obtain brief, high-level descriptions. There are many excellent Web tutorials on how to conduct a CRC session.

The UML

Software development methodologies use graphical notation schemes to express the relationship of classes within an object-oriented system. The Unified Modeling Language (UML) is the industry standard for graphical representation of object-oriented systems. The UML specification is coordinated by the Object Management Group (*http://www.omg.org*). UML diagrams show object relationships, such as the following.

♦ One–to–one

♦ Many–to–one

♦ One–to–many

♦ Parent–child

♦ Composition and aggregation ("is a member of" and "has a" relationships)

Modeling is a crucial phase in large software projects. With sophisticated software models, you can be more assured that the functionality will be complete before implementation begins. UML modeling allows your team to visualize the software design and check it against requirements prior to the costly development phase.

Web Services with XML

A Web service is an application that exposes itself to the world, allowing its features to be utilized by any other program through standard protocols over the Internet. Web services can be automatically invoked by other programs over the Internet. Programs that invoke a Web service are referred to as clients. There are several different protocols that are used to enable a Web service to communicate with a client. The most common method is SOAP, which stands for "Simple Object Access Protocol." SOAP sets the rules of engagement that govern the transactions between a Web service and a client.

By exposing their data and functionality, Web services make it easy to integrate disparate applications that may reside on multiple platforms and networks. The beauty of Web services is that they can be built as a "layer" on top of existing systems without disrupting the underlying code. Web services provide a mouthpiece for any Web-enabled application, allowing it to share its data and functionality with the rest of the world using XML as the common denominator. Web services have several major uses.

- *Application integration.* Running on intranets, Web services within an intranet can integrate business applications running on disparate platforms. For example, a .NET client running on Windows 2000 can easily invoke a Web service that allows it to interface with a legacy order entry system that could be running AS/400.

- *Business-to-business integration.* B2B Web services allow commerce partners to conduct transactions regardless of their native systems. For example, a supplier's inventory management Web service might permit its buyers to automatically check inventory levels before an order is sent by the system.

- *Commercial transactions.* These Web services allow vendors to sell content and data directly to clients over the Internet. With Web services, the "customer" is actually another application instead of a human end-user. For example, a news organization creates a Web service to allow other Web sites to automatically pull the latest news stories for a transaction-based fee.

Content Management Systems

A content management system (CMS) allows content to be published intelligently to large Web sites. Web sites that use a CMS are usually database driven, in that all of the content is published dynamically to Web pages from a database where it resides. A CMS generally provides the following features.

- Editorial workflow tools
- Content creation tools (creating, editing, archiving, and so on)
- Content publishing
- Content personalization
- Web page templates

By using a CMS, editors can do the following.

- Create content with desktop applications and Web-based interfaces
- Aggregate digital assets
- Integrate with applications developed in-house
- Automate and manage the authoring, approval, and publishing of digital assets

♦ Define personalization rules to better target content delivery

♦ Modify content taxonomy to create a more intelligent and responsive site

♦ Stage content and manage versions to improve integrity and security

♦ Enable a consistent look and feel of the information architecture to Web sites across the enterprise

Leading CMS Technology Vendors

♦ BroadVision—*http://www.broadvision.com*

♦ Interwoven—*http://www.interwoven.com*

♦ Macromedia ColdFusion—*http://www.macromedia.com/software/coldfusion*

♦ Microsoft Content Management Server—*http://www.microsoft.com/cmserver/*

♦ Vignette—*http://www.vignette.com*

Digital Rights Management

Leading-edge content sites provide multiple levels of membership and access, segregating content into several buckets.

♦ Free content (often advertising-supported, with paid areas ad-free)

♦ Free members-only (membership is free and is used as a vehicle to promote opt-in newsletter sign-ups)

♦ Premium membership

♦ Subscription-based (provided in various combinations or bundles)

♦ Pay-per-use (usually supported by a robust search engine that delivers synopses or samples of the paid content and shopping cart mechanism)

"Premium" or paid content sites rely heavily on Web site metrics to evaluate and tweak pricing models. There are several digital rights management (DRM) vendors providing a layer of content servers that protect content and allow bundling of users and groups. This software facilitates information commerce, the controlled distribution and sale of information online. DRM systems allow business owners to easily "package" content offerings, change pricing and business models on the fly, and administer complicated access rights across multiple types of users and groups.

Appendix C

Useful Web Sites

Rather than list the tremendous number of sites devoted to project management, we have selected our favorites. These sites are the most useful for the job.

Project Management Sites

Gantthead: A content and community portal specifically for project managers.

http://www.gantthead.com

PMBoulevard: A resource center offering access to a virtual project management office (PMO), online training center, extensive knowledge center, and personalized online consulting services.

http://www.pmboulevard.com

Project Management Institute: The leading nonprofit professional association for project managers. PMI establishes project management standards and provides seminars, educational programs, and professional certification.

http://www.pmi.org

The Project Management Center: A portal to online project management resources.

http://www.infogoal.com/pmc

ALLPM: Forums, jobs, templates, and other resources.
http://www.allpm.com

4PM.com: An extensive free library, including articles, tools, and techniques.
http://www.4pm.com

Web Development and Technology Sites

CNET's Builder.com: A fairly technical portal dedicated to bringing software developers a fresh, real-world perspective. The management section contains excellent project management tips.
http://www.builder.com

Internet.com: For the "hands-on," everything you need to know about Web technologies, aggregated.
http://www.internet.com

Tech Republic: A content and community portal for IT professionals with excellent e-newsletters. We recommend the *IT Consultant* newsletter.
http://www.techrepublic.com

Graphic Design and Information Architecture Sites

Design Management Institute: Articles and techniques for managing designers as well as articles devoted to the design process.
www.dmi.org

Jakob Nielson's Web Site: The blurb at the top of the usability guru's Web site says, "Usable Information Technology." Well put!
http://www.useit.com

Glossaries

Whatis.com: A great reference site for technical information, and it also features an excellent searchable glossary of technical terms.
http://whatis.techtarget.com

Wideman Comparative Glossary of Project Management Terms: Don't laugh. Pay this site a visit to bone up on all the latest PM geek-speak, and you'll be the life of the next launch party.
http://www.pmforum.org/library/glossary

Hybrids

A List Apart: For people who make Web sites. A fresh, always frank, and often hilarious collection of articles covering everything "from pixels to prose, coding to content." Updated monthly.

http://www.alistapart.com

Webmonkey: Now part of the Terra Lycos network, Webmonkey is one of the first Web development "how-to" sites. Reading a cross section of Webmonkey articles is like getting a lesson in the evolution of Web design and development.

http://www.webmonkey.com

Recommended Reading

In our advocacy of an interdisciplinary approach to Web project management, we recommend the following reading list for those of you who find yourselves marooned on a desert island populated by natives who have no concept of software development process.

Brink, Tom, Darren Gergle, and Scott Wood. 2001. *Usability for the Web: Designing Web Sites that Work.* San Francisco: Morgan Kaufmann—ISBN: 1-558-60658-0.

Burdman, Jessica. 1999. *Collaborative Web Development: Strategies and Best Practices for Web Teams.* Reading, MA: Addison-Wesley—ISBN: 0-201-43331-1.

Castro, Elizabeth. 1999. *HTML 4 for the World Wide Web: Visual QuickStart Guide, Fourth Edition.* Berkeley, CA: Peachpit Press—ISBN: 0-201-35493-4.

Cato, John. 2001. *User-Centered Web Design.* Boston: Addison-Wesley—ISBN: 0-201-39860-5.

Doucette, Martin. 1999. *Microsoft Project 2000 for Dummies.* Boston: International Data Group—ISBN: 0-764-50517-3.

Fields, Duane K. 2001. *Web Development with JavaServer Pages, Second Edition.* Greenwich, CT: Manning Publications—ISBN: 1-930-11012-X.

Friedlein, Ashley. 2000. *Web Project Management: Delivering Successful Commercial Web Sites.* San Francisco: Morgan Kaufmann—ISBN: 1-558-60678-5.

Nakano, Russell. 2002. *Web Content Management: A Collaborative Approach.* Boston: Addison-Wesley—ISBN: 0-201-65782-1.

Project Management Institute. 1996. *A Guide to the Project Management Body of Knowledge.* Upper Darby, PA: Project Management Institute—ISBN: 1-880-41023-0.

Shneiderman, Ben. 2002. *Designing the User Interface: Strategies for Effective Human-Computer Interaction, Third Edition.* Boston: Addison-Wesley—ISBN: 0-201-69497-2.

Siegel, David. 1997. *Secrets of Successful Web Sites: Project Management on the World Wide Web.* Indianapolis: Hayden Books—ISBN: 1-568-30382-3.

Taylor, Allen G. 2001. *SQL For Dummies, Fourth Edition.* New York: Wiley Publishing—ISBN: 0-764-50737-0.

Tufte, Edward R. 1990. *Envisioning Information.* Cheshire, CT: Graphics Press—ISBN: 0-961-39214-2.

Tufte, Edward R. 2001. *The Visual Display of Quantitative Information, Second Edition.* Cheshire, CT: Graphics Press—ISBN: 0-961-39214-2

Wysocki, Robert K., Robert Beck, Jr., and David B. Crane. 2000. *Effective Project Management, Second Edition.* New York: Wiley—ISBN: 0-471-36028-7.

Yourdon, Edward. 1999. *Death March.* Upper Saddle River, NJ: Prentice Hall—ISBN: 0-130-14659-5.

Index

Note: Italicized page locators refer to tables and/or figures.

Also Available from Addison-Wesley

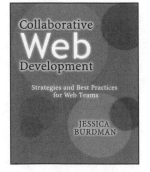

0-201-43331-1
272 pages with CD-ROM
© 1999

0-201-65782-1
272 pages
© 2002

0-201-65786-4
240 pages
© 2000

0-201-72149-X
816 pages
© 2003

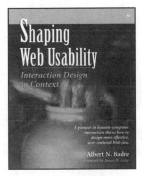

0-201-72993-8
304 pages
© 2002

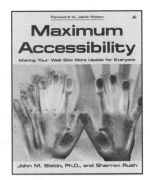

0-201-77422-4
640 pages
© 2003

0-201-73063-4
384 pages
© 2002

inform**IT**

CD-ROM Warranty

Addison-Wesley warrants the enclosed disc to be free of defects in materials and faulty workmanship under normal use for a period of ninety days after purchase. If a defect is discovered in the disc during this warranty period, a replacement disc can be obtained at no charge by sending the defective disc, postage prepaid, with proof of purchase to:

Editorial Department
Addison-Wesley Professional
Pearson Technology Group
75 Arlington Street, Suite 300
Boston, MA 02116
Email: AWPro@awl.com

Addison-Wesley makes no warranty or representation, either expressed or implied, with respect to this software, its quality, performance, merchantability, or fitness for a particular purpose. In no event will Thomas J. Shelford, Gregory A. Remillard and/or Addison-Wesley, its distributors, or dealers be liable for direct, indirect, special, incidental, or consequential damages arising out of the use or inability to use the software. The exclusion of implied warranties is not permitted in some states. Therefore, the above exclusion may not apply to you. This warranty provides you with specific legal rights. There may be other rights that you may have that vary from state to state. The contents of this CD-ROM are intended for personal use only.

More information and updates are available at:
http://www.awprofessional.com/

The latest versions of the documents on the CD-ROM, as well as additional templates not included here, are available for download from this book's Web site at *http://www.realwebprojects.com/*.